DOWN UNDER ROUNDABOUT
AND UP THERE

Down Under Roundabout and Up There

PAT BUCKLEY

Copyright © Pat Buckley, 2003

First published in 2003 by
Kirriemuir Publishing
25 West Cliff
Preston PR1 8HX

Reprinted 2004

All rights reserved
Unauthorised duplication
contravenes existing laws.

British Library Cataloguing-in-Publication data
A catalogue record for this book is available from the
British Library

ISBN 0-9546406-0-8

Printed by Biddles Ltd, King's Lynn

Foreword

Pat Buckley was widowed at fifty and since then has travelled, usually alone, but always independently.

She has related these trips in letters to her friends and it is some of these which form the basis for this book.

It is lightweight, with the only serious stuff being confined to the back

Her daughter wanted to be married in Thailand. This was postponed, but fortunately too late for the author to cancel her nine-week trip.

In the month before she travelled, she tore a ligament in her knee, which subsequently developed a life of its own.

The author apologises for any lack of continuity, inevitable with a collection of letters which is personal and therefore subjective. She has made every attempt to be accurate within the limits of her memory and of her knowledge at the time of writing the letters.

Acknowledgements

My thanks go to Clare and Michael, Sue and Peter, the letter recipients, who persevered valiantly. Also to my many friends who have listened, read and discussed this project *ad infinitum*. To all who brought it physically to fruition. And finally my family for their love and encouragement.

Cast of Characters

Pat Buckley

Roy
Deceased Husband

Paul
Andy
Gavin
Caroline (Caz)
Vicky
Their children

Paul
Caroline's boyfriend

Sue and Peter (Wales)
Clare and Michael (Preston)
Recipients of letters

Chen, Yen and Charlotte
Chinese Hosts

Lynley, Dale and Jean
New Zealand Hosts

A Dishonourable Guest Arrives

Xi'an, China
09/03/03

Dear Sue and Peter,

Welcome to China.

No matter what people say I will never believe it was my fault I was standing outside Beijing Airport in the middle of winter in a silk dress with light snow falling on my head.

As I boarded at Hong Kong I took no notice of all the others in winter clothing. I thought they were just being cautious.

Even as the captain welcomed us aboard I felt no alarm, but as he informed us that the weather in Beijing was zero degrees centigrade and light snow, I felt a slight frisson. Had I been misinformed? Apparently so.

I stood at arrivals, facing my hosts, with a trolley full of mismatched cheap luggage (intentionally so), silk dress and short sleeved linen jacket.

I realised I had spectacularly dishonoured my country. I was not fit to travel. How had this come to pass?

Well, Charlotte (remember my Chinese student?) when she invited me to Beijing last December, as she and her mother were my guests, had blithely informed me that the temperature in March would be thirty degrees centigrade. 'That hot?' says I. 'Oh yes,' says Charlotte, 'it can be very hot in China.'

Charlotte is twenty-three, has just got a good degree in Business Studies in a foreign language, and I trusted her. I now realise, as the Americans say, she didn't know shit from shinola.

You may, and you wouldn't be the first, wonder why I didn't look up weather conditions on the internet – who he?

Well, back to Beijing Airport. Charlotte's parents, Chen, the father, very good English and Yen, no English but simpatico, greeted me with flowers and many hugs. Yen had visited my house, had seen the sort of car I drive, and I think was very puzzled when she saw my luggage. She was expecting M&S matching at least.

There's a very good reason for this. My hotchpotch of small cases is never locked, is never stolen from and I can lift every one of them – just. You see it's not worth risking your job to rifle through a case where the owner can't afford matching, which is why Posh Spice lost her Gucci luggage – too obvious, you see.

After they'd got over the culture shock of my arrival, Chen and Yen took me to lunch, which sort of set the scene. We are always dining. I don't know how the Chinese keep so slim, they consume far more than I do, every stick-thin one of them.

So this meal, which consisted of about twelve dishes, had Peking Duck, something which was a fish's stomach (a bit like tripe to look at) and all sorts of other things I didn't ask the provenance of. At some meals though you could tell it was a bird by the head or the feet. I suppose it's no different from our serving fish with the head on. I never got the opportunity to try snake, perhaps that will be an Aussie delicacy.

A DISHONOURABLE GUEST ARRIVES

If it didn't get lost in the translation, we were at the restaurant where Peking Duck was invented – I think.

Once they realised Charlotte had slightly misled me about the weather, as soon as lunch was finished, we were off to the indoor market, bustling with designer copies.

Instead of heading straight for the coats, they were sidetracked by a luggage stall. Much muttering between them and pushing of a massive 'smuggle your granny' type of suitcase up and down the aisle. I assured them I was quite happy with my hotchpotch and as a redeeming feature I did have two matching Harrods hand baggage. It was a very hard sell to get them to agree to disagree that my baggage was perfect for me.

Accompanying us was Nicholas, a family friend, who was at university in Beijing.

We proceeded to a handbag stall. Apparently they had noted my handbag. It is an Eagle travel bag (Paul gave it to me before India). It is small, compact and does the job and as I found to my cost before India it needs a minimum of four days' usage before arriving in chosen country, otherwise there is panic writ large on my face as I wonder in which of the fifteen zippered compartments the tickets, passport and money are located. I know I have them, I just don't know which compartment they live in. I'd had seven days' practice this time and I wasn't about to give it up easily. The bag being proffered was big and impressive-looking and in a country where honour is important it was beginning to look like this could be the most dishonourable guest to have ever graced Chinese shores. The awkward squad had arrived. I must have been a big disappointment to them.

We arrived at the coat stall. Various duvet types were being inspected. Now as you know this is not something I'm ever to be found dead in. I managed to steer them towards one I would be willing to wear – slightly fitted, mid-brown, almost ankle length, detailed cuffs, quite classic. One was found in my size. Glances were passed, much talk between them, then negotiations began on the price, which always consisted of us walking away and the first one to blink was the stallholder. Got for half original price. I later found out this was £40. Then I was told it wasn't suitable for the Great Wall. We started again, duvet coats at the ready. I had to choose a colour, knowing after the Great Wall I would never wear it again. And do you know I was right? I left it in Beijing for Grandma.

I was already overweight on the airlines, definitely couldn't take it. Now you know when I say I am overweight on the airlines, I do mean my luggage? Nothing else, you understand?

By this time, Nicholas was beginning to resemble a packhorse, but I could learn to live like this. Someone to pay for my shopping and then someone to carry it. Bliss.

On we moved relentlessly ... did I want sunglasses, sneakers (Reebok), a fleece, Chinese version of furry dice? The latter I acquired, but it took three turns of the market before the stallholder blinked on this one.

Then Chen, who by now had got the hang of the dishonourable English guest, stated with no argument, 'My daughter wishes to buy you silk jacket'. Since the daughter wasn't there I had to give in gracefully and chose royal blue.

Honour satisfied, we moved to the next stall. I, who could shop for England, had to avert my eyes and show no interest in anything.

Nicholas and I were ahead of the others and he asked, did I like cats? I gave my usual stock answer, that I prefer them to dogs. So he stated 'I get you cat'. I remember the feeling of panic as I tried to explain that I still had sixty-two days to go, I had nowhere to carry it, our quarantine rules were very strict, where would I keep it? Still he insisted. Perhaps he meant a toy cat. I saw fur sticking out from one of the stalls, but on approaching saw only dogs. I turned to him and he said he must buy my cat, what pattern did I want. 'They come in patterns?' 'Yes, cats have many patterns, choose one.' Oh yes I see, up there, a kite ... relief until I have to explain that it is too big to fit in one of my sad little cases. He is visibly disappointed.

As our visit to the market draws to a close I am curious about my 'new home'. Surprise then when Chen checks me into a four-star Oriental Hotel. I should have realised as their address is Room 909 etc. Of course, it's not just a room, it's a two-bedroom, two-bathroom apartment. They are well off by Chinese standards, two cats as well. In fact, probably well off by our standards, allowing they are living in a comfortable apartment in the main part of Beijing. In London it would be a very desirable property.

Thinking about it, this was exactly the size of the apartment in India and fourteen of us shared that some of the time.

The most amazing part was, Chen signed the credit card receipt for all my extras, gave me the vouchers for four days' breakfasts and a ticket for the Great Wall the next day, Friday. This is because Chinese hospitality demands that all their guest's needs are met by the host family. They do what they can, according to their financial circumstances.

After Charlotte arrived home from work we all went out for dinner, the usual Chinese banquet. Dozens of courses and you just whizz the table round. Much laughter, talk and bonhomie. Charlotte had only just started her new job on Monday and so couldn't take time off. This was her first job since her degree and although she wasn't enjoying it, it was a much-needed job. More news later.

Love,

Pat.

The Grand Old Duke of York

Beijing, China
10.03.03

Dear Clare and Michael,

For the Wall I had to be ready for 7.30. Due to jet lag this was easy, but I didn't arrive back to the hotel until 6.45. Exhausted was not the word. I'd to be out at 7.00 for another banquet.

Change of tack, this time it was a Korean restaurant. We were going to have one of those mini BBQs on the table (so popular in the Korean restaurants in London). This was changed about every five minutes, presumably to stop it smoking.

My hosts had ordered beef and pork. It came in thin strips about an inch wide. We all took whichever meat we wanted, put the seasonings on we liked, turned it over and ate it with various vegetables.

I'd noticed that they had dog meat on the menu, but whether because of my English sensibilities, or because they didn't eat it themselves, it wasn't ordered. I don't think I could have coped with that. But somehow I can manage to do it to 'Babe in the City'. It's enough to turn you vegetarian.

As I haven't seen you for a while you won't realize I have a gammy leg. Tore the ligament in my knee. It's a lot better after osteopath visits but I still have quite a limp. Hoppalong rides again!

So to the Great Wall. Now, as you probably realize, the Wall is not on the level, there's a great deal of the

Grand Old Duke of York about it, as it follows the mountain crests. Quite a good thing though, there is a little railway for getting to the Wall itself. Railway perhaps is a misnomer; it is a sled, plastic à la Asda, and just as brightly coloured. You sit on it at ground level; they fasten a shoulder restraint (like the Pepsi-Max) and off you go. That's fine, but coming down, I was told you slide down. The helter-skelter sprang to mind. This time the sleds were together and it reminded me of the Wild Mouse at Blackpool. On one side there was netting to catch you but unfortunately if you or the company of sleds left the track, there was more chance of concussion as every six feet at the back of the net were metal railings to hold the netting in place. Health and Safety would be on to it in England in a flash. I've just realized, Chinese people using it would be OK. Only Westerners are big enough to hit the railings, locals would just fall in happily to the net.

On the Wall there are always the eager ones who want to 'do it' from every angle. They go to the top, very impressive, quite dramatic, come back down a little and then ask someone (me) how to get to the other side much lower down as 'there are people on it'. For some reason it was an anxious American woman who asked me this. She must have thought I knew what I was doing. How she got that impression I've no idea.

My outfit did not inspire confidence in anyone as I was tightly rolled in slate grey quilting and resembled a pale duvet that had got into the dark wash by mistake. My limp was moderately pronounced by now. I think I was the only person without a rucksack, which must mean I wasn't a tourist. No camcorder, camera tucked well away. So I was giving away too many clues – she had to pick on me.

On the way back, in the middle of the road at a busy intersection, a man with a broom was busily sweeping away and the traffic, no matter what speed, was avoiding him. Do you think there is a part in their Highway Code and driving test which caters for this and they fail at their, and the workman's, peril?

On the Saturday I visited the Summer Palace with Charlotte, Nicholas and a friend, Mr Lu. After so long of calling him Mr Lu I asked could I dispense with the title, so he became just Lu. Within minutes of arriving at the Palace, I'd been decked out as a Chinese bride, had had a Polaroid taken and was on my way.

The canal, as we crossed the bridge, was frozen over. There were shops and cafés on either side. Its name is Suzhou Street and it was modelled on Suzhou, a city on the water in Southern China.

The Palace itself, as you can imagine, is stunningly beautiful, especially in the snow, which melted as we visited. By the time I reached the lake, I was wearing a short-sleeved jumper. I think the funny looks I got were because I was European, not because the Chinese were wrapped up like mummies and I looked like I was ready for a normal English summer.

A complex of buildings on Longevity Hill is intended to give you a feeling of strolling through a picture and the Marble Boat, also know as the Clear and Peaceful Boat, is made of massive stone slabs. There is also a Garden of Harmonious Pleasure. I'll say this for the Chinese, they certainly know how to carry a name.

We were there nearly all day and watched the lake thaw out in the sun.

A Bronze Ox was erected near the eastern dyke. It was cast so as to control floods. There is no record to say if it worked, but it must have been cheaper than the Thames Barrier.

At the hotel in Beijing there was very cheap reflexology (quite brutal compared with English type) and massage but the best has to be the hair wash – $7.50 wash and blow. For that, you get a full head massage, back and shoulders. Out of this world. They start by giving you a dry wash. They put the shampoo on top of your head, add just a tiny drop of water, then the massage starts. Rinsing is the usual way. Usually, it's boys who are the hairdressers but I shall keep my eye out in case girls are allowed.

By the way, the street sweepers are mainly women. Another thing I've noted is that on building sites and while farming, some men wear suit jackets. Whether these are second hand clothes and it doesn't matter, I haven't found out.

It's only when I was leaving the hotel for the airport and Chen and Yen started to laugh as the porter wheeled out my luggage on the trolley that I realised how ridiculous it looks. Ha, little cases, they must now realise they have a true English eccentric among them. We are a dying breed. As the recipient of such lavish hospitality I was relieved I'd taken a Royal Doulton tea set in old English country roses that they'd admired in England. I also bought them a nice piece of jade. Let's face it, we English aren't used to receiving so much for free.

In Chen's car there are now two golden bells, trimmed with red and green satin ribbon, bought at Barton Grange Garden Centre at Christmas, and he is the only person in Beijing with this version of 'furry dice'. It is quite a status symbol, that and the fact that he's just got a new top-of-the-range Audi. People still ride bicycles in Beijing but not too many.

Most drive foreign cars. If you can afford a car you don't want a Chinese one, so German and Japanese do very well. Could be an opening here for a British franchise. They liked my Rover 75 when they were in the UK.

On the Saturday night, Nicholas' parents were taking me to dinner. He was hoping to stay at Rose Cottage when he finishes his degree next year, and this was to clinch the deal. All that pack-animal stuff in the market was to impress me. Two other business acquaintances joined us so there were nine of us. They'd hired a private room at the restaurant and I think the presence of all these business tycoons was to make sure the deal proceeded smoothly. Nicholas was placed next to me. His English is very good despite giving me a patterned cat trauma. His parents own their own medical company; another friend had a string of restaurants. The other one was the one who was there to charm me, for all I know he probably owned half Beijing. I have found that some of my wit does translate quite well and gets laughs all round, but it took all my composure to keep a straight face when he said (and Charlotte's Dad translated), that I was very beautiful, I was just like a film star. Now I know they like Western looks because we are different and remember, I hadn't started taking the Chinese medicine, but I wonder if they meant a Bette Davis in old age? Anyway, I did the Clara Bow pose and fluttered my eyelashes, laughed and hoped we were all in on the joke.

Apparently for Nicholas to get in my house will be a coup for him. He doesn't want to live with Chinese students as they speak Chinese all day. He wants to improve his English. Poor love, Lancashire accent and all. So he's booked in for September 2004. I don't think he realised how easy it was to get into my house, but I do understand. His parents were anxious, just like all of us; they want to make sure their kids are OK, especially thousands of miles from home.

Despite the fact that I was being entertained and taken sightseeing all over, I couldn't wait to be on my own. It's just something about me. I prefer to choose when and how. The control freak coming out again.

Later

Well, now I am on my own. Just arrived in Xi'an and checked into a five-star hotel. Quite luxurious; only two days here though. I have just returned from inspecting the Terracotta Army, which was the whole reason for visiting China. Just as good as you'd imagine. You can get really close. The visit takes about two hours and there are no boring bits. I hired a private taxi to take me, and then a guide at the entrance. Much better than trouping round following a guy with a flag and being told when you can go to lunch. The guides, usually female, are specifically trained when they have finished university. They are fiercely proud of their country and regard it as an honour to show it to visitors.

I wanted to get some cherry tomatoes on the way back. I tried sign language, then I drew one, tried to explain the colour. In the end we resorted to modern ways and the driver rang up the switchboard on his mobile and she explained to him what I wanted. I'd already had one aborted attempt and found myself in a Chinese medicine market, but at least I got the market bit right.

Much later: 4.00am

Everyone is very friendly and the educated teenagers try out their English. I have been here a week now and thought I'd finished with jet lag but have just found I've slept twelve hours – 4pm to 4am. Well, I needed to diet. I can manage without one dinner. I think it's because I had to be out all over the place at various times in Beijing and have not relaxed naturally until I arrived here in Xi'an. I think it's time for those cherry tomatoes.

It's now 5am and peace reigns throughout the hotel. No one knocking at the door to make sure everything is all right. As it happens, when I arrived it wasn't and I had a room change. There was something suspicious lurking on my bathroom floor. I have since had a bouquet of flowers presented by the housekeeping delegation, the manager, her second-in-command and a tiny girl peering round the offending door of said room, followed half an hour later by a bowl of fruit and profuse apologies. In England, I'd be lucky if they acknowledged it, but this is the Chinese way. They do not like to be dishonoured. There are many times such as this when you realize you are still in a communist country, but in Beijing you would never know. It has such beautiful new buildings, and so few people ride bikes any more. Top-of-the-range Audi and VWs everywhere. Sensational would be the word for much of the architecture, even Prince Charles would approve. They look like they are almost ready for the 2008 Olympics. They could have taken 'Floodlighting your Buildings' as an Open University course and come out with a first with honours. The streets are so wide and it's as though you are in the middle of a vibrant, bustling Western city, but with better buildings. I have to be truthful – not much is old, but the Forbidden City, Summer Palace and the like have been well preserved. Someone who visited five years ago said none of the new buildings were there then. The whole city seems to have been rebuilt.

Just found out breakfast served 4.30am onwards, so I'm now replete. I was the only person in there, so they put on some music (orchestral sounds of 1960) and I was a teenager again and sitting in a Chinese restaurant. Quite nostalgic. Very peculiar. Almost surreal.

I have swapped my paperback copy of *Hotel du Lac* for half a dozen pieces of writing paper. I arrived with Chinese for hello and now can converse fluently so long as I'm 'not interested', I'm 'thanking them' and I'm 'full up'. My accent is quite good which makes them think I'm more aware of what is going on – maybe not a bad thing.

I've had another sleep – just an hour this time – now I know how all these people feel in BUPA Homes for the Elderly. It's still only 10am. I've just negotiated an extra two hours of room use to tie in with being picked up for the airport.

I've used the same taxi driver to bring me in, take me on tour and take me out to the airport. I find this inspires a fine loyalty and I get looked after like royalty. And I know he'll have enough to keep his family this next month. Also I judge the competence of the driving on the way in from the airport as not all taxi drivers are safe. Once he's passed this test, not charged me too much, I don't have to worry I'll be at serious risk of injury from his driving.

I went to the Hot Springs at Xi'an and it is a beautiful spot. The water is just nice and warm but not for bathing in (I'd taken my cozzie just in case). I took many photos because the trees were such a beautiful colour and the blossom trees were out. On closer inspection, I touched one of the mauve blossoms – artificial, wound round the branches, quite expertly; in fact the branch of the artificial greenery was the most realistic thing about it. So what do you know, the beautiful coloured leaves of the trees were not brought on by hot springs but by kind permission of the petrochemical industry. Blatant plastic. A taxi driver who was wandering around said he'd seen me arrive and as he talked to me said quite disgustedly, 'They're plastic', as though he couldn't believe they'd try it. From afar though it had the desired effect and I've got the pictures to prove it.

This hotel is a high-rise, very dramatic, massive and the rooms are gargantuan. Mine (basic) is big enough to house a small village out here, plus visiting relatives; in fact, they'd probably rent out space as well. I know when Chinese students come to the UK they are quite happy to share between two the box bedroom at each house. A normal large room they view as home to six people. My friend said when they rented one of hers, so many people were coming and going, the neighbours thought Hong Kong had declared UDI in it.

As I say you don't have to read all this, they are just my ramblings, due to jet lag, body over-usage and Heaven knows what else.

Just file it.

Love,

Pat

xxxxxxx

A Bit Like Lego

Guilin, China
12.03.03

Dear Sue (and Peter),

I've found out where the Chinese get their love of gambling. It starts very young, on the roads. The main road running through Beijing has children as young as seven, with satchels etc. blithely walking alongside the thundering traffic by the central reservation, bobbing about and waiting for a chance to cross, while they joke with each other. There are no pavements which makes me think the children shouldn't be there, as it is a dual carriageway.

I'm sending some of my letters to Clare as well, so the onus, I hope, doesn't seem too great. I don't expect you to plough through all the letters – you can be selective and decide when you have four hours to spare, to read one.

You should see me with chopsticks now. I can even reach across and help myself from the whirligig in the middle and still reach my mouth with it. I couldn't do that two nights ago. This is not as impolite as it sounds. Everyone else does it and I was only copying them, which is what my children used to say to me and they *still* got in trouble.

I realized how used to them I'd become when yesterday, at the airport café, they gave me knife and fork and the amount of rice festooned about my tablecloth gave testimony to the fact I was going native. I couldn't use the damn things. I'd more off the plate than on it.

That meal in itself was an eye-opener. The menu was in Chinese and English. I decided on green beans and dried radish (lovely) and honey pork. The pork arrived first, it didn't look the right colour, but hey, it's been honeyed. I picked up my first lot, tried it, there was a great deal of bone, bone I didn't recognize. I thought it can't be pig's snout, but it was something's snout. I started to reassemble the slices, a bit like Lego. I could see the bill. Perhaps because I was travelling I was a bit slow – but pork it wasn't. I'd pushed and prodded (are you reading this over breakfast? hope not) some bits were too soggy. Bloody hell! It's a duck bill, the soggy bit was the eye. Once I'd sized it up properly, I don't know how I missed it. So I'd got the duck's head, which has taught me never to trust Chinese translation. I just finished off the veg and left this beautiful delicacy on the plate. I think they got the honey bit right though and they made a very nice job of slicing it to fool me!

Charlotte had asked me 'Why not move to Beijing and teach English?' What, and forget how to use a knife and fork?

I've arrived in Guilin. It is just gorgeous. Before I left, someone wrote to say they were visiting Hong Kong and would like to spend just two days in China. The travel advice was go to Guilin – as it is how China is depicted on postcards. The beauty of it is, it is all natural. The reason I picked it was because I'd read all about the river and mountains and seen the photos.

This morning, I walked from my hotel along the lakeside into the town. I stopped at a restaurant in a side road on my way back and tried to make myself understood. A young schoolgirl (about fourteen) was passing and she started to speak English. I got out my map of Guilin and they all gathered round. Even an old lady from the back came out. Much consultation again and recommendations as to where I should go. The girl and I then walked back to my hotel together. Of course, they are very proud when you admire their city. This is the most relaxed I've been. It is just the right size, yet houses 4,600,000 people. Where, I wonder? I arrived last night and they told me I had a river view. It was dark, floodlit and beautiful. I am so pleased I have three days here.

So far this trip, I've not felt as exhilarated as I did in India. I think this is because until Guilin, China hasn't felt foreign. Also last time I hadn't booked anything; it was daring, risky and unplanned.

I've just boiled my kettle so I can wash the strawberries (40p) I bought this morning in a side street market. Got some cherry tomatoes (25p) too. The boiling of the kettle as soon as I reach my room has become second nature to me, to provide safe water. Perhaps the government can pay my pension here and I can move as soon as possible and have a comfortable and revered old age. Blow the knife and fork.

I am so glad I am not on a tour. The Great Wall finished me for that. Twelve sodding hours, half that time visiting emporia where, if you're not careful, they rip you off. I was told by my friends, 'only pay half the price'. We visited a Chinese medicine laboratory during the lecture, where the doctor was asking questions as he imparted knowledge. 'If you drink a lot of water and lose weight, what would be wrong with you?' and so on. After about three questions, he said, 'And what if you are yellow all over?' Now, being politically incorrect, I was just about to call out, 'You're Chinese', thinking he was joking and someone said – jaundice. I was quite pleased I'd kept my mouth shut. I feel if we British can laugh at ourselves, the rest of the world can reciprocate.

I volunteered to be checked (they put their fingers on your pulse). I was told I'd high blood pressure and a little raised cholesterol. I'm not surprised I'd high blood pressure, I'd just finished scaling the Chinese version of Everest, namely the Great Wall. I'd still got my gammy leg (not as bad though) and recently I'd been eating fried food (namely Chinese food) – so raised cholesterol. Even though it looked like a laboratory, it was in fact another shop, so I bought some medicine and if I look like Joan Collins when I come back, it's worked. If I look like Dawn French, Chinese food has worked.

This morning I got my new camcorder to work. This is no mean feat as I left the heavy instruction book at home, just photocopied three pages on re-charging the battery and how to start it. No one in my family wanted the job of showing me how it worked. I don't like having to read pages of instructions. I've managed to charge it, load it and start it, albeit in night mode to begin. Now it's OK and I've been out with it. I'm taking it on my river cruise tomorrow. I think it has something of the Blair Witch project about it – you know that unsteady handheld camera stuff.

Chinese babies, who are toddling, have their own little window on the world. They're wandering along and they see something they're interested in, bend down and their little pants part to reveal two plump half-cheeks. Charlotte says it's so they can pee easily and I'm too polite to ask about other arrangements. Winter and summer it's the same. It looks so cute.

I'm just going down now to book my river trip for tomorrow. It's negotiable and I want to go privately, but only at the right price. I think I'll have to do a bit of walking away to get that. Surprisingly, I didn't see any trips advertised downtown this morning. Usually they're all over the place. I think I'll dine by the river tonight. It's safe to stroll round afterwards so I'll camcord the floodlighting – I hope. I won't post these letters until I get to Hong Kong as I'm sure from here it will take weeks. I think, from what I gather, Hong Kong runs just the same as it did before.

I saw someone today on a bike with an umbrella. It has rained (very soft, and a bit Irish) on and off all day but you don't notice it. It says in the blurb that they get monsoon rains as well. Presumably when it's hotter.

Hope you receive this safely.

Love to you both.

Cox and Kings It's Not

Guilin, Guangxi, People's Republic Of China
13.03.03.

Dear Clare and Michael,

I can't believe I'm writing this, but I've just come back from dinner and to get Peking Duck ...

Well, let me start at the beginning. I decided at lunch I would dine with a view of the floodlit lake tonight. I asked my hotel and they got a cab to take me to a five-star hotel. When I reached the restaurant, the maitre d' decided they were full. You see, it was only for one. So I wandered back a bit and realised I knew where I was, (I was a bit chuffed here as it was dark and I'd only walked about two miles in total at lunch). I'd seen a restaurant then which had a large Father Christmas in the window saying 'Happy Christmas'. Now, this isn't as significant as it would be in England. They just think it's a nice sign with lots of red on it for good luck. If a restaurant were still displaying Christmas greetings in March in the UK there would be serious grounds for concern, if not alarm, but in China it did not put me off. I found it again and went in with the usual, 'Do you speak English?' Blank looks. Nervous laughter and I was passed on to the next person, but very quickly ushered upstairs. They had a live one. Still no English. They seemed very keen to entertain me so I followed them into a large private room. I pointed at myself and signed 'only one'. That was OK. Sat down. Curtains were drawn back and I was facing the lake and opposite the musical fountain and a gazebo. Boats were sailing by all lit up. Up till now, it had all gone quite well. Not only was I welcomed but they'd given me my own room away from the men who all were smoking. I had gone from the least wanted diner to the most highly prized diner within thirty minutes.

The menu came in Chinese characters. The only pictures were of a lobster and a whole suckling pig. I said vegetables – giggles. Duck, Peking Duck? 'No duck.' I mentioned chicken and one of them repeated it and seemed to like the idea. She went to the kitchen and came back with hieroglyphics on a pad. 'No chicken.' I said duck again; puzzled look. I said, 'You know, *duck*', and flapped my arms and quacked. They all fell about. I was entertaining them, not the other way round. Still no duck. Pork, oink oink, suckling pig, small piece. They were very happy and went away chirruping and giggling.

Half an hour went by. The door opened and shut now and again and the girls giggled and disappeared. Then a plate of pork ribs came in, closely followed by steamed kale (enough to feed a small town). Such smiling all round. I started by trying to avoid the fat. Halfway through, in came the Peking Duck. A massive tray of it on a bed of rice, with hand-carved carrots into orchids and the usual accompaniments for Peking Duck. The last time I had it there was some duck on it. This was just beautifully crisped skin; a lovely colour. I stabbed at the rice piled up over what I hoped was the rest of my duck. Just rice, but to prove it was genuine duck, the head was nicely glazed on the side. Four pieces was the most I could eat. Then they brought me in a plate of fresh fruit and the watermelon rind had been sculpted to form a waterfall over the fruit. I had a bottle of water and as Michael Winner would say, 'That set me back £7.' I left them a tip of about £1.60 and they were excitedly chattering and giggling about it as I left. I don't think – no, I'm sure, they'd never had a tourist in there before, but I'm sure they'll be looking out for them in the future – and I like to think I'm doing my bit for Anglo-Sino relations. I should also add that while this assault on my dignity was going on, I was wearing my royal blue silk Chinese jacket, with my lime green trousers – not exactly attired to fade into the background, even without the quacking. Old Macdonald had nothing on me.

I know I always scoff at people touring with Cox & Kings (or it could be Abercrombie & Kent or Hayes & Jarvis), but I'm willing to bet any on a tour round China they never had to quack to get their food. Then again, if my life proceeded normally, whatever would I write about?

As I've come back to my room on Friday night (breakfast to you), there's a message from Ms. Zhing ChanJun and a telephone number. She's the girl who tried to help at the lunchtime restaurant. She liked meeting me and talking in English, and would I be her friend? Does she know her friend does duck impressions? I've just rung the number and eventually someone answered. I asked for her, best accent, there was a silence. I tried a few times, different accent each time. One or two noises were made on the other end. Eventually, they put the phone down. They'll be able to dine out on that in Guilin and the story of the funny foreign phone call.

I've just brought back a brochure on Guilin Li River Folk Custom Centre. A beautiful pagoda and a girl in colourful regional dress graces the front. The blurb is in Chinese but the few items I have understood make interesting reading. 14.50 – cock fighting; 15.30 – horse fighting, dog racing; 15.50 sword-ladder climbing, fire purgatory; 21.20 – cock fighting in the Folk Theatre. I think the rest of the folklore is fairly innocuous stuff, but how can I be sure? Their 'innocuous' could bring about palpitations and hot sweats in the rest of us, including the men. It makes Morris Dancing seem a job for fellows with beards and flowers on their hats.

While I was on my wanderings yesterday, I went into the impressively large (three floors), Guilin Department Store. As I was leaving, a young lad in his best suit tried to drag me over to his stand. He wanted to clean my shoes. He was going to have to be a very good salesman. These shoes, which have climbed mountains, paddled in the sea and are incredibly comfortable, started life as a very smart pale green suede and when events happened to them and they looked scruffy, I polished them and now they are two shades of green leather. He had three cohorts all smiling and eager, so I put my foot on the pouffe offered, and, giggling, they brushed the seat and mimed sitting down. He did the least disastrous-looking one first (he had been well trained) and asked me to compare. I think that's what he wanted but he could have been telling the others that nothing was going to work on the other one. Since I am a sucker for youth and eagerness, I paid just over £1 for my 'pure leather cosmetic clean'. One of the chambermaid's tips is going to be in kind.

The trip today down the river was very beautiful but that doesn't seem to say enough – evocative, stunning, touristy, misty, ethereal, unique. I'm quite sure there's nowhere in the world which has this mountain shape. China only has it in this region. I was using my camcorder (Oh! How Roy would be proud of me. He used to say, 'Keep her away from anything technical') on the river and couldn't understand why I could only get either the river or the mountains, but not both. I wondered where the zoom lens was. I looked all over and pressed many buttons. Even if I'd brought my photocopied instructions (which I hadn't), they didn't cover zooming. I asked the Taiwanese guy sitting opposite and he showed me where it was and you've guessed, I was half on zoom. How can that be? You would expect to press zoom and when you stop pressing, it unzooms. The switch said M or L. That doesn't say zoom. So then I could get river, mountains, cormorant fishermen all at once. Well, I think I got them because a light started flashing and the Taiwanese man said when asked (it had been going a bit by then), that my battery had run out, so I don't know how much I got, or whether I got any. Thank goodness for my panoramic camera. The old ways are the best. Well, they are if you manage to load your film correctly in the first place. I really need an idiot-proof camera, but you know what they say: 'Make it idiot-proof and someone makes a better idiot' – which could be me.

The Taiwanese man was with a woman and friends. Whether something had happened or this was usual, his girlfriend, opposite me, looked like she was just about to mutiny. No matter what he or the others said to her, her expression remained one of bored disinterest.

She pointedly ignored him, first plucking her eyebrows, then she Q-tipped her ears, sorted her nails and looked bored to the point of rebellion.

He didn't seem particularly fazed. Perhaps he was used to it.

Then she used her mobile. Good grief, the woman became almost animated – but not quite. She sort of flickered. Call over, the stony expression returned and that continued the rest of the trip.

I wonder what he'd done.

As I've said before, I think I'll move here because I want to be revered in old age. It's either here or India and unless it's the Himalayas, India's too hot.

There were water buffalo along the riverbank, little villages, and cormorant fishermen. They train the birds to fish for them and then give them back some of the catch. Generations of cormorants have been doing this without twigging they're being taken for mugs. The young cormorants are raised by chickens while their parents are out 'working'. And I used to feel sorry for birds raising cuckoo chicks. Have you seen the size of the cormorants? The fishermen put a chain round the cormorants' necks so they can't swallow the fish. The fishing is done at night with a lantern hanging from the boat, which gives it a romantic look.

It's about a three and a half-hour cruise and the usual Chinese food, you know, more than you can ever eat. I had chosen to go privately to and from the boat to give me a chance to stay as long as I wanted at Yang Shuo. This is a Western/Eastern town where I was told 'everyone speaks English'. I don't know where they got that from as I had as much trouble there as anywhere. There are French restaurants, English tearooms and Italian spaghetti houses, all manned by Chinese people. A bit incongruous really. The part of town devoted to this was quite quaint if a little obvious. One thing I noticed as we motored up the river – one cruise ship following another – that those boats on the way back were getting ready for the evening cruises. Someone sat at the back (I never got round to learning the names. I think it's the stern, but don't ask me about port and starboard), peeling vegetables and on the ones which really had their act together, the tablecloths had already been washed and were hanging over the rails, drying. (People are brought back by bus.)

In Yang Shuo I went in the Blue Bird Café and ordered a café latte. I should explain that the Blue Bird Café's *raison d'être* is to serve every coffee you can think of that the modern traveller requires. After coffee, food is well down its list, but asking for the latte threw this girl. There was only me at their pavement café and after about twenty minutes, I found her again and she said the coffee was coming. It looked OK when it came but latte it wasn't. Cappuccino in a glass – probably; undrinkable definitely. Then I asked for the tourist bus station. I'd been warned not to go to the local one, so I went in CITS (China International Travel Service) – they sold me a map – I found the tourist bus area on the map but they insisted it wasn't the right one and there was only one bus station, sending a young girl to show me the way. When I got there I'd to look for my driver's number plate. One or two drivers called out to me and I couldn't remember what mine looked like and of course they were all touting for business. Eventually when I showed one driver the number I was looking for he pointed way over – I presumed he meant the tourist station, so I went in the Information centre and they said I was ten minutes away so I got a taxi to get my taxi. Why is life so complicated? From now on, I'll trust my instincts. After all, I am the traveller and they're sitting in an office in a backwater in China, what do they know?

I've just remembered something I read. 'If evolution works, how come a woman only has two hands?'

I've seen my first Chinese dog and despite the fact that they should be Pekinese, they look remarkably like Indian dogs, which makes me think that their ancestors, like Pavlov's dogs, must have had a bike.

Guilin has so much water in it and round it, it makes Venice look rather arid. There are many paddy fields, the soil is red clay, but they seem to make a great job of the vegetables. On the way back, I saw a few things which raise comment. One was a hen, sitting on a massive pile of gravel, as though incubating it. Perhaps this has a similar advantage to the cormorant fisherman but I haven't figured it out yet. Could warm gravel go farther? A motorcyclist with his pannier and on top three Canada geese, looking remarkably unconcerned as though they were enjoying the day out, on the side two other geese hung limply upside down, on the farther side two more live geese watching the world go by. Not a care in the world. They are probably distant relatives of those other colossal brains of the bird world – the cormorant.

Another insight into Chinese life – Chen (Beijing host), answered when I asked why a new government and said they'd brought in younger men. The next day the *China Post* (English language paper), showed resumées of the most prominent ones; there was only one woman, but without exception, all were older than me. One was born in 1904. I presume the previous government had everybody born in the nineteenth century. You see what I mean about being revered in old age in China? No Bambi Blair here. He'd still be licking stamps in China.

Great gnarled pieces of tree or tree trunks are prized in China. They make carvings but often just polish them and the more intricate and delicate the arrangement, the more desirable.

Later

Well I've now worked out why I was the only one in the Western dining room at my hotel two nights ago and again tonight. Thought I'd grab something quick so I could get off into the night with my newly-charged camcorder. I had the Chinese version of mushroom soup and chose braised beef with raisins in red wine with mashed potatoes. The mash was lovely, broccoli fine, raisins luscious, the beef I couldn't cut with my knife. I didn't want to choose something else, so I think I left the chef dishonoured and ready to slit his wrists. On the first night, the chicken was tough but I hadn't the heart to tell him and thought it was a one-off.

I headed into town, as I should have done all along. It was Friday night and the place was buzzing. The Chinese love illuminations. They are everywhere – looks like Times Square, New York. Shops all open until at least 10pm. Cute baby trousers (probably with a window on the world) were only 50p. After I'd walked a bit, camcorded and weighed up the situation, I chose a restaurant near McDonalds. Everyone was sitting on the second floor and it looked a happening place. I found the only stairs and entered. Yep, the most happening place in town, unfortunately the average age was twenty-three. I think I was the only

Westerner in town. I certainly didn't see any others, so I was a bit of a curiosity – again. Many of them said hello in English and then giggled. Like everyone they like to show what they can do. The maitre d' spoke excellent English and when he had shown me to my table, gave me a card and told me to go round with it and choose what I wanted, pay when I leave. I'd died and gone to heaven. I was going to see the food, be able to point and make sure I got what I wanted. No quacking involved. First thing I saw was duck. I looked all round the plate to check for unsuspecting appendages, but it seemed like leg and a bit extra. I chose two small dishes of veg and a fresh strawberry drink. I had a view of the town, the lakes, the neon lights. The atmosphere was great, but when I'd finished with my chopsticks, I was rather greasy. I haven't worked out how to take the skin off the duck with them yet. Perhaps I never will. I arrived at the cashier and asked for a napkin. Maitre d' promptly said two yuan and put it on my card. I didn't like the feel of this. He'll probably charge me for their having to wash my dishes next. Then the cashier said 23 yuan. That's less than £2.30. Suddenly, I didn't mind the napkin, life was rosy again and every table I passed said goodbye.

Halfway along the main drag, a voice said hello. I was just a bit wary as I don't know if Friday night has any significance for women walking alone. He was only young and very confident. His accent was great and he wanted to practise. I think I needed it more than he did. We chatted all the way along the road. He was very good-looking, personable and fifteen and he wanted to be a tour guide. His after-school English coach is a tour guide and said you make lots of money – so how come he's teaching

English for extra money? I told the boy to be a lawyer or work in finance, but his loyalty to his tutor was total. Can't win 'em all.

They have had a really good idea in China; at major traffic lights, high in the road, is a green signal. It is the number of seconds left before the lights change, so if you're far away, you'll know it's no good putting your foot down. Must help road safety, although in China, I realised jaywalking is compulsory so I was in my element. It's just as well I don't walk very far in the USA as I would soon be arrested.

I walked along two lakes recording, needless to say, the only person doing so and never once felt I was in danger of being relieved of my camcorder. I was also out in a short-sleeved shirt and felt just right. I could never travel in a group. Just think of all the experiences they miss in their sanitized hotels. It's feeling that you don't know what's going to happen next that makes life so interesting. No matter how fraught, it's all worth it and until things start to go wrong, it's fairly predictable and just another holiday.

Here in Guilin the only other Westerners I have seen have been on the boat trip and in the hotels. Certainly none downtown or in the side streets. As I wandered down the back streets, I could hear a saxophone being practised. It was playing 'Tinker, Tailor, Beggar man, Thief'. Seemed a bit weird but it was quite haunting. Nursery rhymes must travel well.

I visited privately (i.e. I got my own taxi), the Reed Flute Caves. I was dropped in the car park as the heavens opened. I had my newly-bought umbrella and I had to run the gauntlet of stalls on both sides and eventually went through the turnstile. I think it's to keep the sellers out. Further in, there are more sellers, this time it's the big boys, tree carvings and so on. I should think they'd paid serious money to be beyond the turnstile.

I missed the entrance, back-tracked and the rain had stopped. Signs of the old regime here in the way the crowds were 'controlled'. Forty people each time, then the tour starts. Can I go in by myself? No, you need a guide as she switches on the lights. Twenty minutes later and we were off. She had a loudhailer and I began to worry. I don't like being herded and the shepherds I'd come across only ever had a crook, loudhailers weren't allowed.

I have now found out how they get that voice on British Rail stations. They hire an English-speaking Chinese person and give them a loudhailer.

The lights she had to switch on were coloured and a red one came on and shone over a certain stalagmite and a yellow on another. Trouble was, there were about a dozen such groups and by the time we hit the big one (Mother of all Caverns), there was a fair ding-dong going on to be heard. Coupled with Communist – sorry, socialist jokes, it was deadly. The caverns themselves were beautiful – big, loads of water, 'tites and 'mites to gladden the heart. I love caverns, but it has to be subtle. I could have spent a day there. As it was, I left my group and joined the next loud hailer round the back of them.

Don't slip on those stones, am I meant to be walking on these? and I was up to the next group.

I finally joined four groups ahead of my own, but I could hear her coming. It was like the advance of the Daleks. That's it, that's what they were – Daleks. I raced out into the fresh air just before Dr Who needed to rescue me. If anyone missed me, I never heard and they let me leave the country that night.

On reaching daylight, a monsoon rain had just started. I put up my pinky-mauve umbrella and set off on the trek back and reached my 'private taxi' with hair and shoes totally soaked. Eventually, my brolly just gave up and let it all through and do you know what? Those sellers were still after me.

I have a method I have developed – an enigmatic smile in the manner of the Mona Lisa. It's there, just playing around my lips and I understand no language spoken to me – I never make eye contact, but hope I'm walking along in a non-aggressive but positive way. I work on the premise that if all else fails and it gets too much, I can always say 'bog off' viciously enough and everyone will understand from Kathmandu to Bali. Let's face it, if Mona Lisa said it to you, you would be shocked as well.

You will not be surprised to hear, I'm just developing repetitive strain injury. I can feel it affecting my wrist. Does American Express cover me for this? I think I should really be attending a hypochondriac's convention, not world travelling.

One of the downsides of being permanently overweight on the airlines is the constant worry that anything other than adding to my already overflowing wardrobe will send it into the danger zone for excess charges.

On my last morning wandering in Guilin, the rain, as I said, was steady. Other than enjoying the atmosphere, being among the locals conducting their business, there was a nagging thought as I walked.

All I could think about as my shoes became waterlogged and my heavy linen trousers began to soak up the rain nicely was what bad luck for this to happen when I was leaving that afternoon and had no chance to dry them.

In the market on the back streets of Guilin they had live fish, quite big ones, in plastic basins full of water. The vegetables were beautifully set out. I would love to have bought some but as I was leaving in two hours, the last thing I needed was to be even more overweight with a load of sodding vegetables.

How mundane could I get? But these are the thoughts that consume you as the departure time gets nearer. Until you've checked in your bags, tension reigns.

And so as the China Airlines clerk duly charged me £10 for excess baggage – the only time I paid it – I blamed it on the shoes. Water weighs heavy you know.

I don't know if you remember that saying about fathers wanting to move next door to the man who made traffic cones so their daughter could marry his son; well, it's changed. It now has to be the man who makes speed camera signs. They are all over China and they are exactly the same as ours. The same firm is making them! Go to Companies House and find out who the MD is and move quickly. His son may be a suitable match for one of your girls. He may like budding punks. This is your chance – don't miss it. This must be the best financial tip you will get all year. In the meantime, hope the invention is going OK Michael.

Love,

Pat.

Mountaineering in Hong Kong

16.03.03

Dear everybody,

Well to Hong Kong. It was as eventful there as everywhere. Hotel in Kowloon, free bus to the ferry for Hong Kong Island hourly so if you missed that you could take a bus for three HK$ for non-air-conditioned. Four dollars for air conditioned. I didn't bother as I was more than a little worried I'd get on the wrong one and the fact that I was saving a dollar would have been of little consolation. Hong Kong *was* steamy —only twenty-four degrees (unusually high for this time of year). Now where have I heard that before? but in a city that can be claustrophobic. Roy never told me how steep it is. He used to visit it regularly when on the Ark Royal. On Hong Kong Island it's mountainous and we're only talking small island there.

As I said it was steamy, but I persisted and on my first day I walked from the ferry in the general direction of the Man Mo Buddhist Temple. I had a map, but a map does not show hills or severe inclines. I think anywhere else they'd class this as mountaineering but not in Hong Kong. I met this American couple, who looked like back-packers but turned out to be locals. Been there nine years and once they'd completed the paperwork, they would be citizens. I was asking directions and they seemed surprised I'd walked from the ferry. I was OK with the directions, till he said, 'You'll see these steps at the top ...'. I stopped him there and said there'd be no steps, dehydration was almost setting in. I'd seen an escalator going up in the middle of the street (how quaint) and asked could I use that. Sure, he said, so I ascended. There are warning signs about holding on due to steep incline. I tell you, anyone with a larger rear end than their front end is in serious danger, gravity being what it is, of bowling over backwards and scattering all behind them as skittles. Anyway, I went off at an alarming angle and hung on for grim life and finally found the Temple. Not at all like I'd imagined. I didn't feel at peace like you normally do in similar places. I was conducted round by a very eager young girl; there was a poster saying 'the young volunteer scheme' in place. I bought my incense sticks and tried to light them – you see, it's not just technical things, it can be anything. This young man helped me because by this time I was covered in a yellow pollen-like substance from the sticks. He asked if I was Buddhist. I said Catholic. He said he was nearly trained to be a Buddhist but would like to be a Catholic as well. He doesn't seem quite to have got the hang of this religion thing unless he's so far in advance of us all, he's a philosopher advocating a joining of all religious faiths for the greater good. I may have met a genius or he could just have been a very confused young man. Oh yes, and I saw those steps. They rose almost vertical like a pair of ladders in the racks (pre-purchase) at B&Q. They made the ascent to Montmartre look like a trip to the lowlands of Holland. No wonder they'd an escalator.

All over the streets that day (it was Sunday), there were hundreds of women and young girls. The noise was deafening, they were sitting down at the ferry stop and the bus station, all the side streets and the parks. They sat on newspapers or tablecloths and were having picnics, playing cards, painting each other's nails, doing hair, sleeping. They seemed to be in groups of four or five. I found out later these are all the maids, mainly Filipino, in Hong Kong and Sunday is their day off. They seemed to take over downtown.

I stopped in one grassy square. I sat down next to a woman and we started to chat. She said she was a Filipino and when July comes, she is going home and then she'll go to Hawaii. The reason being because the government is now taxing them, so it's not worth working for what money they get. I then found out that the government has taxed the families who have maids and these people have taken it out of the maid's wages, which is not how it was meant to work. Their employers have told the maids it's the government's fault. Someone in the ex-pat community filled me in on this.

The second day saw my taking a trip across the harbour to Aberdeen fishing village, where all the people live on their boats. I believe the boats are typhoon-proof although no one told me here, or is it the harbour that is typhoon-proof? Is it typhoon-proofed in the same way Sheffield is a nuclear-free zone? (If the bomb ever drops will it bear this in mind?) Therefore does the typhoon know?

At the harbour, there is every designer shop you've ever heard of. The genuine article. How can they make a living when Hong Kong is the biggest rip-off of designer goods? You can buy copy Louis Vuitton bags for £10.

I took a tour the third day as I was leaving Hong Kong soon but true to form I said I'd make my own way back. This was a good idea as I met an American woman, whose husband had just arrived to join his firm. We hit it off, buying clothes, so we went to lunch together. Before we parted she warned me if I started to cough or run a temperature, to consult a doctor immediately as there was a nasty bug about. The ex-pat community was just beginning to get alarmed. I said I'd heard about it via the BBC World News and I'd take care.

On the way round on the tour the driver pointed out a yellow net at the beaches. This was a shark net as they'd lost a few swimmers last year to sharks. The bit that got me though was a boat bobbing up and down just outside the netting with a makeshift sign saying, 'Water Skiing Tuition'. Could this be the Hong Kong version of meals on wheels?

The pool on the roof of the Hong Kong Hotel had a sign saying 'closed because of winter'. I don't know how hot it needed to be to open the thing, but in England twenty-four degrees is usually as hot as it gets.

You know how addicted I'd become to hair wash with automatic head massage. I went to quite a chic salon two doors down from my hotel. One of the boys was very with it. Designer glasses (or copies), great clothes. There seemed to be a debate after the wash as to which boy would do it and I'm quite sure the 'with it' boy said, 'I'm not doing it, I'll kill it.' My hair is not my crowning glory, but this was only two days since the quacking episode and I was still fragile.

Keys here are electronic and on returning to my room the bathroom light wasn't working. I rang housekeeping and they did it while I was at dinner. But as soon as I entered and put my electronic tag in the electric slot, the bathroom light went off again. Rang housekeeping again and this giant gnome arrived. All smiles, aged about thirty-five to forty. He explained to me that I'd put the card in upside down – one way for the lock, another for the slot. As he was telling me all this, he kept putting his hand on my backside, patting it and stroking it. Now we British, as you know, are very polite and like to give people the benefit of the doubt (except Saddam Hussein) and as he waltzed further into my room and went through everything electrical, he touched my arm, back and rear again. I was ushering him towards the door and dodging his hands as much as I could. I looked like I was doing the Paso Doble. I got him out of the door and like a good old Brit I was still smiling and being polite instead of telling him to bog off.

I mulled it over that night and finally, I became indignant. How dare the little squirt do that? It wasn't his just being friendly; he was a little pervert, albeit a Hong Kong pervert. I went to the assistant manager's desk the next morning. I'd tried to explain at reception but they had just smiled and said, 'You want housekeeping?' I explained to a charming man, Peter Chu, (Assistant Manager), that housekeeping was not to go into my room again until I'd gone at 11am the next day. I told him why. Apologies of course. The thought of that guy near my knickers turned me queasy and his final shot on leaving my room was, 'You go to sleep now?' I assured him I would and jammed a chair underneath the handle of my door. Sweet dreams!

Also, offered in the hotel brochure, Goran would visit you in your bedroom and give you a massage. The only Goran I know of is a big guy who plays tennis and is definitely male. After the housekeeping octopus, I didn't dare risk someone who was being *paid* to put his hands all over me.

I don't know if you've heard about the virus that the WHO has given a warning about. It appears to be travelling via the airlines. It started in, that's right, Hong Kong, then Singapore and guess where I was about to fly into? Many of the local people arrived at the airport sporting face-masks and kept them on all through the flight. I have to admit, I tried to buy one but everyone thought I wanted a facemask (the sort that goes stiff and makes you look ten years younger). They presumed I was one of those Westerners who was always having facelifts and liposuction. After two attempts with the same result, I gave up. It's a form of pneumonia, which is highly contagious and with a high mortality rate. The official name is SARS.

Another useless little fact I learned is that in China, the ratio of male to female is 40:1 and in Hong Kong it is 1:14. So the guys in China come a-looking over the border.

As I was leaving the hotel in Hong Kong, dragging my usual hand luggage, I thought someone had kicked me in the calf as I collapsed. I was like a footballer (or a hundred metre runner when they realise they're beaten), pulling up. It was due to carrying all the linen trousers and jackets back from the other side of Hong Kong the day before and my camcorder (which this time, had run out of film). As chance would have it, a nice couple from Gloucester were there and they helped me. We were together for five hours as they were on the same flight to Singapore. They were the first people I felt I gelled with this holiday. They saw me on to my flight to Bali waving me off like a long-lost relative. We've exchanged addresses and we will have to see what happens. So, at Singapore due to increased security, I'm going through hand baggage check and have to unload my hairdryer, snorkel and mask. It's taken off to be X-rayed again and I'm given the all clear.

As I drag my leg, two Harrods bags, handbag and camcorder round to the departure gate, I pass a woman, all chic French 'casual', and I grimaced a bit at her and do you know what the French *vache* said to me in her Sacha Distel accent? 'You 'ave too much.' Talk about stating the bleeding obvious, but not only had she a husband running round after her, she probably hadn't gone from zero degrees to thirty-eight degrees. It's too much to ask, but I hope on reaching her destination she has no air conditioning.

As I looked around, I realised I was the only person catching this flight who was not dressed as a hippie backpacker (excluding the Frenchwoman). Most seem to be travelling alone and the middle-aged guys in either shorts or linen pants and a two-colour neckerchief twisted round. The latter seems to be *de rigueur*.

When I checked in at Hong Kong where there seemed to be no air conditioning, the Qantas clerk declared me overweight. Who – me? Let me weigh your hand baggage. Horror of horrors, everything that weighed over two ounces I had put in there. Nobody had ever suggested that before. I was also carrying a bag with my Beijing coat in it. I threatened to put it on – even though the air conditioning was making a bad job of it. I insisted one Harrods bag was my handbag, so she weighed the other and declared, quite satisfied, that was too heavy. I tried to look surprised, but my acting skills are dodgy without air conditioning. She said some had to be removed. To where? Oh yes, my handbag and then Jean and Arthur (the Gloucester pair), appeared and it was all OK so long as he carried it. The fact that it weighed over the prescribed allowance for overhead lockers due to the fact that it could concuss someone seemed not to matter.

I'm not at my best at airports. For someone who likes travelling as much as I do, this could be a small problem. I think it's to do with the air-conditioning – when it's working. It's like visiting Toys-R-Us. I feel distinctly off in there and can't make decisions – or perhaps TRU is simply as big as an airport and is exhausting. So in airports and TRU I find difficulty with my thought processes and that leaves me vulnerable. Not an adjective people who know me would easily associate with me.

As I looked round as we boarded for Bali, the only things missing from the middle-aged hippies were worry beads and surfboards.

Singapore to Bali was almost empty but I noticed for our meal, we got a proper knife and fork. This may not seem strange to you but on the Hong Kong to Singapore flight we were given plastic 'in line with airline guidelines for security'. How come all the respectable middle-England and Australian good folks were not trusted with metal yet all the dropouts of the known world are deemed fit to wield metal as they enter Bali?

As I filled in the Indonesian entry form, I had to declare my Chinese medicines. They came alongside firearms, explosives, drugs, weapons, laser guns, Chinese printing and pornography. It had four stars, which meant forbidden. Oh yes, and cordless telephones. I had to go through the Goods to Declare

Channel. I've never done that before. I was the only person there. I thought the guy might make a meal of it but I'd put on my form they were tablets and not raw medicines and I think he wondered why I was wasting his time. No eye of newt – then you're in.

Getting into Bali was slow due to all the checks. Immigration seemed to be taking everything into account but I don't think middle-aged grannies were top of their terrorist classes.

As it would be a long flight, I decided to wear Dr Scholls flight socks. The fact that I had lime green mules and they were sexy black was not deemed important as I could be travelling with a DVT in my calf, but we won't think too closely about that. As I put them on, Arthur laughed and I realised I'd more in common with Britney Spears than I thought. I only needed the figure, the pout and the bunches. He thought more St Trinians. How nice of him! This is where I think I lost my street cred, with the surfers and the French *vache*. I could have got away with it but for the lime green mules.

Tai Chi with Blossoms

Bali
Wed – 19.03.03

Dear Clare and Michael,

When I arrived last night around 10.30, I just flopped into bed. The hotel guide said before 8am is the best time in Bali before it gets hot, so I reached breakfast by 7.30. You should have seen the number of people about. Tai Chi here; lengths of the pool there, beach jogging; power walking; insane buggers! I was surprised no one was coming along shadow-boxing.

The air here is like velvet at night, and during the day there is a little breeze at the beach and so long as you don't overdo it, it's lovely.

I've now had a poke around town (or a stretch of road as it appears to be here). I went in the shop where the lady doesn't bother you. It's much easier. This being Bali, pestering shoppers is a national pastime. If it were an Olympic event Thais and Balinese would be the only ones in the medals. Just been for another massage. I could get addicted to this.

The grease appearing on this page heralds dinner as I've just put my Avon Skin-so-soft spray on as an efficient insect repellent. I tried the garden pool today but as it's 1.65 meters I was too scared to go in, and that's from someone who's just booked to go white water rafting again.

I went for snorkelling lessons before I left home.

Well, it's been the snorkel, mask and hairdryer in my hand luggage that's set alarm bells ringing. I could have hired out here but I didn't fancy using one everyone else had been using.

It's funny here – 14,000 rupiah to the pound. You think you are parting with a fortune and it's hardly anything. The figures are soon up in the hundreds of thousands. The Balinese are pleased to see people. It's quieter than normal which makes it pleasanter for us visitors. After another day sunbathing, I can take it here better than Wales.

As I said, I'm going white water rafting. I'm going in the afternoon because it's not as fashionable and therefore cheaper. If all goes well this time, I intend to go again at the extreme sports centre in New Zealand where bungee jumping started, but I won't be doing that, I might dice with death over rapids, but if I want to dislocate any area of my body, I know many ways that are free, without having to pay for it.

This is what happens to people who don't speak fluent Balinese. They end up writing on reconstituted toilet paper. I hadn't my glasses with me and there was no sign of writing paper; either the Balinese are not big writers or there is a special shop I've not found and I'm not likely to find. I asked the assistants at the supermarket (no air conditioning, hotter than outside and I was wilting). This apparently was the cheapest but it said Kertas CD Bulky Folio, Khusus Stensil Kwalitet Terjamin, which roughly translates to four hundred sheets of the worst quality computer paper, not suitable for writing on. I've already asked for extra sheets of paper at the hotel but I wanted to be independent. So now I am. I even have emergency loo paper which is probably just as well, as public loos don't provide it and the skill of managing without it (as advocated in a guide book I have read) is not something I intend to master. In another week I'll be able to walk into a shop, as a Pom, and ask for writing paper and presume they'll understand me.

Now, you may think I'm daft and you wouldn't be the first, but the sun here on the equator doesn't seem as hot as Wales. There are two reasons for this statement; first, here I can stay out in it and not burn and secondly, in Wales, I have to shelter from the rays and only do my legs. Can't stand my face getting full sun. Strange or what?

I have a cottage in the most luscious gardens right by the sea with Hindu shrines throughout. I can hear the surf crashing in. Last night was a full moon and I sat at the beach restaurant (echoes of Shirley Valentine), with the surf, and the moon overhead shining across the water – cicadas were making their usual noise but a real racket was being kicked up by something else. I was informed by the receptionist that it was geckos. Now, I like geckos ever since my head-on meeting in my room in Goa, but noisy mine never was. Fast, or immobile, and very loyal, but noisy, never.

Despite being almost on the Equator the humidity here is not as bad as the North East Coast of USA (or Eastern Europe last June). For the most part it's bearable, but you wouldn't want to train for a marathon, not unless you were carrying five litres of water and were a bit of a sadist. I am rather pleased. If I pace myself and don't walk too fast, I can go shopping. The only thing I don't have to do is buy anything as the act of carrying anything weighing more than two ounces brings beads of perspiration to the brow. On my first venture out by the time I'd walked a hundred and fifty yards, been in two dress shops, called at a cash machine and bought apple juice (two litres), I had to have a cab back to the hotel. I looked like a turkey cock.

I've seen my first cat since leaving home. It's ginger and white and has a two-inch tail which just sticks out and because it has legs as long as Naomi Campbell, its arse is stuck right up in the air. I've not stroked it as it looks like it has an attitude a bit like hers.

As I said there were all these middle-aged women about doing Tai Chi with blossoms behind their ears at 7.30 am. I felt I was among a load of poseurs at the best, but since then, everything's seemed normal. I met a Danish woman, Susan, and she said, 'Where's your blossom?' and promptly shoved one behind my ear. It didn't stay long. I felt a bit of a wussie. The blossoms fall all day and staff are constantly sweeping them and the leaves off the grass. The grounds contain a garden pool and a large pool, on the beach, with the obligatory sunken bar. So while swimming and sunbathing, I can stare out at the coral reef or come inland and just contemplate my navel in a peaceful Hindu setting. The grounds are spectacular and very beautiful – there is a library in the centre and an art gallery, open on all sides of course.

Masseuses are at the beach end of the gardens but the downside is, but for a flimsy raffia curtain, everyone can see you. I notice the security guard seems to think he should walk round the back at an appropriate moment. Even I told him to get lost. But perhaps even more disconcerting is that there are three beds and you may find yourself next to a man in the nude. Now, I don't mind seeing his, but he's not seeing mine. With that in mind, I've found a salon across from the hotel and no blighter gets to see your bits and pieces – and it's cheaper. Like dying and going to heaven isn't it?

According to the Lonely Planet Guide, lone women have to watch their step for beach gigolos. They say it is best to invent a husband who is arriving later. I don't think Roy would mind, after all it's in a good cause.

While I'm away Andy's in charge at my house. Heaven help me. He's on ant patrol. He's been told where they come in, where the spray is and what will happen to him of they take over.

You know, in an English hotel, (you must remember before you had children), how if it says breakfast is till 10am and if you arrive at 9.59am you get as long as you want till you've finished? Well, in China and Hong Kong, when they say ten o'clock, they mean ten o'clock. The lot gets moved and very quickly. I came down at 9.50 one day and ended up looking like Everest was before me. I'd fresh fruit, toast, preserves, egg, bacon, and tomatoes. When it's all together like that, it just makes you seem greedy and we all know I'm not, well, not really.

Saying that, I'm off for my dinner now so we'll have to see how the alcoholic drink the waiter serves me (free) affects me.

Later ...

It's now 9.30 and I have to admit the only thing missing is someone to take an after-dinner stroll with. Although the gardens are lovely and lit, it is still a bit funny to be walking round them and along the beach on my own. It is quite safe to walk on the beach here at night, the mugging goes on in the daytime by all the sellers out to make as much money as possible. I don't think it's changed since before the bomb, but now I feel slightly ripped off and think, since the tourists that are here are going against government advice and have had to sign disclaimers and inform their insurance company, the least they can do is give us a break. I say this as one who was ripped off by the hotel masseuse to the tune of 360,000 rupiahs. I know this is only £25.50 but by their standards, it's a small fortune. I dine three courses at the hotel for about £5. If I bothered to go along the strip (the road outside which runs parallel with the beach), I could even get it for half price. Anyway, now I've found the beauty shop with air conditioning there's no stopping me. The beach woman was expecting me every day. Well, she can whistle. She charged me 150,000 for a manicure and the shop wants 70,000. No one gets a chance to do me twice.

Bad news, I think Naomi's bought it, unless all the cats are ginger with long legs. There was one by the side of the road as I was shopping and it won't be going anywhere with attitude again. She must have played chicken once too often.

Going to get an early night tonight.

White water tomorrow afternoon.

Love, Pat.

Typhoid on Legs

Sanur, Bali
Saturday – 22.03.03. –
First Half

Dear Clare and Michael,

This is the first time I've been able to unpack. The luxury of it. I didn't know the half I'd brought and here I am adding to it.

I'm off-peak white water rafting. If they pick you up after 1.45pm it's nearly half price. It sounds deeply unfashionable but half price is half price and the trip is as long. Twenty-seven rapids which, in the rainy season, may rise to Class IV. I've got a checklist of things to bring. It says nothing about water wings. I only feel brave, I'm not really. They give you a life jacket. I presume I can't drown. I'm even getting a crash helmet this time. In the Himalayas they're only for softies.

When I checked in here, the first cottage had the most awful smell. In India, unless it was four-star, this was normal and so you get used to it. It seemed to be coming from the air conditioning and it smelt like typhoid on legs and because of it I slept on and off all night. Before breakfast, I talked to this Canadian guy and he said it was unusual. So I got a room change. I thought he was an Australian, but even if I didn't recognize his accent (for Heavens sake, I'd lived in Canada for two years), I had it by the time I set off to my cottage.

It would appear many Germans come here, judging by the library – but the scaredy cats aren't here now – either that or they're just more generous at leaving their books than Aussies or Brits. I'm reading Dirk Bogarde's autobiography and I hope to donate it as I go. Ideal holiday reading – nice and gentle. This is meant to be my R & R time after all the hectic sightseeing.

I thought it would all be honeymooners, but it's mostly middle-aged women. I'm not disappointed by the size of their bums, mine fits in nicely here just at the right end of the measurement. In fact, I feel quite sylph-like some days. Don't think I will when I'm rafting. I'm likely to be the oldest, fattest, least fit, most scared rafter of all.

Susan, the Danish woman, showed me some bats in the palm trees asleep during the day. They look quite large. I'd seen them flying at night but wasn't sure they were bats.

As I watched high tide today I saw something moving ashore. There were one or two people swimming and one or two surfing. As it got nearer, I saw it was a huge tree trunk – about fifty inches diameter but only about five feet long. If it had hit anyone, they'd never have survived. And this is the sea I'm considering donning my snorkel and mask and exploring? I'll be having a rain check on that, especially if I've to go out of my depth. I've also seen a pram on the esplanade – no sign of the inhabitant but I think it's on its holidays.

Later:

Last night, I passed the Swastika Hotel. I'd seen it advertised and someone had just used it as a landmark for me, but, surprise, surprise, the German

Consulate is just opposite. The sign on one side of the road reads, Hon German Consulate and the other says, Swastika Hotel and Bungalows. Is someone pulling their leg do you think? Nobody here seems to appreciate the irony.

As I sit here waiting for my pickup for my Nemesis/rafting, I am carefully reading all about how much insurance they have, even up to the ages of seventy-five or eighty, so I'm all right for a few years then. The nice thing about this lot is they have showers and towels at the end. In the Himalayas, it was, 'Bye, see you' as you staggered dripping wet with your shorts chafing your legs nicely.

As you wait (time in India was about five minutes from ringing to their arriving and another five minutes to being water-bound), you tend to wonder is this the last time I'll see this room? Will my family mourn me? Will they even miss me? Will I end up in hospital? Just as well, there's no wedding in Thailand at the end. I wouldn't be very popular turning up like 'Return of the Mummy' – literally. I'm going to tell the organizers that if I end up in the drink, this will be a first and I'm not sure of my reaction. It's in their best interests to safeguard me. They don't want the publicity.

To make today a normal day and as I waited, I've been indulging in what I do best, other than arranging holidays and that's retail therapy. I'd decided which ones I was going to last night – boutiques with air conditioning and changing rooms and a mirror. These may seem a necessity but are not guaranteed in Bali. I piled out of one shop with great stuff in a designer bag – five items for £36. The next one was four items – £35. On the point of collapse, the last manageress was fanning me with her phone book, then I did my marathon stint of trying on everything in my size and I returned back for midday. I'd been out since 9.30.

Instead of my hanging around the open-air lobby, the desk is going to ring me when the pick-up arrives. It's any time between 1.30 and 2.15.

Can you imagine the faces of the others in the raft when they see me limping along? I'm saying nothing about the dislocated shoulder or the carpel tunnel syndrome. I will manage. I just need to be on the left, in the best position not to fall out. I don't mind getting wet. I get wet in the log flume and that water is filthy. At least this is coming from near the active volcano and should be sterilized.

I've not opted for the volcano trip as I reckon anywhere giving off heat at these temperatures has to be avoided. Otherwise, I'd be fascinated. Nature and all that raw energy. I'll stick to the rafting.

Because this is a Hindu island, you have to step over all the offerings people leave on the pavement to their gods each morning. They put them in little trays, food, flowers, incense. Roadside shrines are all over the place. The grounds of this complex I am staying at, in particular are beautiful – quite spiritual as they're very quiet.

Just remembered to pack tissues (no loo paper remember) and you never know. The minute you don't take them, that's when you need them. Have just eaten a mini packet of Maltesers as I didn't want to eat before I went. My stomach is rolling; think I may have to eat a second packet. These are my standby when I travel and they don't weigh too much either.

Have just got spare shoes out, the only pair which are sneakers, in case I need these for my adventure.

They've gone mouldy. They smell like mushroom compost. I remember I got them wet through in a downpour in Guilin about a week ago as I was leaving for the airport. They're outside but I don't hold out much hope of an improvement in half an hour. I wonder if the rest of my 'winter clothing' where they were packed is smelling– oh well, I may need more clothes – and I may just have to jettison some I brought with me.

The roads in Bali seem to be good, but the pavements have a habit of disappearing about eighteen inches down and then up I come again. When I got home from where the shops were, I felt I'd climbed a few hills. No pavement is level for more than six feet or so. I suppose it is good exercise but it can't be doing the blood pressure any good.

Surprisingly enough, postcards cost 50p to post here and letters £1. No wonder there is no writing paper in the supermarkets or anywhere else. The poor devils can't afford the postage. All along the strip there are email shops. They're probably just more advanced than we are. I think if it weren't for the tourists, the post office would be out of business.

I've just read a book of articles by Marion Keyes. I've not read any of her books, but she has the same quirky observations I appreciate. She went to Vietnam and by the sound of it, it's going to be interesting if nothing else. She visited the underground hideouts of the guerrillas. They had restaurants and a hospital. As she says, 'no wonder the Americans didn't stand a chance'. Allowing that I don't think they have air conditioning in the tunnels, I will give that one a miss. She said the only 'off part' was on entry to the country. A young lad who looked like he was wearing his Dad's uniform with a sub-machine gun, cross-questioned her as though she were a spy. The article wasn't dated so I don't know if this is current or not.

It sounds though that Vietnam is still very communistic, whereas China isn't, at least not on the surface. China's growth last year was seven per cent, savings rose eighteen per cent and the pundits were saying that so long as the National Debt stays at three to four per cent GDP and inflation is controlled (0.2 per cent last year), the Chinese are going to be the most successful country, I think even taking USA into account, and all this has been done by communists in a free market economy. Makes you think doesn't it? Or did your eyes glaze over just after eighteen per cent? You know me, I love economics.

Oh well, time to put the rafting gear on.

Love, Pat.

I've got the receipt to prove it

Sanur, Bali
Wednesday 22.03.03
Later

Dear Sue and Peter,

Well, as you can see, I made it back in one piece but I don't know about Roy. I resurrected him halfway towards the rafting venue.

My young driver was telling me he hadn't seen the bedrooms at my hotel. Were they nice? He did not earn enough money to stay at the hotel. A bit like our asking to see Holiday Inn rooms really – he would like to see one. He whinged on for so long that suddenly Roy had a job to do. He was to pick me up on Thursday at the airport. No more mention of bedrooms, but it still gave him one hour to try and flog me ... Elephant Safari? Wild Bird Sanctuary? Gold? Silver? I was a captive audience.

On the way there, we'd gone through a monsoon downpour. You could not see in front of you but the last of the red-hot lovers kept going, beeping his horn. I was wondering if the rain had swollen the river.

Remember I'd chosen the cheapest afternoon excursion. Well, there was only me on it. I ended up with two guides, Wayan and Made (pronounced Marday). One life jacket, crash helmet, waterproof bag and one oar. I had not forgotten anything from the Himalayas but this time 'boom boom' meant hold on for dear life.

Equipped with all my stuff, I started down these steps. I hadn't realised I was going down the mountainside of a rain forest. There were over four hundred steps and I feel no need to doubt them. Hoppalong was beginning to appear again.

No matter how long I descended I only seemed to be able to see the top of the canopy quite a way below. I could hear the river but although the noise was deafening, the canopy didn't appear to be getting any nearer. My heart was sinking further with each step. Going this far down only meant I had this far to come up.

After about fifteen minutes of steps, paths, twists and turns, some by death defying plunges, the river appeared, a raft and a smiling second guide.

I warned Wayan not to lose me. Well, I don't think there was any chance of that. The first rapids we hit, fifty yards downstream, I flew off my perch and landed on the bottom of the raft with a seriously wet bum. My feet were in these footholds and the gammy leg felt like it had been concertinaed. When we reached calm water I released it gingerly. No earth-shattering pain, so no harm done. No matter how often I repositioned myself, oar in hand, the next rapid we hit jolted me back to the floor. Given gravity and the size of my posterior, I realised unless we all capsized I was in no danger and stayed where I was.

Most of the scenery was stunning, sheer cliffs on either side and no other way of seeing this. I managed to retrieve my camera from the dry bag just in time to get an iguana leaving the shore and swimming off, but not before Wayan had said it was a crocodile. I'm not that gullible.

By this time, Roy had developed a new career.

Growing like Topsy. He was in Malaysia. What was he doing? Involved in finance, works for a bank. (Roy's only relationship with a bank was his overdraft.) How long has he been there? I was getting good at this – two weeks. He picks me up in Bali and we go to Australia. I just hope for Roy's sake he enjoys it. Oh yes, how many people work for Roy and I? Slight falter here, before I came up with six. How many children? How many girls? I think they will be beautiful says Wayan, but at least he's not asking for a conducted tour of my bedroom. Made says nothing but 'boom boom'. Don't think his English is up to much.

This time, I am determined to get a picture of me in full flow on the river. I have brought twenty frames in my camera. In the rain forest, Wayan points out the hotel where Mick Jagger and the unfortunate Jerry stayed on their honeymoon. Remember the wedding that never was on a beach in Bali? Crafty, wrinkled old devil!

It's a two-hour trip but there seem to be more than twenty-seven rapids. There is hardly any time when I can use my oar; it's nearly all 'boom boom'. So I give up and abandon all pretence of making a difference to this expedition. They seem to be managing very well. I now feel like this is another part of R & R. When I get back, I'm going for a pedicure. Promised myself if I didn't end up in the drink or incapacitated in any way, that's what I would do.

As we near the end, some areas have villages coming down to the river; there are a few rope bridges across the gorges but one, which I took to be broken, is angled at sixty degrees on purpose. It still looks very holey in places and people traverse this carrying sand bags on their heads. There appeared to be a small business with pulleys to extract the sand. Just round the corner, I said 'More sand'; 'No, that landslide.' Well, it looked like sand to me. I'll give it two months and they'll be bagging it up off up the rope bridge – unless of course it's holding back the rest of the mountainside.

As we docked, they both got out and left me in the raft. Best Maggie Thatcher voice, 'Don't dare lose me.' Big grins all round and I scrambled to safety. I was absolutely drenched due to the waterfalls we'd been under, as well as the 'boom boom'.

You know how I said this was a civilized trip? Now, that may have been a bit of an exaggeration. I didn't have four hundred steps back up, but there were just two hundred. I thought I would pace myself, but as I started up on my own (the boys stayed at the raft station), clutching my camera, dripping Ayung River everywhere, there was a queue of guys all selling wooden carvings. They were descending the steps in droves.

I'm not at my best in the middle of a rainforest, on the equator, climbing two hundred steps plus steep paths, and saturated from head to foot, fending off salesmen. I passed them all by waving my hand saying 'no, no' and not making eye contact. They let me by, because of course, they knew where I was going and they knew they could catch me anytime they wanted. I tried to put a brave face on it, and the fact that I had no money on me helped.

I set off at quite a good pace but knowing I would slow down soon the higher I got. Now I know how the oldest, weakest one of a herd of wildebeest feels as the predator stalks it, waiting for a falter or sinking to earth that separates it from the rest of the herd. Except in this case, there was no herd. Half the work had been done for them. They were talking among themselves as if they were on a school trip. Eventually, I had to stop to admire the view, but in reality, to put a bit of breath back and drink some water – oh yes, that's right, the water is at the top of the mountain waiting for me in a locker. The men caught me up and tried again, but very good-naturedly, I kept up my front and then said, 'No money.' One guy wanted to trade my designer sunglasses for the only piece of carving among about twenty I didn't want. It was hideous. At least I think that's what he wanted, but he could have been wanting to show me what it would look like in my hotel bedroom.

As they passed by, I was relieved and expected them to wait for me further on. I stopped just twice more and was quite pleased I wasn't too out of breath. Let's face it, I'm not used to climbing a mountain every day. As I got nearer the top and houses started to appear, a little girl of about six and boy about four were collecting blossoms which had fallen into a stream. She answered when I said hello but I think that was the extent of her English – either that or she didn't speak to strangers.

As I reached the top, someone from Adventure Bali came to collect me. I think they were waiting to shut up shop and go home and I was the fly in the ointment.

I was shown into a changing room. I came out and asked where the shower was. 'You want a shower? Have you brought a towel?' 'The brochure says hot shower and towels.' So I got my shower and then they'd to wake my driver. He'd had two hours to kill dreaming about the next tourist's bedroom.

Lonely Planet warned about this, but made out it is beach gigolos. From the conversation I have with the staff here at the hotel, it seems more than likely to be them or tour guides. Some staff seem over-friendly and I think with only a little encouragement, I'd have to buy condoms. Still, I mustn't worry, Roy's arriving Thursday, but I have taken to wedging a chair under my door handle. Cottages are very nice but if they only have an ordinary lock and are isolated, it's as well to be sure.

You know how I said I'd twenty pictures and wanted one of me *in situ* on the river; well, by the time I'd taken M. Jagger's love nest and it said 'three left', and you have guessed it, they'd all gone. Perhaps I'm fated never to be filmed rafting. Not to be outdone, I've cut out the twenty somethings, all good-looking, rafting and having fun, from the brochure. Anyway, I've got the receipt to prove I went, bet I'm the only person who sat in the bottom on her bottom for most of the time, though can you imagine if there had been six others. Would I have knocked them all over as I flew through the air?

I had a good look at Bali as we drove through the central part of the country. When I mentioned how prosperous it looked, nice houses, the driver said most young people lived with their parents and two grandparents because they couldn't afford their own house. But as I pointed out to him that is the Hindu way.

There is a cremation (that's right, a cremation) party tomorrow and the hotel desk said I could go if I wanted to. According to the guidebooks, this is a very spectacular thing (not for the person involved it isn't), and tourists should try and see it. I've seen pictures and the cremation pyre which appears to be paraded, decked out with flowers and tinsel is about fifteen feet high. There is even a postcard showing this. They're very proud of their cremations. I've passed on this and told them I want to go snorkelling. It may not have the cachet of a cremation, but it's what I want to do.

As we were rafting, where the villages reached down to the river, there were two women in the water. Wayan explained that one of the women was pregnant and because she was frightened of an operation, she had to come to the river. Whether this was their version of a birthing pool, I don't know, but judging by the silt and debris I got out of my swimsuit, I wouldn't recommend it. I couldn't quite understand him; perhaps she'd only come for a blessing or similar.

You know the mouldy shoes – well, they've been fumigated. When I got back from 'Pat goes rafting', there was a note on the table on my veranda informing me that 5.30 to 7.30 today, pesticides would be used in the gardens and advising you to stay indoors. This was 5.40. No early warnings for me. The gardens filled with what looked like smoke and I retreated back indoors. I'd only eaten Maltesers since breakfast and I was in urgent need of my pedicure. I didn't know which to do first and now I couldn't do either. Bother me!

Here they ask you to leave key rings at reception while you're out and to make sure you comply, the keys are attached to a big fat Buddha. It weighs a ton and is cumbersome and I find it very easy to obey this rule.

Just to illustrate what a seasoned traveller I am, at Manchester airport, before I got international, I'd had a fruit juice and decided to make my way to the gate for Heathrow. I followed a crowd through Passport

Control and by the time we had all been X-rayed, my hand baggage and I, they discovered I'd come through the wrong gate. I was with bmi passengers. I'd only left home one and a half hours ago and I was lost already. There was great consternation – by now I was airside and not allowed back. My first of very many long treks began, along the back side of Manchester airport. They said to go as far as I could and I would be photographed and to explain why I am there. So there I was, jetting off all over the world and I can't get out of Manchester airport. I got a few odd looks as I dragged my bags in (I must get one with wheels), from the arrivals side. This had repercussions. We're airborne somewhere over Europe or possibly Iraq, when a message comes over the address system. Would passenger, Patricia Buckley, make herself known to staff, as there was a message for her. Only my family knew my exact whereabouts and I said to the person sitting next to me, 'I'm away for sixty-two days. I've been gone three and a half hours. What can have gone wrong already?' Everyone looked as I made my way through first class. Ah, Mrs Buckley – we haven't got you registered, how did you get aboard? I then had to say that due to a mistake (I didn't say whose, but I think they knew it wasn't theirs), I'd entered via bmi and they were probably looking all over for a missing passenger as well. Security alert over – everything balanced – end of story.

Well, sort of. In Hong Kong, I put my ordinary jewellery in a drawer, threw all sorts in, notes for the book, two reading books, cough sweets, and my new tens painkiller (for the leg), shaped like a pen that cost £56. Didn't want to leave a mess for the maids. So far, I'd never used a drawer. Big mistake.

Never gave it another thought until I'm sitting with my seat belt fastened with Jean and Arthur bound for Singapore. Hell fire! Got out the bill quick with their phone number and limped, no, hopped down to see the cabin crew where the last bits and pieces were being loaded. Explained situation and they would ring for me. I went back to my seat. Hostess (senior cabin crew) came and asked me to talk on the phone. They were waiting and the answer would be back in two minutes but they didn't know if they could hold up the flight that long. I stood there at the doors, while the captain announced that everything was ready for take-off, they had been cleared and they were just waiting to clear up one or two things. I smiled weakly at five cabin crew and first class passengers and listened while they decided just how long they could wait before they had to shut the doors. I decided it for them. The embarrassment was awful – I said I'd get the message in Singapore and hobbled back to seat number 38A, which is a long way, if you have been holding up the flight.

Halfway to Singapore, a message came over the tannoy. Would Mrs Buckley contact ground staff in Singapore and get message now from aircrew? Jean and Arthur were quite pleased at this as they said they'd always wanted to know somebody who got paged on board. It gave a bit of excitement to the trip. I didn't like to tell them this wasn't the first time or they'd think they were flying with a celebrity – or a nuisance, take your choice.

Looking back on this, I had got on at Manchester and again at Heathrow and no alarms had sounded for staff until we were well on our way. And this when the country is on high security alert. Worries you a bit doesn't it?

In Bali it turns out there are two Patricia Buckleys staying here. How can that be? Don't they know there's only one? I wonder if the other one, who is Australian, has an eventful life as well. Tell you what – if she flies to Sydney same day as me, that'll give Qantas something to think about. Bet the tannoy will be hot then. Imagine P. Buckley in 28b and 58F. One of them must be a terrorist. Do you think they'll choose me?

Since all this happened re my jewellery, I've had faxes flying back and forth between the hotel and me and the upshot of it is, I've asked them to keep the books and post the rest to New Zealand. I've only just realised that that includes a packet of cough sweets. The hotel's Senior Assistant Manager has now taken over; perhaps they feel they owe me one for the touching up I received at their hands.

And all this is before I found out that that hotel in Kowloon where I stayed was where the SARS virus started in Hong Kong. Hong Kong of course seemed to be the worst affected region, not only a housekeeping octopus but a killer virus to boot. So you see not all my adventures are sporty. I live life on the edge, medically as well, even when I don't know it.

Back to Bali, there is something nasty in the woodshed as they say, but in this case, it's the beach. I've seen it on the Maine coastline, Californian coastline and far too many in the UK to mention, but there is an odd unidentifiable line of something at high tide. No, it's not unidentifiable; it's probably just what I think it is. I went paddling one day and wasn't too happy then, so on the advice of Chic Salon of Sanur, I'll snorkel further north. She says the sea is clear there. Sanur is not clear, so you see; there is no such thing as Paradise.

I'm glad you're enjoying good weather in the UK, nice to think of you all out in shorts. If they'd fifteen degrees here, I think they'd put their jumpers on.

Saw children coming back from school today (Saturday) at 5pm. They were all in the same uniform reminiscent of the scouts and carried small plastic buckets, even on their bikes. I think they put their lunch in them. Guide book again, says Bali is the most educated part of Indonesia.

I've seen an ad for a Montessori school and other private ones. House prices seem cheap but there is not much in the way of jobs here which doesn't include tourism and everyone keeps saying the war in Iraq is keeping people away and of course the after-effects of the bomb. I told them people returned to New York; they will return to Bali, but they are very worried.

I know I've not related this so far, so to catch up on my departure and the *real* reason BA hadn't got me aboard.

On transferring at Heathrow I'd forgotten how far it can be to the gates.

I started on what was to be normal for me, a hard slog, dragging my cases after me as my limp became more and more pronounced.

As I was on one of the walkways, an electric trolley passed with a driver and two white-haired people and their luggage. They looked very pleased with themselves. Suddenly I wanted white hair and an electronic trolley. There looked to be no pain involved, torn ligaments were catered for.

And, just as suddenly, one appeared at my elbow and the driver said he'd wait for me at the next gap.

Was my guardian angel working overtime? Perhaps not, but some concerned person on the security cameras had seen me and decided I wanted hauling aboard. Pride didn't come into it, it was either this or a serious injection of morphine to dull the pain.

Everything was decided for me and I was not about to argue. A wheelchair was provided for the final leg (excuse the pun) and even just carrying my hand baggage on my lap, the weight of it gave me considerable pain.

So I entered the plane in a wheelchair. Ignominious or what? I didn't care. In my ignorance I presumed once aboard I'd be pain-free. I could rest for eleven hours.

As it was an overnight flight, after supper all the lights went out and everyone except me went to sleep. I wasn't free of pain unless I was lying down.

I did everything in my power to mount the golden stairs to get a nice bed as advertised by BA. The hostess was really sympathetic, but told me there was an auditor on board and they couldn't risk it. They're only allowed to upgrade if it's full.

They recommended I use a wheelchair again at Hong Kong as the senior hostess said it was just as far as at Heathrow. Since I didn't expect to be seeing my fellow passengers again, I agreed.

In Hong Kong the poor woman pushing me worked at the airport and by the time the hand luggage and I were in the chair, she could hardly move it. She was built like a racing fly. I offered to get off, but she wasn't having that.

Shirley, the senior hostess, said she'd arrange for me to stay at the Regal Hotel at the airport. I was booked into a hotel in Kowloon, and allowing I'd be up at 4.00am to catch my flight, it wasn't worth travelling an hour into town and then back again. It was already 11.30pm.

The beauty of it was, the Regal was just out of the airport door and along a wide glass corridor and you were in their foyer. You could even use the airport trolleys for your luggage all the way to the hotel. This seemed highly civilised to me.

I was dropped off in my chair by the helper and Shirley, and Shirley checked me in. I don't think I could have got better service even if I'd gone up the golden stairs. Finally Shirley gave me her card and told me if I got stuck at all during my trip to give her a call, as she had lots of contacts.

As she left me in my silk dress she probably thought I had a nice warm coat in my baggage for the Chinese winter. How wrong can you be?

See you later – Love,

Pat xxx

Recycling Little Visitors

Sanur, Bali
Sunday – 23.03.03.

Dear Sue and Peter,

I have little visitors; they come in the night and they visit the bathroom. They are not roaches; just medium-sized ant-like things about one and a half centimetres. (How European can I get?)

The first night, when I got in from dinner and put the bathroom light on, they were running frantically in all directions. Luckily, I'm quite good at this, so they were dispatched between tissue down the loo. There had been about a dozen. Later that night, there was one still wandering around the toilet pan and in my innocence I presumed I'd only stunned it. The next night, nothing, so I presumed I'd got the whole family unit including stepchildren – Oh no. The following night two more foot soldiers were looking around. Middle of the night and there was one which seemed to be partaking of the water in the loo. I began to wonder if they lived there. Remember all those stories about rats in the loo? Next night – nothing. It's as though they have a visiting pattern of every other night. Last night again, toilet pan visitor. So now, at night, before I sit down, there is a thorough check of all visible surfaces. You need to feel confident on the loo!

I've just time to confirm with Adventure Bali that I sent 60,000 rupiah for my river guides' tips. I've an odd feeling that lover-boy driver may not pass them on.

Later ...

Tried a bit more retail therapy but not too successful. The only thing in the linen nightdresses and lace shop was a blouse my Granny would have loved. Nothing else was over a size ten. I wondered why they weren't too eager when I entered. Their eyes, which view Visitors in terms of cash-till and walking ATMs, had already assessed and dismissed. Nothing worth getting into a sweat about.

The snorkelling is booked for tomorrow. The guy at the desk said to me, 'You are sporty?' Not so as you'd notice pal, but if I want to do something, I can be.

Got a film developed today – rafting etc. It's not brilliant and it's definitely not got me on it in my rafting gear. Jagger's hotel looks OK though.

I then went to the tailors to get a sarong made into a skirt. Due to size of posterior, they never go round to meet twice.

By the time I arrived at Madeleine's boutique, I collapsed dripping through her air-conditioned, door, and she offered me a seat and a cooling face wash. After half an hour recovery time, she'd wondered how I'd got in such a state. I explained, no air-conditioning until now, except the lace shop and I wasn't in long enough to feel the benefit. The strip is a long way if you don't keep cooling off. All the drivers beep at you – they want you to hire them, then if you take no notice, they call out. I feel like I'm in a red light district without the potential of making a profit.

So I have ordered some trousers from Madeleine's and if I don't like them, I don't have to have them.

A blouse as well. Nice way to do business. She's having them made to fit me exactly, given that the XL they'd sent her had a twenty-four-inch waist. The skirt I got at another shop is medium. The only size I've not been in is small.

Went swimming this afternoon and got myself noticed. With my sunglasses in place I was just going down the side steps and I slipped. I thumped down on the next step edge and submerged. Due to my snorkelling training, I did not panic (nor open my mouth to breathe) nor flap my arms to emerge quicker. Roy would have been proud of me; pity I couldn't do it while he was still around. All he ever saw was a scaredy cat. I surprised myself – I came up and I knew I'd have bruising but no one would see it. There was only one other person in the pool and she came to commiserate. You feel such a fool. The sore bum just added to the indignity.

Anyway, we got talking and she'd been to the Barrier Reef and once she's asked her husband if he could remember, she'll give me the name of the tour which took her snorkelling. Every cloud has a silver lining. Grief, I'm beginning to sound like my Grandma, not even my mother – but Grandma.

After this, I set off for the ATM. I was looking on the other side of the road and they'd made a monster, some kind of mauve-coloured, seven-legged, four-tailed and one basket head type. No matter how peculiar or ferocious the design, they always get a basket head. I was so busy looking, I disappeared down eighteen inches of no pavement. This is not a good day to try anything dangerous. I'm not fit to be let out. Perhaps a night's sleep will improve me. I've to go off at 9am tomorrow snorkelling.

Found also, due to the time difference, Sydney could be eight hours away. Time for Britney to do it one more time.

Went for a whole body massage for £6. In a salon. Civilized. No men in the altogether; just me starkers and a fantastic masseuse. I'm sure even I could hear me snoring. The radio was on in the salon and I could hear Rod Stewart's 'Sailing', Queen's 'We are the Champions' ... golden oldies – Bali's version of Radio Two.

I think when they recruit security for the hotel beach venue, they tell them it's not too good a salary, but the perks are great. As much female nudity as you can take, so long as you slink round the back regularly when the massage is going on. In fact, if you just patrol the beachfront you can still get an eyeful. They're probably queuing up for the job. It could be handed down from father to son or have a waiting list like Eton.

You will have noticed that as I'm not talking to too many people, I'm using the lavatory writing paper for my verbal diarrhoea.

I found that if I came back to my room once I overheat and spend twenty minutes cooling down, I manage nicely.

Later in evening

I'm all ready for snorkelling – early wake up call. Cozzie on the side, towel, mask, in case I can't get my act together too early, and chair under doorknob. No bathroom visitors tonight, but I think it's their day for next door.

I notice I arrive at Sydney at 7.40am. What an uncivilized thing to do to me. I presume there is only one flight per day to Sydney and this is it. God, I'm an awful writer. Sometimes when I read it back, even I don't know what I've written.

Our hotel complex came alive tonight. So far, it's been rather genteel. Six Aussie women were quite loud but in a nice way. They were the bigger bum brigade with one exception.

Tonight, a group of young lads was fooling about on the beach. Shouting and laughing. As they were throwing sand and ambushing each other, there was every likelihood of tears before bedtime. At the same time, two couples came by along the walkway and as they looked at the menu, it was clear they were way ahead of everyone else at the party. As they passed my table, the nice good-looking one smiled and said they were only going to have their appetizer here as they were on a pub crawl with food thrown in. I wish they were staying in my complex – they would have really livened it up and people wouldn't have to rely on my falling A-over-T to get their entertainment.

Back to Hong Kong – just got some pictures developed as said and I've taken one of a wall. It has its own registration number and the person responsible for looking after it in local government. I do hope it doesn't catch on in the UK or our council tax will go up.

Today, when I went into two boutiques and the beauty salon, they sat me down and as I said, one gave me an ice facepack, the other two shops fanned me as I sat down. I must have looked like I was going to pass out before I could conclude our business. Even the tailoress sent me to the bar for 'cool drink'. Since I am on the other side of my face, I don't realise how alarming it is.

Have just had a big shock – beetle once again, not roach, but big, sitting minding its own business by my wardrobe. Now swimming towards the South Pacific. Well, I sincerely hope so. Does it have friends or family nearby? Will somebody come looking for it; how many and was this a baby one? Perhaps it was looking for the 'ants'. When you are fixated by bugs as I call them, there are never any answers, only questions, like, will it be in my suitcase to Sydney on Tuesday, taking the family on a free flight, courtesy of Pat on an away-day? An air miles special.

Will I sleep any easier having posed these questions? As I captured it, it had wings, but I didn't notice flippers. It took five goes to get to the loo and even then, it was a lucky aim as it left my souvenir postcard of the Great Wall of China. Touch and go whether the whole hoo-ha started again in the confines of the bathroom. Ants I can squash; this one, I was too squeamish to deliver the *coup de grâce*. Far too big and chunky. I'd have been shuddering for two days after if I'd squashed it – after the sort of day I've had, I needed a break and this must have been it.

I've looked at the steps where I submerged so gracefully and if I hadn't gone under in the deeper part, I would have caught my back on the next lot of steps, so I think I was lucky to get away with a bruised backside.

At Madeleine's boutique (remember the one with the ice face pack – she was Australian of an uncertain age), I tried on a white lawn shirt and as I put it back on its hanger, through the material, I could see this enormous, moving bug at the top of the shoulder, inside – and I'd just taken it off! Ugh. When said bug shot out, it whizzed down to the back of some cushions. It had a very strong resemblance to my long distance swimmer of tonight.

Oh great, I've got a little gecko. When I say little, I mean it. This beetle could have swallowed it. The gecko is about two inches long and very, very thin but to me, this is my new friend. I'm watching it with interest and if it plays its cards right, I may introduce it to the bathroom.

Morning

Well, this is it – this is what I've been training for. Snorkelling in the ocean where my feet can't touch the bottom. Just writing it sounds scary. I expect to go through with it. My moment of truth, but I'm not going over the side without a life vest and a Buddy. I know all the signs for if I'm in trouble, and now I don't flap my arms any more in panic, will I remember to do the other things? The chap who trained me at Hutton Baths said I could do it. He said he wouldn't be surprised at anything I did – I'm not sure which way to take that, but he said he expected me to be a skier – well, how wrong can you be? I never even had roller skates. Much too dangerous said my mother. The only time I tried ice-skating at nineteen years of age, I did better on the carpet before I hit the ice.

Later

I am officially a snorkeller. This may not seem a big deal to anyone who doesn't know me, but I've just rung Caroline at work, where I knew she'd be on ansaphone (as it's 3am UK time) and told her of my triumph. Cock-a-hoop, as opposed to turkey-cock.

Memo to myself – do *not* put sun cream or Avon oil insect repellent on before going over the side of a boat. The poor fellows trying to get me on and off had a job on their hands. No matter where they got hold, I was slippery – all their grips on me failed. I'm not good at climbing on board even in the shallows, because it reminds me of the metal fence near church, when aged nine, I tried to climb over and straddled it and then just swung over and blacked my eye. I had a very bad headache all day and went to bed with my favourite book at the time – Little Women. I always associate Louisa M. Alcott with steak, butter, headaches and a feeling that I'd burst my nose. I can feel the pressure now, just writing about it.

So, we've established I am not a gymnast by any degree. The metal ladder climbing in was no problem, it was as I hit the top and was straddled and my foot wouldn't touch the bottom of the boat. Louisa M. Alcott swung into memory as I sat there explaining – (this would not be the first time today) that I'm not very good at 'straddling'. They were very patient and eventually I was reeled in. I'd got my snorkel and mask ready; they had provided size forty-two flippers (which surprised them – they had given me thirty-nine to start with. Don't think they thought women had that big a foot – even thought they could see I was a strapping lass, as they say in Lancashire).

I watched as we headed out, first by punt and eventually engine. This is where I got startled. Punt, I could see the bottom; engine is serious – you're looking down thirty feet. I questioned them – is it shallow at the reef? Oh yes, you can see coral at one metre. One metre suits me – I am taller than one metre. But three metres – not too happy. I don't do three metres. The guide book said, just like my diver guide, coral at one metre.

Before we left land, I insisted on a life-jacket, so you may be wondering why I was twittering on about three metres. It's a question of confidence. Give me a set of figures, a problem involving high finance, or any quandary regarding money and it's as likely or not I'll solve this problem. I'm confident. Once my feet can't touch the bottom, confidence, logic, equilibrium are replaced by panic, semi-hysteria and a lot of flapping of arms. Not to say flippers.

Oh yes, flippers – well, due to sun cream, body weight and flippers, I could not get over the side. This was the first problem to be solved, terror would come into it later.

To snorkel. First, just straddle the boat (in your flippers). I tried – then they said, just drop into the water. Did they know what they were asking? I said I'd try the ladder. It seemed more secure. Ah – but the flippers – you can't use a ladder with flippers or so I found out – I did try though.

When I was at my snorkel lessons, I wasn't too happy with the flippers. They were just like nail extensions; they got in the way and did not feel part of you. So most of the time I snorkelled without fins. So now, off came the fins. I approached the ladder – it was almost like a scene from 'The Graduate'. Everyone encouraging me, but in the end, only I could do it. I could hear my breathing. Once I got down the ladder, Made, my guide said just look down in the water and leave go. I can never remember in my life shaking like a leaf. Oh, but this time, I did. I could have been given an award for shaking and trembling, teeth chattering. I was first class. If they had been giving badges, I would have got gold.

I got my snorkel going, dipped my face in the water – I could see the coral, a bit dusky, not myriads of colours, but I could see fish, which *were* myriads of colour. I could also see that the sea was very deep. I could see down about thirty feet and then, nothing. Made said 'Let go of the ladder, you can't sink.' Oh, if only I believed him. Where's the Swiss Banker? I'll negotiate with him. I'm on his wavelength.

Gradually, after about five minutes of my telling Made he didn't know what he was asking me to do, I let go of the ladder for about one second. Grabbed it again – this time, two seconds.

Once I felt I was happy with my breathing (it was six weeks since my snorkel lessons), I gradually moved away from the boat with Made by my side. I had established that he knew I was a panicker and might grab him without good reason. I find it is always good to get your own ground rules accepted, even at thirty metres.

We went off – I kept very near the boat – just going round it really. About every five minutes, I would panic as water was either in my mask or snorkel and I couldn't expel it. Made was grabbed. At any other time this could have looked like a middle-aged woman just taking advantage of a beautifully honed body, but I have to admit, I'd have grabbed Cyril Smith if he'd been around.

I was feeling quite relaxed (thanks Paul, my tutor, you did a great job) and getting further away from the boat. I knew I had half an hour and wondered how long I would last.

Made was pointing out the beautiful fish, which really showed up the coral as just a big mushroom bed, dusty beige-looking, and I saw a very big starfish. Many of the fish of different varieties seemed to sport black and yellow as their team colours. I even saw angel fish. I was quite satisfied this was only about ten minutes out to sea. I had not travelled hours to see them – I will have to at the Great Barrier Reef.

As I got really brave, I headed to deeper water. Still grabbing Made every seven minutes or so now. Then he guided me back toward the boat. I'd asked the 'driver' to take a picture of me in the water, so that's why he guided me back. I'd lasted half an hour, but I have to be truthful, I was exhausted.

All I had to do then was climb back into the boat. I did suggest if the worst came to the worst, they would have to tow me back behind.

It took me as long to get back in as it did to get out. I was still slippery and they couldn't quite get a good hold on me. I kept my snorkel firmly in my mouth as I climbed the ladder, just in case gravity and the bum took me backwards.

On board, I felt whacked – I think it was mental as much as physical, but I don't usually swim for thirty minutes non-stop.

Since I have got back, I've had to lie down in a darkened room to recover. I sound like a Victorian spinster – Elsie, where are my smelling salts?

Think I may give Caroline's answerphone another ring, as it is now 4am UK and I've got to tell someone about it again.

Triumphant I am, but I now realise I should have bobbed about in the life-vest without mask and snorkel just to get me used to the feeling and realise I can't sink. You see, logic wasn't working. It only works on terra firma.

I've managed to get pictures of the fishermen in the lagoon. Some standing, some with a boat, but quite a few snorkelling and towing a polystyrene box which holds the fish. You don't think they were catching some of those beautiful coral fish do you?

As we set off, the driver filled the petrol tank and then threw the plastic bottle into the sea. They don't seem to be looking after the environment and I think that's why the coral looks a dull brown/beige colour. Or am I just a tourist that wants everything pristine and me to be the only visitor and therefore, no pollution?

Love, Pat

One Slipped and Another Sluthering

Bali
Monday – 24.03.03.
Later

Dear everybody,

Have just talked to Sue and Peter; will ring Michael and Clare later to see if they are being bombarded with missives. I have posted eight today. But I'm posting from various points to hedge my bets.

I write when I come back to cool down. It serves two purposes, although I'd be quite happy if I only cooled down.

Met a man today and do you know, he checked me out as I got out of the pool? This was very flattering for me because I think he's only about forty. Blane from Atlanta, Georgia. He sounds like something from a Barbara Cartland novel. Anyway to get back to this checking me out. Rising like Venus from the waves, adjusting my cozzie as I go and making sure the tummy is in the right place and nothing is protruding from the top of my thighs is not my best profile. If I had to think of the worst one, I couldn't. Ah well, it's nice to know he looked. We'd been chatting in the pool; he was here on business. His firm have their main outlet in Bali for seafood. Today, he'd been checking the tuna and swordfish. Perhaps that was it – he was checking to see how many steaks I'd make.

He stood, later on, in the shallows with his laptop on the sunken bar counter and tapped away. As he said, it's a hard life but someone has to do it. He travels the world quite a lot – almost as much as me. He did not seem too impressed, Sue, about my snorkelling feat. Then again, he doesn't know what a jelly-belly I am. Oh yes he does, he saw me leaving the pool.

I got bitten last night. The first time since I left home. The only night I didn't put Avon spray on – I was getting blasé – only my foot, but in three places.

Back to Blane. I suppose he could have been Blaze, but I think that's more your Mills & Boon – he is divorced (seven years married) – no children. His wife travelled with him and didn't like it after a while, so just stayed in Georgia. As he said, they weren't exactly slumming it in the hotels. I managed to teach him one or two things (nothing like that) – things like – 'One slipped and another sluthering'. For those of you not familiar with this quaint Lancashire expression, it correlates with one sandwich short of a picnic or the elevator doesn't go all the way up. Its reference is to slates.

I must be due some sugar levelling because I'm beginning to lose my ability to spell. My heavens! Time for dinner. Will Blane mosey along? I should imagine, having checked me out, he'll run as fast as he can in the opposite direction, thinking, she looked all right from the waist up. Had a thought. What if Blane is spelt Blain as in chil ...?

Later

Well, I think I've scared him off sufficiently now.

He was at reception as I was asking the directions to the kite shop for the grandchildren. Up to now, I've not tried to shoo him away, but once I said grandchildren, I realised I was playing my ace. I think really I just wanted him to show an interest to make me feel good on my snorkelling day. A bit like getting a gold star, excellent and 10/10 altogether.

Normally when I go to dinner, our resort is the only one with a floodlit beach, but it's all darkness tonight. Do you think something is up (or, in case I get published in America, something is going down?)

Despite my hotel meals, I have not put on any weight, nor, despite my massages, 400/200 steps, snorkelling, have I lost any. Mustn't grumble.

The restaurant at the beach is twenty-four hours. I'm tempted to go and see who is there at 4.30am, but I'd probably be surprised as many get up early to watch the sunrise.

I am desperately shortening sleeves on all the shirts I've bought in a bid to make them lighter – six sleeves equals one whole shirt, twelve sleeves equals two shirts and so on. I have been driven to these measures by the fact that I was grossly over the limit coming and I've been putting Bali back on the road to economic recovery with a zest. The economics in this are simple – leave behind six non-essential toiletry items and it equals new trousers and maybe even a skirt. There's a forlorn group of items on my dressing table waiting for the chambermaid tomorrow. One peacock blue nail varnish, hardly used, hand spray cleanser (kept forgetting to use) for travel, one soap/emergency rations, just in case and carted around continents, and a never-used leg and foot gel. Now, I've never worked out how to use the gel. By the time you have covered your feet and legs and you are nice and sticky, so are your hands, but because your feet are sticky, you cannot wash your hands. A decision has to be made re sitting and waiting with sticky hands or padding over your carpet and making sure its fibres are soothed and cooled as you go. Sort of defeats the object. And finally, the aromatherapy oil purchased from the beach masseuse on my first day at a grossly inflated price. The heat fries my brains. I have already donated my Lonely Planet Guide to Bali and Lombok to the library and the front desk has stamped it. Dirk Bogarde never made it. My Lonely Planet Guide (1997) was purchased full price in 2002 from a bookshop in North Wales. They must have been glad to see me. Apparently, Bali is not the top destination for the North Welsh – or if it is, they don't need a guide and they are not lonely.

There are proper children here, five of them arrived at the dinner table with four parents and squealed with delight. They had just arrived and I'd seen the fathers at reception, asking to change rooms and wanting an upgrade. Do you think one of them got my old room? By the time they hit the dinner table, the fathers were each clutching four fat Buddhas and telling the wives they'd move the bags while the kids ate. Three of the boys went off to the loo and there was an almighty shout of 'There's a frog trying to climb out of the toilet.' Someone at another table shouted, 'Well, let it!' The mothers were calling shush to the children and one of the dads was dispatched to sort it out. He took his Buddhas with him. He didn't return for five minutes and then reported back to the wives. I never found out the fate of the frog but I think I'll double-check the bathroom tonight.

Talking bathrooms, I was up earlier than usual for my snorkelling trip this morning and as I went into the bathroom, just scuttering round the door was one of my little visitors, looking for all the world like he'd just spent a night on the tiles. Didn't he know it wasn't my room's turn last night? Anyway, they better not mess with me tonight because I can snorkel, which means I can do anything. Grief, I'll be trying walking on water next.

I realise now the reason my rafting guide was called Wayan was because he was first born; the next is called Made (which I thought was Mardi) and the next Nyoman. After the fifth or is it fourth, they start again with Wayan. They say it doesn't lead to confusion but since, as a mother, whenever I called one of my children I often did not get the sex of the child right, never mind the name, I think it would. I could go through the lot before I had it. Don't think it matters male or female, as my hairdresser is called Nyoman. At first, I thought she said Norman and you see I wasn't so far out; it's a unisex name she has got.

There is no need for an iron out here. Of course in my opinion, there is never any need for an iron, but that's another topic. You get out your creased shirt, skirt, dress and put it on and by the time you hit the restaurant if you walk slowly enough, there is not a crease in sight. Eight minutes does it nicely.

I have been finding out more about this cremation celebration. In some cases, they bury them and it's years later that the cremation takes place. As it's expensive, sometimes a few are done together. (I do hope I've got this right, I don't want to insult anyone). If it's a very big important person, the pyre can be so big that it takes fifteen to twenty strong men to carry it. It is paraded around the streets and it's not just flowers, but tinsel, shiny objects and anything to make it more attractive like ribbons. Yes, as you can imagine, someone has to have the job of disinterring the body and one would hope it's a few years and not a few months, although no mention is made of mummification. After the ceremony, the eldest son has to poke around in the ashes to make sure no part of the body remains. I should think this is a time when a woman or girl would be glad their chromosomes favoured them for once. I've not found out what happens if there is no son. I'm afraid if I show too much interest, someone may tell me all the details are in a book in my bedroom and they'd be happy to explain personally.

I'm fast becoming an expert on toasters of the world, but the one here is something else. I put in my small pieces of continental type bread and because they're small, they don't pop out. Once I've rescued them from the fierce heat (no idea where the setting is on this one), I've to flick the switch and hope only one comes out at a time as I've to catch it. This morning, I managed to catch two at once. Shades of ping pong or is it badminton?

Tomorrow, I think I'll have it untoasted. There is something a little nerve-racking to what should be a peaceful start to the day, if you're dodging back and forth like Martina Navratilova on a bad day.

It's nearly the witching hour, which means 10pm here. It's when my little visitors come out to play. And – yes, there it was playing chicken across my bathroom floor and not making it. Don't mess with the Mama. Another one on its way to join the food chain of the South Pacific. Where is my gecko? He can manage these. No sign of the frog yet. Time to do another bathroom sortie. It's like being on patrol at Fulwood Barracks.

Anyway, back to the job in hand. De-sleeving shirts. It's amazing how many you can pick up when they're in linen or fine lawn for £10 each or less.

I am buying up Bali, as I believe in Thailand they only go up to size twelve. I can believe it, as my daughter hasn't managed to bring anything back that fits me (and believe me, I've tried), unless it's a sarong.

Judging what I said earlier about the cost of postage and lack of writing paper, if I send any more letters, there could be a public enquiry re the overload on the services – but what am I thinking? This isn't Britain – no third world here. Everything runs on time. Taxis ordered are always there ten minutes early and connections to take me rafting or snorkelling come early as well. Even in this heat. Don't know about the railways. Actually, I've never seen a train while I have been here, but you can bet it won't be the wrong kind of sun. Their lines won't buckle, people will turn up for work to run the buffet car – monsoons won't stop them!

For my last day, I raced up and down to dressmakers, boutiques, banks and post offices. Booked a full body massage for 5.45pm followed by a cream bath – the head, shoulders and back massage – steamer and then blow dry. As soon as it was finished, I was off to the airport for the 11pm flight.

The taxi driver was waiting outside the hotel as I left for the beauty salon. There is so little work they wait where they know they have it. On the way to the airport, he said some days there is no business at all. Many, many people in Bali are worried. They pray to their gods to help them. He said he'd pray I came back next year and brought others with me.

The girls at the beauty salon took my address and want to keep in touch. They asked if I had email. How come even hairdressers who say their salary only covers living, they cannot afford to travel, have email? Am I falling behind completely?

The final night before I left, I had black rice pudding. I was curious. I could not eat more than half, it was very rich. I asked how it was made, as it looked like molasses plays a part. The waiter said they boil it for three hours. You can taste the husks in it as well. But I don't think I've got to the bottom of its ingredients.

Gave the chambermaid all the toiletries and about three hundred sheets of A4 reconstituted toilet paper. She was delighted for 'her children'.

My bill for the week (excluding one breakfast and one lunch), was £42. It is incredibly cheap. That also included £7 charge for using room until 6pm.

In all my time in Bali, I never heard a voice raised in anger. They are very gentle people. The maddest anyone got was probably me when chasing visitors around my bathroom.

The previous day to my leaving, among all the shopping and eating, I'd managed to fit in some sunbathing. By now, I knew the best position for the sun mid-afternoon. I got myself established nicely, suncreamed up and something landed on my leg. Pink seeds. A very fetching bird, reminiscent of a finch, don't ask me which one, was high up in the tree above me. No matter how attractive it was, it was shitting on me. I didn't realise how often finches 'go' – about every three minutes on average. A direct hit every time. Then another came and they started doing it in tandem. They could even have been competing – well done Marlon. I'll just see if I can get down the front of the halter top – nice one – try for the legs now – we've really got her going. So I gave up and retired defeated, gracefully. As we all know, we English are quite good at that – retiring, gracious in defeat.

I should imagine, Clare, you dread my phone calls, for verdicts on the letters. You're living real life, daughter with broken arm, getting meals, working, and a mad woman's ringing you from surreal Bali, demanding a critic's response and complete analysis and a ten point plan as to where she is going wrong.

On leaving at Bali airport, I had an hour or two to wait and I was alone on a run of four connected tubular like chairs. Just as I was about to go as the flight was called, I must have moved and the whole lot tipped into the air. I was saved the ignominy of sliding onto the floor as I redistributed my weight and they crashed down again. I gathered my belongings together and made as dignified an exit as possible under the circumstances and I think I was as surprised as anyone as I'd been there ages. Must have been that last Malteser.

See you in Australia ...

Love,

Pat

A Bridge Too Far?

Sydney
25.03.03

Dear Clare and Michael,

Well, I twitched my way to Australia. Why do any flights have to take off at 23.00? On the whole flight, I seemed to be the only person with their light on. As the hostess passed a couple of times, she checked in case there was anything she could get. I desisted saying a king-sized bed and a pillow filled with sleep-inducing herbs. But I didn't want to swap my sleeping companion. Yes, I slept with a man. Unfortunately he was 27A and I was 27B, but on the looks-front and hunkiness, he scored 10/10. Actually, he was very nice and charming. Yes, a charming Aussie. He'd been to Bali to buy furniture for his new house he'd had built just out of Sydney. He also had a place in Sydney. The price of the furniture was a thirtieth of the Aussie cost; even with shipping and insurance costs, it hardly made it cost more. Now I know it's a lot further to UK than Oz but the wood is fantastic and the carving beautiful. I may need another trip to Bali to check out the furniture and prospect of importing. Well, that's my excuse. You see, I never priced the furniture – big mistake. I didn't even check out the price of a four-inch carving (due to being overweight etc, etc). Another visit is a must, I'm sure.

When the hunk woke up, he said he hoped he

hadn't disgraced himself. I said no and I would happily write him a reference. He told me about the position of the hotel I was staying in. and some tips on where to go and where not.

I arrived at Sydney about 4am my time, 7am their time. By the time I'd cleared Red customs control again (yes – Chinese medicines but also now, a Balinese kite – it has wood you see) and I taxied into Sydney, it was 8.45.

As the taxi dropped me, he said it was the best hotel in Sydney. Hopes were high. No little bathroom visitors here then.

Reception was very nice and as a result of non-smoking request, she said they had a special offer of upgrade to executive floor for about £12 per night. I was already in a deluxe room, so I declined her generosity. She then said the only non-smoking was executive, but not too good a view. So I'm here now on the twenty-ninth floor. The lift sounds exactly like a train moving rather fast. Great anticipation as I entered. Thank goodness I'm not in a standard room. This would be standard in a Chinese four star. As it's a Sydney four star, I expected more. The bathroom is so small two people wouldn't fit in. The wardrobe is a single, the other being taken up with tea-making and a fridge. The bedroom has a king-sized bed but other than having a large space to walk across to the bathroom (the space is three times the size of the bathroom), it's a Post House hotel room. *All* my other rooms have been bigger.

I immediately visited the restaurant for breakfast. It's the worst one I've ever been in. Absolutely soulless. I shall never dine in there again. I felt like I'd entered a downmarket cafeteria from the 1960s. The design of the place was terrible along with the food.

Anyway, since then, I've had a duvet day. Had a bath, just enough room to towel myself afterwards and retired to bed around 10.30am. Woke up at 8pm. Now watching TV. Ordered from room service, boeuf bourguignon and cheesecake. Got beef burger and cheese platter. Had another go. Nice girl came and said I could keep the other meal if I wanted. Probably should have done. Both courses were extremely rich. I'm getting a bit like a sumo wrestler; you know, eat and sleep, eat and sleep.

I'll be up early tomorrow I should think, in time to sample one of the two restaurants recommended by the hunk in 27A for breakfast. Nowhere could be worse and Sydney has a reputation for some of the finest dining in the world.

Thursday

Breakfasted at Feline's. Sounds good doesn't it? Italian, but got served by a girl from Devon. Just been in Australia three weeks.

On my boat trip round the harbour I decided to visit Manly, a rich enclave of Sydney with its own beaches and centre. I liked it very much. Quite small after Sydney. A woman I talked to on the ferry back said when she'd been to the Barrier Reef recently, she couldn't snorkel because of a typhoon. Her son lived in Manly. She was French Canadian on a visit, which she did frequently.

Also that morning on the subway I'd met two young Brits. One of each. They were staying for a year but hadn't managed to get jobs yet. Could it be they were busy sightseeing and not throwing themselves too enthusiastically into job-hunting?

I decided to check out the bridge today and they invited me through to see Simon. Nice young guy in a suit – which in Australia means management. I mentioned my leg, said it just twinged a bit, but nothing about the dislocated shoulder. Thought it best not to mention the trapped sciatic nerve and the vertigo. He said he was sure I'd be fine to do it as I sold it to him via the white water rafting trip etc. I was most worried about the zoot-suits. These are pale grey to blend in and cover you from head to toe. I haven't dressed that warm since a particularly cold February day in the Cairngorms. I could see me passing out with heat stroke before we left the training building. It was quite hot in there and you'd all this climbing up and down vertical ladders and making sure your safety harness could be unsnagged by yourself. I needed enclosed rubber-soled shoes. I only had the mouldy ones which I washed. Whereas before it was mushrooms, now it was Stilton or was it Danish Blue? He said if I hadn't shoes they could lend.

I booked my climb for 1.55 because 'Simon says' the breeze is at its coolest around 3.00 when I hit the bridge. Mornings can be humid. I've only just found out you can do it at night. They give you a miner's lamp. I think we'd enough to carry. We had hooks for everything. Can't wait for tomorrow.

Friday

Today I kidnapped a very nice woman on my way to Bondi Beach for breakfast. (This is almost like name dropping, but I was only two stops away on the Metro.) First of all with my 'go anywhere paid for ticket', I chose the bus as I could see it went all the way to the beach and the train stopped at a junction and you'd a bit of a walk. After breakfast I intended just looking at the beach and the bodies beautiful and would walk along on the edge of the surf. Apparently there is a lovely cliff top walk between there and Bronte Beach, takes about forty minutes. I felt this would suit me as I had to be back to my hotel to get my sturdy Stilton shoes and jacket etc for the bridge climb.

I got on the bus; the driver said I'd be quicker on the subway as it would take him until 11am (it was 10.10am).

So I duly got off and made my way to the station. I looked around and couldn't see exactly which line I needed (again) so decided to ask this woman. As is normal for me I had asked another a visitor (from Brisbane). We went so far together and then had to get off to change and we were getting on so well, she decided to join me. Her daughter was here for a conference and as her husband was away working she'd come along for the ride, she was even staying at my hotel. Her name was Hetty, fifty-five, her husband a builder.

At the next station we asked the railwayman (in the main booth) who said which line we wanted and pointed the direction.

Hetty was a bit worried as she only had a two-stop ticket. It was a double decker and we went up for the view. We passed the opera house/the bridge and kept going.

Although we were talking fit to burst I kept an eye on the time. I was hungry and I said to Hetty it was taking as long as the bus. Eleven came and went and I was feeling indignant with the bus driver, but then again, Hetty and I wouldn't have met if I'd used the bus.

We started to climb into the hills and eventually there was only us two left.

Hetty had made a few remarks about being kidnapped and said she was definitely not letting me have her mobile.

At 11.10 I decided to see a driver and guard at the rest station. As it happens we were next door to the driver and he got out at the rest stop. The guard told us this was the terminus and the driver had gone to the loo.

We were at Berowra and not one Sydneysider I talked to afterwards had ever heard of it (unless it was my pronunciation or accent, or both).

By now my cheeks were turning hollow and even Hetty, who'd had breakfast, was hungry. We raided the machine on the platform – I got a drink but the driver came back as Hetty put her money in, lost it and had to rush back.

The guard said we'd be back in Sydney for 12.30. I'd to be at the bridge for 1.30 and I'd got to change and get back again, also to eat.

Hetty said she'd never gone as far for $2.20 – nor had as good a time. Of course she wasn't used to what normally happens to me. I wasn't too surprised. Annoyed, but not surprised. We decided it had made coming to work worthwhile for the guy who sent us the wrong way. Possibly how he got his kicks or maybe my accent saying Bondi sounded like Berowra. We'll give him the benefit of the doubt.

Eventually we saw the suburbs of Sydney and then the opera house. I decided I had to get off to change trains and raced up, but Hetty said she may stay on and go to Bondi. She'd wanted to do the bridge but I knew you had to book in advance. So, with hardly a farewell, I was off. I decided against returning to the hotel and taking any more trains, so I walked to the bridge area. This is called The Rocks and it's

Sydney's oldest, quaintest area. I found one Lowenbrau restaurant and a nice young lad came out (he could have been twenty-five – thirty though) all dressed up in leather breeches and bib, the usual Black Forest garb they think tourists want. 'And who got you ready today?' said the Prestonian wit. It could have been the accent, but something got lost in translation and he didn't appreciate it. He also took no offence, but laughing at himself was not part of the Lowenbrau training manual. Unlike us Brits, who find endless occasions to laugh at ourselves e. g. rafting, snorkelling, the half-day out to Berowra and so on. We can make fools of ourselves anywhere. Most occasions present an opportunity.

Suitably fortified I arrived at the bridge offices, halfway up a hill only slightly breathless. This didn't appear to be a good omen.

I was just ten minutes early. Someone checked me in and said did I want to go earlier and get it over with? Bit like turkeys opting for Christmas on 30 November.

So you see, there was room for Hetty. I chose to go earlier and everyone of the group was a backpacker – except for me. I noticed the group before me and after me had golden oldies on them, only mine had just me.

Not having gone back to the hotel, I'd only got open sandals, so they sorted me out a pair of shoes – thank goodness they didn't rub. Zoot suits appeared and the girl was a good judge because mine was a perfect fit. So I went off in borrowed shoes, socks, zoot suit and my own knickers. A three and a half hour endurance test. We'd had to go into a prep room, where we signed disclaimers (are you reading this American Express?) and blow into a bag to see if we were alcohol fortified.

So that's another of life's hurdles completed. I walked to the to the top, all 1,440 steps plus inclines and meshing. There were twelve of us, seven English, one Aussie, three Papua New Guineans, and the leader of the pack – a nice personable chap called Edward. It's three and a half hours of training, equipment, and of course practice climbing. It is technical but I managed it. A lot to remember. You get a safety harness, radio and earpiece, special connectors for your sunglasses and everything has to be connected via a big ring at the back of your neck on your zoot-suit. Nothing has to fall. These are grey suits we all have to wear so we don't stop traffic. (My mother always said I would.) You are over, under, and by the side of eight lanes of traffic and a railway line.

The safety harness is about fifteen inches long and you attach it to a metal rail which runs alongside the walk. The harness is not to stop your falling, just to stop would-be suicide jumpers from going over the top.

Imagine the ignominy of dangling fifteen inches below the parapet when you want to make a big splash. Your fifteen minutes of fame at the end of fifteen inches of harness. You'd make the papers, but for all the wrong reasons.

The metal rail, which as I said, runs the length of the walk, was what took so long to get the walk established. Until it was in place and proved it would work, the walk could not be opened.

Allowing how much it must have cost at the beginning, no wonder they put a debit through of £57 on my Amex. I believe they were in profit after two years though. The Bridge Company, of course, is private and for your money you get a certificate and a group picture.

My gammy leg had been playing up and I wondered how I'd be. I think tomorrow morning, I'll know. Just a bit stiff, although when I left the restaurant tonight there was laughter as it took me a second or two to get a fluid movement going. We'd all been chatting about it and they'd all done it, then again, they were about twenty-five years old.

Just after the start as you are walking along the parapets, you stop. The guide said every time he and any of the other guides took a party up the Bridge (every twenty minutes) they stopped at this exact spot. Now, he said, look down and remember you can't see that woman just walking to her lounger, because that hotel boasts that its rooftop swimming pool is the most private in Sydney. He said he couldn't think of one which got more attention. We were near enough not only to see the woman in her bikini but if she'd had a leg wax and how recently.

It almost was as hard coming down as going up. My leg prefers up. The hardest part was where you were totally on your own and you had five lots of vertical ladders all angled side by side, and it was difficult transferring one to another. Everyone said both up and down, this was the worst. I get vertigo now and again, but this time nothing. The top is exactly double the height of the opera house. All I can say is that the pictures are so good – and remember I don't take good pictures. I'm having them copied, then laminated and they'll be all over the house. I look about thirty-five. Shows what leaving your family behind and taking on a challenge does for you. It was only Edward the guide taking the photos with an ordinary camera. I've not been airblown like Jane Fonda etc., or is it fly-blown?

The nice thing was half a dozen of the others invited me back to the pub. We had a kangaroo pizza. I tried not to think of Skippy, it was very good. They had a crocodile one but I could not order it because they'd put it on a coconut base and I really hate coconut. So I had to give that a miss but I could get crocodile at the Great Barrier Reef.

On a totally different subject, in a very expensive boutique here, when I was very overweight baggage-wise, the woman said to send it by sea. She said it was cheap. She did it for clients all the time. So, today, Friday, as I came in, I asked the concierge where the nearest post office was. He said next door in the underground supermarket. Then the crunch came; they are shut both Saturday and Sunday and I thought the UK was bad. So here I am now with letters needing weighing and a small suitcase ready for the off. I'm lumbered with the lot until about Cairns. Ayers Rock is Sunday/Monday. Will I have time to post anything? I will if I stay in Alice Springs, but not if I want to see the Rock (now called Uluru).

The hotel I chose in Sydney was at King's Cross, a bit like Montmartre in Paris. Boho, red light, nightlife. This used to be the place to be, but now the concentration is at the harbour, near Circular Quay. All the big hotels, Intercontinental, Sheraton, are there. Everything seems to leave from there. I paid £30 for a three-day ticket, giving me access to trams, buses, trains and ferries.

I leave on Sunday – the hotel, part of the Millennium Copthorne Group, closes Monday to be turned into flats. I've never closed a hotel before.

There was a paragraph in the paper about the staff. They had staged a seventy-two-hour strike earlier for a proper redundancy package. This time though they'd settled for what had already been offered and they're all jobless on Monday. But do you know, everyone is really nice and helpful – you would imagine as it is, they'd feel resentful, but you'd never know they were closing (unless you count the breakfast and the caféteria).

Oh yes. The Aussies love Fergie. On the radio in the taxi, they were reporting on her father's funeral. They were saying what a true lady she is, a really great lady and I wondered if it were the same Fergie we knew or were they talking about Alec Ferguson. Do they know something we don't?

See you later,

Love Pat

British Rail, Oz Style

29.03.03

Dear everybody,

Today, I went to the Blue Mountains – on purpose, not by accident. It would take me a day to get there and back.

When I got to the station it said there were works on the line (does this sound familiar?) on 29–31 March. This was the twenty-ninth. Due to this there would only be a bus service from Penrith (yes, definitely sounding like BR) to Katoomba. Allow thirty minutes longer each way.

Although I invariably look like a pack horse or worse when I'm flying, at least this time I only had my bag with camcorder and camera in. Some poor people were going on holiday and had loads of luggage to cart off trains and on to buses.

I like looking at scenery from a train, it gives you a feel for places and people. From a bus it's an even closer look.

We passed a Museum of Fire leaving Penrith, which looked like it had been a victim of the same. It didn't encourage you to go in, there was a peculiar smell going through Penrith. Is it the bus or the town? I am not a happy bus traveller.

On reaching Katoomba I found a nice café bar called Zuppa, which had wonderful, freshly made food and freshly made juices as well. Katoomba Heaven.

It all looked very genteel with a decidedly Victorian look. It appears the whole area was developed for Sydneysiders to escape the heat of the summer around 1863.

I'd expected a peaceful day in the mountains. The journey out took three hours instead of two hours and on the way back the bus stopped at every mountain village. This I normally would have enjoyed but after so long, you just yearn to get back. I ended up exhausted. The bridge climb was not as tiring as this.

At Café Zuppa the waitress said Echo Point was just down the road. As it was a nice day I decided to walk. It took fifty minutes and I thought I'd never get there.

Echo Point is where you see the three sisters rock formations, three of them and they're a bit alike. So logic related them.

I wasn't as daft coming back and caught the bus. Ah but, I didn't then progress to the next stop. That was too simple. The map shows one – twenty-three stops. In order. You're meant to get on and off the bus as you come to the next thing you want to see.

Well, they don't work it like that. Each time you go back to Katoomba and start again. Everyone who got on asked the driver and he seemed to have trouble. Then I found out why. One or two buses actually move on to the next point, but he wasn't very sure which they were or when they were due. He went to look at a board propped against the bus stop. It measured about eighteen by nine inches.

I decided the class dunce had been allowed to run amok with the timetable when all the others were on an open day to the university of their choice. Evidence of this was confirmed by notice on the board which said, Satuday. More evidence when the driver said you had to work out which side of the road you need to be standing. If you do manage to catch a bus on the right side, the driver has to consult a timetable to tell you if you're right.

Has nobody been to Disneyworld where the train just goes round in a circle?

Anyway, due to the timetables and having to allow longer to get back, I only managed to do one other sight in my seeing before leaving.

This was good though. I went down the almost vertical railway. An engineer who got on said this wasn't physically possible. We were all tipped backwards and because of the forest canopy, the train's see-through roof was just skimming our heads. It was all very spectacular. You come back by cable car, which gives stunning views of the forest. In between the train and cable car is an ecological path with observation posts and dotted with posters giving information. Quite calming if you don't know you've to sort out your bus as you leave. Blue Mountains because of the blue haze made by all the eucalyptus trees.

All the eateries in Katoomba looked good. Many offered organic food and really unusual stuff.

From Katoomba it was only an hour's drive back to the station but one chap must have used the loo. I didn't know there was one.

Anyway, he was strange for an Aussie. Mark Phillips look-alike, older and with a thin, black moustache. He came back towards the driver and said 'Hey mate, there's no paper and no water.' What the driver said I didn't hear. Probably 'No worries.' Well there were worries. No water and no paper and this guy is sitting among us all and I'm wondering how he managed. I kept a very close eye on him at the station and made sure I got in a different coach.

I didn't want to be late back as the previous night I'd had to use my room key to access the hotel. I don't think I've ever done that before.

The previous evening I was too late for the night cruise and as a consolation prize I decided to eat at Level 41 (it's actually on 42) with views over Sydney.

As I was quite late, all the window tables were taken, but the one I was at was quite good. The maitresse d' said could she just explain the menu. I knew what was coming because the guidebook put it into the very expensive category. She had a set menu at night; three courses $120.00, about £40.00. I said fine.

Actually it was six courses and including two glasses of wine, bottle of water and ten per cent tip, it came to £50.

Now my kids can spend that on a night out, so I refuse to feel guilty. It was my consolation prize.

First course I had warm, rare duck salad, but the canapés before were oyster and caviar.

After the duck, a small cup of asparagus soup. Then I chose lamb and a pissaladière. The latter was too strong, but the lamb was great. Then along came apple jelly and strawberry coulis. I then had white chocolate marquise with raspberries. The staff even brought me some short books on Sydney and the bridge as I was on my own, which was thoughtful.

After my soup, a table came free at the window and just as I was thinking should I ask to move, the maitresse d' suggested I might like to. When I got there the opera house, floodlit, was immediately below. Bliss.

Anyway I'm not having any more of those dinners,

I'm going to try and economise in Thailand.

The first morning I left my hotel in Sydney in search of a decent breakfast, and I hadn't got half a block when I saw these sandals to die for. Now I couldn't have them as they have a thing that comes up between your big toe and the next. So I tried them on in my size and decided which would be the better size for Vicky.

I told her about them and she said, 'Are they the sort of present I've to pay you back for? Have you kept the receipt?' This is a normal conversation between Vicky and me.

As I left Sydney from the domestic terminal, it was great. There was an oyster bar, fresh pressed juices. In comparison San Francisco circa 1996 looked like an outpost of darkest Africa.

Since I thought that though I've been through the Sydney International Departures to New Zealand and that was awful. Just one café. As bad as San Francisco.

At the domestic terminal, a bowl of fresh fruit and fresh apple and carrot juice was £3.20.

At my favourite restaurant in Sydney, the waiters, gorgeous looking but too beautiful to be true and obviously gay, were charming. They were very quiet the Thursday night and Saturday night I was in. They said it had been like that since the war started. When I said goodbye and that I'd enjoyed my food there, he said he was pleased he'd been part of my holiday. See what I mean about charming?

Bridge Climb facts – the majority are Brits. And on that note, goodnight.

How many camels did you say?

Alice Springs
Sunday – 30.03.03

Dear Sue and Peter,

Boy! It's been a long day. This morning, I was on the twenty-ninth floor in Sydney and by lunch, I was in the outback on the third floor. The worst of it is, now it takes me twice as long to get from my room to the lobby than it did this morning. I've got lost twice, but I'm easily confused.

I booked a taxi to take me downtown, all six or so streets of it, to buy a fly net. Yes, you're right, a fly net. More about that later. When the taxi arrived to collect me, I suddenly realised I hadn't got any cards or money. I'd changed my bag for the third time that day. Travel bag, pool bag, day bag; so the money was in my pool bag. It took me ten minutes to get it, and I'm only on the third floor, which is the top floor here.

Downtown, the search was on for a fly net. While I was by the pool, I'd seen some people coming back with bushranger hats and the women hadn't got corks dangling, they had pale green netting all round, and I remembered as soon as I left the airport, the flies were all over me.

As you might be expecting me to say, this is not usual for this time of year, but they are particularly bad due to the unusual weather conditions which have let them breed. Why, everywhere I go, do the weather conditions try to break all previous records? Does it know I'm coming? So, I've been assured they will be gone in the next month or two. That makes me feel much better.

I had booked to go quad biking in the outback for two hours. That was the reason I had to go into town. The shop in the hotel only had a hat with net. I couldn't see my being able to get away with net, hat and helmet with visor. Not without looking a wally. To go quad biking, I have to be up at 5.50am because the animals are around first thing and it takes an hour to get into the hills.

I am not going to Ayers Rock because travelling time is nine hours return, even by car. I wanted to hire a plane but they only do a minimum of two people and although the guy was really nice when I rang him, I told him I couldn't wait to see if there was another punter on their own, willing to pay £200 for their own plane, four-wheel drive when we got there, lunch and a view of the comet crater, plus many more wonderful sights and sounds, as promised in the brochure.

Instead, tomorrow I go into the outback visiting various sights and phenomena in the Western Mac-Donnell Ranges and then the next day I do biking.

In the evening, I'm going for some 'Bush Tucker', i. e. I'm going to sit round a camp fire and sing bush songs, have a bush BBQ at the cattle drovers' camp, find out how to throw my boomerang and make damper bread. All that and back by 9.30. I think it's an Aussie version of the Mediaeval Banquet. Instead of serving wenches, they have hardened cowboys slinging your food at you as you check to see what dangerous insect is crawling up your trouser leg and how much longer you have to live.

Tuesday

So I went into the MacDonnell Range yesterday morning. Pat and her net. Was I ever glad I'd got it. Just a couple of people didn't have them – everywhere they'd asked, sold out. It's official, there is a plague of flies this year. At least if I were in Egypt, I'd see the Pyramids.

Even so, the scenery is quite stark and beautiful. Danny, the guide, was Aboriginal – friendly. Many facts and figures. When the powers that be built housing for the Aborigines, they moved in, promptly took out all the windows and generally trashed them. David Gulpilie, the Aboriginal star of Crocodile Dundee, Walkabout and quite a few others, was a local. He now lives near Darwin in a Humpy, which is the normal house for native folk. A hole in the ground with a corrugated roof on stilts. It stays cool and protects generally from the elements. No windows though.

Aborigines never worry about tomorrow. If they have enough to eat and clothes to wear today, that's as far ahead as they'll think. When David made Crocodile Dundee, he got £14,000 (about), he gave it to his mother and she shared it among all the relatives. That's the Aboriginal way.

There are many Aboriginal people nearby, but they are all different tribes and speak different languages. They do not intermarry between tribes. In Alice Springs, they have their own school. It helps because they have no written language of their own and can't benefit properly from normal education. Their communities are dry, so once someone takes to the drink, they're expelled which explains why there are so many Aboriginal drunks about Alice Springs. As soon as I arrived in town, an Aboriginal woman came up and asked me for money. I must have looked like new blood. In his book 'Down Under', Bill Bryson noticed all the Aborigines in Alice Springs were ignored by the rest of the population, which are mainly white Australians and he inferred it was because they were Aborigines. But they are ignored because they are drunks and, let's face it, most of us avoid the alcoholics and drunks in our home towns. So it's not prejudice, they'd probably ignore white drunken Aussies as well.

Aborigines, by nature, do not live in towns. They live in the outback and when they go Walkabout it may be because they're drunk, but it's usually because it's a tradition and because they can.

Despite all the problems facing the Aboriginal people, many are now becoming doctors, lawyers, artists, actors. White Australians seem to be divided 50/50 between those who like Aborigines and those who do not. It seems to stir up deep-seated feelings either way.

To get back to the Aborigines; a story I heard from an anthropologist who lived with them as a child. He says Aborigines do not understand whites and of course, vice-versa and illustrated with this story.

A white man is replacing a fence. The sun is very high. He rips out the old one and has to dig deep for the replacement. He is feeling it. He looks over, and under the shade of a tree an Aborigine is sitting, doing nothing. He is angry and thinks, what a good-for-nothing is the native.

The Aborigine now watches as sweat pours off the white man. Why are white men so stupid to work during the hottest part of the day? He should sit in the shade, it's cool. The white guy thinks that it could be a good idea to offer the Aborigine some work as he may be unemployed. He goes over and says that if the native guy will come and help him, he will employ him and give him a proper wage at the end of the week and he can then go into town and buy food, clothes and anything he wants. He may even open a bank account. Imagine that, a bank account with money in it. All his and after a while, when he's saved up enough money, he will be able to retire and do what he wants – he can even sit under a tree all day. The Aborigine looked at him.

Do you know what the Aboriginal word for whites is? – ants – presumably because we're always rushing about. From their point of view a reasonable comparison. But I know, because I've read, that a scientific study found that ants are lazy. They scurry about for five minutes and for the rest of about an hour they skulk under leaves doing nothing. Do you think the queen knows? Is there a union? Is it the equivalent to the British Leyland tea break? I know when I've found them in my kitchen they're usually hiding under a canister or similar. I thought it was so I couldn't see them, now I know it's their fifty-five-minute tea break.

Aborigines have many wives and husbands. They have a very simple and at the same time, complicated system of preventing interbreeding. As they are such small tribes this could be a problem. They have four different family names and move around in a circular direction so that only every third generation you come full circle to your nearest that were. If I explained it in detail you'd think I was wearing crimplene flares, have grown a beard, with a wide shirt collar and tie (kipper) and you'd tuned in to Open University circa 1974. But it was very interesting.

There are no widows or widowers. When you

marry, your wife's sisters become your wives also and for the woman, her husband's brothers are also her husbands. Therefore, no widows or widowers. No infertility either. No can do, don't worry, I know a man who can.

I think one of the reasons natives don't worry past today is because of all their wives, it wouldn't do to dwell on everything. And imagine the women. 'Will you be putting that shelf up today Brother No 1 or should I ask one of the others?' She'd be given the run-around by them all. Everything would be done at the last possible moment – a bit like married life in UK really – so we're not so different after all.

Anyway, back to my morning trip in the ranges. I managed to see four black-footed wallabies, about fifteen inches high. One looked pregnant and stared back at me, quite unfazed. Seeing rock wallabies is a bit like saying I saw a blackbird. Not as common as sparrows, but not rare either. So, no 'I Spy' marks for that.

Danny said that a while ago, two hundred camels were brought into Central Australia and they were such successful breeders, that there are now more than 100,000 or 600,000, depending upon who you believe (Discovery Channel says 500,000). Well, I didn't see any of them. They're not small. Where the hell were they? Wild horses, kangaroos, seen them all, but 500,000 camels? Someone's pulling my leg. Now, we passed a camel farm, but a farm is a farm. Apparently camel is now appearing on menus, but they've got a humane programme of shipping them back to the Middle East (coals to Newcastle), just as if they've used Oz as an incubator and breeding ground. The trees are their favourite food and they're decimating them. The only problem is they ship them back alive and the camels are too tall for the ships, so it's still to be sorted. The wild horses are also rounded up. They provide pet food. I believe we do the same – is it the New Forest or Dartmoor?

On my morning trip (yes, back to that), we visited and walked to some beautiful gorges. For the last one though, it was high noon – thirty-seven degress, flies (remember the plague) everywhere and I was pacing myself for the evening BBQ. So as the others wandered off to see Standly Chasm, named after a self-sacrificing teacher of Aboriginal children, I bought a postcard of it as we were at the billy stop – see how easily I'm sliding into the language – and sat down with an ice cold bottle of water and contemplated Danny slaving away over a hot billy and getting out the 'light lunch'. I look rather fetching with my dust-coloured hair, green netting, topped off by my camouflage skullcap. Yes, that's what the netting has. I suppose they had to finish it somehow. Drinking's a problem though, you have to beat the flies at their own game. Quick, up with the net, thrust bottle inside, tip, swallow and out again before they twig you've left an opening by your hand. Odd times, one entered the forbidden planet, but generally, I was quicker than they were. Of course, I've only got head to neck covered and they still land on the netting and the rest of my body. I wait until I can't see too much and I have a good shake and a flick but not enough to bring me out of a sweat. They seem to think I'm a sun bed. Sitting here in the shade watching Danny, I'm beginning to feel an Aboriginal moment coming on. Just as well I'll only be here forty-eight hours or I could go native and then go walkabout. My family wouldn't be surprised. They're probably waiting for something like that to happen.

Hollywood has also been here making a film and the locals were quite amused when they went down to watch it being made. I think it was at a place called Emily's Creek, near Alice Springs.

They had a mechanical kangaroo. Danny, the guide, said to us the place is full of them and they have to make a mechanical one. Then again, the mechanical one would do what it was told.

I saw no evidence of Skippy's intellect among the 'roo population. Bouncing idiots could be a better description. They seem to think a good bounce will beat a car any day. Numerous tales of wild horses and 'roos going through car windows. Sometimes the passengers are lucky, sometimes not. The animals never are. Locals don't like driving at night and avoid it where possible. They regard it as dangerous, mainly for themselves. If they are out, they travel quite slowly, so they can stop.

Coming back, we crossed over the Todd River. I'm sure quite a wonderful sight in full spate, but alas, bone dry. It flash-floods when the monsoon rains come down from the north – rises to about five feet if the bridge they've put across is anything to go by. As it is, it's a quick route out of town.

Had to do some serious shopping yesterday afternoon and sunbathing. The night before I passed a closed shop in town – the clothes were just me. Did I hear anyone saying I was fifty per cent overweight already?

So the BBQ. I was Saga'd really. I got on Danny's coach (he of the morning trip) and found myself joined by about fifteen others of a certain age. The certain thing is, I was the youngest. These people were seasoned SAGAs, but not from UK, just

Australia and US.

Then she got on, the group leader, grabbed her microphone and proceeded to inform us all what she'd arrange for me that night. I got the full spiel. She was nice enough, but as we know I don't like microphones, loud hailers or people raising coloured umbrellas to get my attention. I want to be left alone.

We got there in daylight and there would be about thirty or forty of us from two mini-coaches.

Pat Brennan, a weather-beaten guy about fifty, gave a display with a boomerang and we all could have a go if we wanted.

I watched and waited a bit, some guys did quite well, some didn't. Most of the women having a go were so-so. One or two hit the ground immediately in front of them as did some of the men.

I then tried and Pat Brennan sort of arranged my fingers just so, and angled it as shown and on a good day I'd have taken down a bird for our supper. I don't think kangaroos would have to consult a therapist about the threat I posed. The speed mine went at, I think the 'roo could have caught it and sent it back. Still, I didn't disgrace myself and it went up and it did come back.

As an English woman, I'm afraid to say I'd be better with a boomerang than a bow and arrow. They really do fall at my feet. Robin Hood would never have had me in his gang. Ned Kelly, well now you're talking. I have the makings.

After this, Pat Brennan again gave a very amusing, with many anecdotes, talk on making damper bread. This is just self-raising flour, water and salt, then bake – no proving, nothing. He then put this in a special pot with lid in the middle of yesterday's ashes. Vegemite or Cocky's Joy is put on, along with Kangaroo butter. Cocky's Joy is better than it sounds as cocky is the cook and he, it appears, liked golden syrup. What a relief.

The Kangaroo butter tasted good, not too salty. They only milk the 'roo for three months per year as it has three Joeys per year and is feeding them the rest. The' roo is the only animal that can extend its pregnancy up to twenty-four months in time of drought to protect its young. Wouldn't do for me though.

After his turn with the boomerang and the damper bread, Pat must have decided he'd done enough and he'd keep his didgeridoo to himself.

Later he would be in charge of the steak. It was to be North Queensland beef and he assured us we'd never tasted anything like it.

Then it was the anthropologist's turn. As he'd lived with Aborigines during his childhood, he understood their ways. He used a very simple lecture technique and talked for about twenty minutes. By which time the steak, baked potatoes, salad and damper bread were ready. The steak *was* the best I've ever tasted. No fat, great texture, thick and tasty.

In its turn the bread was delicious. A Scotsman then arrived to sing folk songs and it was the usual singsong participation and we stopped just short of the hokey cokey. Remember it's a tour.

While all this had been going on, I'd been watching the 'catering staff' who totally consisted of Pat, his son (on the bar) Danny (the driver) and Don the anthropologist.

They tidied, straightened and allowing it was four very different men in charge of the whole caboodle it was extremely well run. All the drink was free, the food was good, even the music and for a finale Don took us down with a big torch to show us the stars.

He pointed out Saturn, Jupiter, the Southern Cross and told us how to find south, but now I've forgotten. I'm intrigued by the stars but as it isn't my abiding passion I soon forget.

The upshot of this evening was that I think time and motion would have been very impressed, that is, if they'd not already visited them.

Another thing I learned that night. Ranchers don't know how many cattle they have and when they want to finally round them all up, they make a waterhole and it's surrounded by gates, which are left open.

Each day the cattle get used to coming in for water and gradually they begin to shut the gates until one day, only one is left and then naturally they shut that. They usually have about ten to fifteen per cent more than they thought. It doesn't mean they aren't good ranchers, it just means they've so much land they can't check it all.

I have yet to find out the name, but the bush is now covered in an imported grass. In the olden days, Aborigines and ranchers set fire to grass for many reasons but mainly renewal. That was OK.

Now, the new imported grass burns at such a fierce heat, no regeneration is possible and it's destroying the natural balance of things. Trees are completely destroyed.

See you later,

Love Pat.

Striped Knickers

Dear everybody,

I notice in the Sydney *Morning Herald* 4 April 03 there's a review of a Michael Parkinson show where he'd interviewed Rod Stewart, Natalie Cole and Halle Berry, which must have been shown on Australian TV.

The programme had got quite a savaging, and I quote, 'This is a pointless blend of narcissism and cross-promotion dusted down with evanescent glitter and an avuncular gravitas. For all his fireside charm, Parky is just another tart in a media brothel. Viewers yearning for genuine character and personality should stay tuned for the frozen alien whose activities propel "The Thing from Another World" at 10.30.' Unquote.

Does he mean our beloved Parky? Surely not. Whatever has Parky done to annoy this particular reviewer; his name is Doug Anderson, who rattled his cage? It's really purple prose as well. You can almost see him sharpening his knife.

Television last night had their version of Ground Force, called Backyard Blitz. Not quite as genteel as ours but it tells you what it does. They have two guys and a girl and a gofer. The girl's bottled out because she wears a bra, but also a tight T-shirt ... Don't suppose it gets wet very often though. 'Tommy' is not as overweight. They also have Location, Location. It's just the same except they stage auctions of houses as well. The poor people wait upstairs while it's being conducted. The people who move them out of their house aren't removers, they are removalists. Sounds a bit like saying recycling operative for a dustman.

When I bought my fly net, I took it out of a packet labelled 'Barker's Souvenirs'. How can an item that must be part of any survivalist's kit or for that matter a holidaymaker lifesaver, be called a souvenir? Don't they have any sense of irony? Barker's Buy or Die or Barker's Life's Essentials – anything but souvenir.

Now, quad biking – I was outside for 7am. The hotel did not give me a wake up call, but fortunately, I awoke eight minutes after it was due. It turned out there was only me. I love this one-to-one tuition.

Nick was his name, thirty-six and fit. I'm not interested and I know he wasn't but it still makes it all the more pleasurable if you get an Adonis. His first child was due in May and a rival firm had just set up in town so at the end, I gave him some sales and marketing advice – two pages in all. As I said, if he only uses one idea, it's better than none. He had not thought of the one where every fortnight, his partner rings up as a punter and gets to know what offers and deals his rival is doing. Nice guy you see, not crafty enough. Takes a woman to think devious.

I arrived with my fly net, got my helmet, out came the bike. Quick tuition. Automatic – quite simple really. It had taken us an hour to get out to the oldest cattle station in Central Australia. I followed him, rather hesitant. Quite a lot of stops and starts.

Within minutes, we were deep in the outback as this ranch is quite big and only Nick has the arrangement to use it. So you see, no one – just animals.

At first, no animals were about but as I was getting

used to my machine, it didn't matter, we were only doing about fifteen miles an hour, but the red dirt tracks were bumpy and had some very deep ruts in them. Nick kept looking behind and I was still there but I don't think he realised on a couple of occasions I was nearly up a steep embankment and away or worse still – I nearly overturned. I realised I'd have to concentrate on the steering and the motor would have to take care of itself. It was much easier after that.

We went about ten miles but we had not seen any animals. Remember the 100,000 or 600,000 camels? Still no sign. Reckon they are an urban myth or in this case, outback myth.

Nick knew I wanted a camcording of me quad biking so he stopped and took my recorder and said he would go to the top of this hill and I could roar up the track once he waved. He got to the top, waved and I was off. I was going great when I got there. He said he had something to tell me, he didn't think he had got much of me, because when he waved he'd still to find me in the viewfinder and also the camera had a flashing thing on it. As I had no glasses he identified it as the film was finished. I'd charged the bloody thing the night before as it had run out of charge somewhere else in the middle – can't remember where. Now here I was with another film gone and I hardly seem to be able to use the damn thing. How can the film be used up? It did this in the middle of the river cruise in China.

We went back a bit to go on paths which were so narrow there was just enough room for the bikes and then we saw them – kangaroos. A whole family. Remember, up to now, I'd seen four wallabies (blackbirds). Now although the 'roos are the sparrows of Oz, I was still quite pleased. By the time I'd got my camera out they'd bounced away. Nick then took charge of my camera. I didn't like to remind him he was as good as I was with the camcorder.

A bit further on, more 'roos and when they moved, five of them started jumping. I'd only seen three even though everything is either red dust or greenish shrubbery, they were well camouflaged.

A bit further along the track, we came to a waterhole. Nick signalled me forward quietly. I came as quite as my quad bike would allow. He said 'dingo' and it was eating something. Probably 'roo said Nick. Some other dingoes went off as we went by but one stayed. We watched and Nick said did I see how skinny the one who stayed was? I have to be honest, I was making sure the 'roo it was eating was dead. I'm not very good with Life of Mammals when they do predators. I know they have to kill to live but I don't want to know about it. Nick explained that the skinny dingo was so desperate to eat, it could not leave it even though we were there. This was probably its last chance.

I noticed some birds' nests in the trees and asked Nick if we could get a close-up of a cockatoo's nest. Not that one said I, one of those funny ones suspended. Oh, you mean ants' nests. These ants I like. They have a proper sense of their place in life. Not for them invasion of people's kitchens and gardens. They have the decency to live halfway up a tree. I speak as one who does not know (but does care) whether the ants at Rose Cottage have found their way into my new kitchen. I'd blocked all the places I thought they could get in and now Andy's in charge and on ant patrol. He is not the person I would have chosen but he's all I've got on site. He'd be highly offended to read this, but he would have to admit, ants come way down his list of life's priorities, somewhere around cleaning loos and baths when you've used them. I have spies you see and there have been reports. Caroline says they'll get in industrial cleaners before I return. For goodness' sake, I've only been gone a month. Does it only take four weeks to trash a place? Apparently so.

Back to the ants in the tree. Nick found me a nest, suspended on what appeared to be cobwebs and the shape was a bit like an anvil. I photographed it, then he said he'd break it open for me. This is where it all started to turn nasty. You see, I hadn't my glasses on and Nick got a stick and started poking this very peculiar shaped nest. It didn't work at first. He had about three goes and kept jumping back quickly. It was about head height. Nick asked me if I had got the picture. I said, 'Are they coming out?' He said quick, as he held the stick. I still could not see any and my visor and fly net kept getting in the way of the camera. Eventually, I clicked but by this time Nick was brushing some very mad ants off his clothes. As we came back to the bikes he was stamping his feet. The upshot of this was he had to take his shoes and socks off to clear them all away. He said, 'Are you OK? Are they on your shoes?' No, says I, I'm fine. No answer from Nick.

We came back via the waterhole and a herd of cows – bet you thought I was going to say camels – was on one side including some calves while the dingo was still eating on the other side. I don't think they'd have risked it if it hadn't got its meal.

Back through the dirt tracks, me in Nick's slipstream all the way. At one stage, whenever I turned a corner, he wasn't there, so I had to guess which way he'd gone. This had nothing to do with the ants because he'd been joking when he put his socks back on – at least I don't think so. Actually, he knew I was quite confident by then and I eventually caught him up where it widened coming up to the cattle station. We never went more than twenty miles an hour, but Nick said with the tracks in the condition they were, any faster could be dangerous. Where it was wide enough we rode side by side, which meant not as much dust for me. Once he said we were turning back, I didn't get a good enough lock and had to reverse, so I executed a five point turn. Not my finest moment but at least I found reverse, so I had been listening you see.

There was like a tuck box at the front of my bike with ice-cold water and all my things in and strangely enough, they were all still in one piece and working, despite the shaking they'd had.

I went back to the hotel and all the front desk fell about laughing. 'You look a bit dirty, Mrs Buckley'. Being on the wrong side of my face I could not appreciate their humour. I reached my room and saw something that looked half-human. You know, in those movies about the desert and gold rush and you see the half-crazed old timer still working his claim. Well, other than the extra poundage, I was a dead ringer for one of them. My eyebrows now the colour of red dust, met in the middle, my nose had a big indentation where the visor had wedged my sunglasses, below that it was bright red and swollen. The red dust was in layers as though I'd been tie-dyed and left in the sun too long. My Stilton shoes also had an aroma all their own – and I'm still thinking of a suitable name. I'd worn long trousers, the thicker ones I had packed for New Zealand. I'd taken my towelling beach bag which had been sunshine yellow and now resembled a camel with a touch of zebra. The alarming thing was, this had been in the tuck box.

I stripped everything off and carefully put the lot into 'a special bag'. I'd spotted a launderette at this hotel and hoped they'd have one at my next. Even my knickers had that outback look. I showered, washed my hair and got ready for the flight

As I write this, I am in a window seat awaiting take-off to Cairns – and we are off. Seated in 12C (I'm 12A), is a rather Middle Eastern-looking guy. He didn't seem to have any hand luggage as opposed to the packhorse seated by him. He then read the safety manual and paid particular attention to the life jacket. This flight is overland. He has a look of Tariq Ali (do you remember the Pakistani left-wing student agitator demonstrator? He is now a Channel Four producer). Well, he looks like him and I think he's suspicious. I keep making sure he doesn't try to light his shoes.

Later

We're just coming in to land at Cairns. Just a short flight really and I see I have pick-up this time. How nice. Wonder what the humidity is like. Will my fly net be redundant? Could I sell it at departures to Alice Springs for a huge profit? Cairns is back to rainforest country.

Is the airport big enough to have a connecting walkway, or is it another hot drag down the steps across the tarmac? Had to do that at Alice Springs and until I left today, I'd forgotten how bad it was.

A quick shuffle across with attendant flies. I think they wait for you to land. Thirty-seven degrees. First fly – 'Joe, they'll soon be sweating; pity it's not humid today – quenches the thirst nicely'. I've been told the flies are after moisture. If I'd known that, I'd have made sure they had plenty.

I am pleased to tell you that 12C turned out to be a nice Aussie going to a conference in Brisbane. He worked for a brewery. So, no chance of a redundancy there.

He was grumpy as he boarded so I ignored him, other than keeping my eye on his shoe as I said. As we were landing and I put away the letter I was writing, he started chatting and I could not shut him up. He used to run a caravan park in Cairns. I got his life story. Could be he wanted to reassure me. Perhaps he'd read my mind.

So, about paying the price for quad biking. First I couldn't work out what was wrong. It appeared all that bouncing, jolting and flying off the bike seat had made my heavy cotton pants rub me and I had friction burns on each inner thigh. My knee (gammy one) had swollen and I could hardly bend it. Still, I loved it and I enjoyed every minute of the biking. It was a bit like riding a wooden roller coaster where you get thrown around a lot, white water rafting without the white water or the raft.

As I got on the plane today, a woman behind said she had been admiring my dress. She was American. I said, 'California, Laguna'; she said 'Fresh Produce' which is the label and that this year they are all over Maine where she was from. I got mine two years ago and use it now for all the hot travel. It's got pockets for my tickets and change and looks clean and fresh. Well, one of us needs to.

Love,

Pat.

"3 bag Buckley"

Cairns, Queensland
02.04.03.

Dear Clare and Michael,

This hotel doesn't provide writing paper. It must think having the Great Barrier Reef and one of the world's largest rainforests on its doorstep, you'd be too busy to write anything but a postcard. How wrong they are!

Tomorrow, it's the big one. Now, I'm not as scared of the great white shark as I am of the snorkelling.

I've made *many* detailed enquiries. You'd think the heir to the throne was going snorkelling. I've found out that I can have a line attached to the lines – these, I was told by a very helpful girl selling me the trip, were lines on either side of the vessel; I presume I am then attached to this, so they don't lose me. I can have a buddy à la Bali or I can have a buoy I'm attached to and bob about. The latter seems a trifle sloppy to me. They could lose a buoy and me. We're talking very big ocean here; it takes one and a half hours by fast catamaran to get there.

Did you know the only time I went on a hovercraft, Roy called me Three Bag Buckley? I won't go into details, but I used one before we left Dover Harbour. I've got the odd feeling catamarans are similar, I am not a good sailor. It's 11pm and I'm wondering whether to ring their twenty-four hour hotline and ask re the helicopter. I'm sure these twenty-four hour hotlines are for people like me. Not sure if you're doing the right thing and glad there's an alternative.

Just a thought – do you think the great whites don't bother with the divers and 'free' snorkellers and just wait for the ones coming along on the line? I bet they even know the time you are due. If I were a lazy shark and had developed a taste for humans, I'd certainly wait for someone to come bubbling along, especially if, occasionally, they panicked and flapped about a bit. Add some excitement to the catch or is that kill?

If you look at it from our point of view, they could be like us with the fox and give it a head start. So they may only go for the divers, the brave ones, because they feel they've had a sporting chance.

A TV advert now tells everyone to get ready for the cyclone season. It has a disaster line and tips. One such tip is to tidy all debris about the garden and batten down your eaves.

Suddenly England doesn't seem too bad. At least our debris stays in one place the majority of the time and have we some debris at Rose Cottage.

Contrary to popular belief, Aussie men seem charming and urbane, at least in the cities. In the outback they were friendly but perhaps the older ones were brusque on a one-to-one basis. Not been fitted with the charm offensive pellet at birth then?

Just a quick note this time, too much to do in too short a time.

Love Pat

An Awfully Big Adventure

10 April 2003

Dear Sue and Peter,

I'm at another airport en route to Christchurch via Sydney. You know coach passengers are my bête noir, well a coach arrived as I did at departures. They got off their coach and then milled. They are so good at milling. They mill because they are like sheep, until someone tells them what to do they're clueless. This morning they probably had to have their bags outside their rooms at 7am and someone, a little elf perhaps, spirited them away and as if by magic they appeared on the coach. They are then reunited with their luggage. This is a chance for a MAJOR mill. They can fill the entire pavement with themselves and their luggage. They shuffle and even their luggage shuffles. They're not safe and are determined if they don't run over your toes with their wheels, they will stop you from getting a trolley.

You can tell I've got a strop on, as I had to weave my way through and when I got my trolley, I'd to go on the road past two coaches just to get back to my luggage. They only missed my toes because I'm not witless.

These same people are now having to make more decisions for themselves at the juice bar and the queue stretches forever. Judging by the speed they manage to connect one brain cell to the next, my flight will have departed before I can get a drink.

They're not just one nationality either. It's as though they put something in the coffee aboard the coaches or it could be a temporary lobotomy, reversible as they collect the luggage for the last time.

And do you know this morning I got up my usual amiable self? It took just one look at the 'Down Under Tours' charabanc and its passengers to turn me into a short-tempered, smug, independent traveller wanting to transport them, like Star Trek, to another planet.

I feel better now, got an ice cold watermelon drink and equilibrium is restored, but I don't take back a word about the zombies. When they tell people they're touring Australia, what they really mean is they're being propelled round Australia, being told when to get off, where to go, when to be back, when they have 'free time' (that's probably when they go to the loo without a timetable), when to be up and where to report to. They have vouchers for all their meals so can't choose where to eat. I wouldn't be surprised if they got a set menu. No choice, no stress.

I have watched many 'coach people' and I'm constantly surprised by their attitude to the patronising way they are treated by their 'guide'. It's either patronising or a Butlinesque approach.

Are we happy campers? I can't hear you. Are we happy campers? That's better.

It is a patronising *and* Butlinesque approach I've decided. What on earth could possibly be worse than that?

On to happier ruminations, yesterday was the Great Barrier Reef. I took two ginger pills provided on board before we started and plonked myself down at one of the long tables. There were two boys and a girl at the other end. The tables took ten people. I spoke to one of the staff and then the girl at the table asked where I was from. I said England. She said she already knew that, but which town near Preston? So it appeared they were from Preston too. Out of all the tables to sit at, I'd chosen Prestonians. It would appear no one was allowed at the table without a PR postcode. They were all post grads. Two had even got jobs. One was at BHS and the other at Airline Network, where the rest of our family had booked their flights. Two were going on the trial dive and Andy, who had asthma, was snorkelling. There's a semi submersible too, so everyone is catered for. I was quite looking forward to that.

Feeling a bit queasy. Quite a big swell. Was told that high tide at first reef and low tide at second. Less swell there.

You could hire wetsuits and these were recommended as they keep you buoyant. That's what I need, buoyancy. I'll have one of those, have you got one to fit me? I'm sure we'll find something. I also want a life vest. That's fine. Do you have buddies? Now there were about a hundred and fifty on board and I hadn't really believed they'd have a buddy for everyone. They didn't even have one for me. They've been telling me porkies. And that line I can be attached to. It's two lines on either side of the boat and you've to stay in between so you can be rescued. Rescued? The brochure said nothing about that. Why will I need rescuing? What can go wrong? You've assured me I can't sink. Have I misunderstood? I think I have.

After one and half hours we're out at the reef and slowing. I still haven't left my seat, owing to the swell. The friction burn has improved and my knee isn't as swollen. Quad biking in the outback was only forty-eight hours ago. I go up top to get my gear. My safety number is eighteen. I think they mean rescue number. I struggle into an enormous wetsuit. Made for a sumo wrestler I believe. Then I don my life vest. One of the guys tells me I should wear flippers as it's easier to swim. I look out at the ocean, can't see land, the water is rising over the pontoon and it generally could be described as choppy.

I told him my foot size but once again he must not have believed me as I was struggling into a size four. Someone came to help and brought back size eight. I could get my toes in but couldn't sort out the heel. Someone sorted it. I staggered to the pontoon. The sea in front of it was a mass of seething bodies, flippers going everywhere. It looked like the local swimming baths, first day of the school hols in the middle of a heatwave. There didn't seem to be an empty bit of water to make an entrance among the masses (I don't think they were a coach tour.)

I sat on the pontoon steps. This blonde tanned girl (about twenty-two) said, 'Well, are you going? You're holding everyone up.' Realisation dawned on me, I'd become a tour zombie. I was MILLING.

I tried to explain that I really needed a buddy and I had been known to panic. She looked horror struck. Remember she was an Aussie, born with her own flippers and gills. She said I'd better go with the large ring. This is where Betty or Laura (who cares) takes three other people and tows them around for ten minutes. Then it's someone else's turn. I didn't really want to do this or I might get to like it and the next thing my suitcases would have to be outside my bedroom by 7am. You see it sounds like a tour. The ocean version of a coach. Betty says go here, now I'll take you back. The photographer was in the water. He'd told us to smile and he'd let us know if he'd got a good picture.

I will not be having the photo of me clasping onto a large ring looking like a whale wearing a yellow life vest while another woman on the ring in an even worse state than me struggles for life.

Shortly after the photo, the woman managed to gasp she wanted to go back. So I got five minutes in the water. Great Barrier Reef only a fuzzy view 'down below'. It was so hard getting back onto the pontoon with flippers and the swell of the water. Every time I tried, the water dashed me against the metal side. Capt Ahab was needed again. I needed landing. Someone, it could have been the lifeguard, was looking for people to rescue and decided I'd had enough and hauled me in. I was exhausted. The stress, the swell, the coming back aboard, Bali was a piece of cake.

I managed to get my flippers off (more help) and left my suit on a hanger ready for the afternoon session at the next reef. What next session?

I found the sunbathing deck and dried out. It was lovely, but my tan hasn't improved. All I need is three days in Wales to get browner than this.

They served a BBQ lunch, the ubiquitous steak, sausage, salad. They kept announcing for everyone to take only one sausage, one steak, as there were some people still in the water who hadn't eaten. It was the most worried I heard them since we left port.

Water safety was quite casual. Before I entered with Betty and her ring, an alarm was sounded and the lifeguard had to run to find a pair of flippers and struggled to get them on. He kept saying, 'Is it a call?' Talk about laid back, I'm glad it wasn't me, I feel the cavalier attitude could have seriously jeopardised my water confidence!

We arrived at the second reef about 1.30pm. I'd booked a helicopter trip back and a jaunt of the reef and islands. I'd to be ready for 3.20. I also wanted a trip in the semi-submersible.

I weighed up the water. The swell didn't seem as bad. I went to look at the pontoon. Actually, pontoon is a rather glamorous word for a metal flap with another just beneath it measuring about one metre deep and two metres wide.

There was hardly anyone in the water. Those that were, were well away from the boat.

Time to don the outfit. I decided to go down the steps. There was no bossy, exasperated blondie heckling me. I took my time. A woman came out of the water similar to myself and she'd been using a half-moon polystyrene thing. I'd tried one in Austria at the spa. I asked her if she could swim and she was exactly the same as me – never out of her depth. She'd only got her costume on and a half moon and was ok.

I thought about this, kept the outfit on and grabbed a half moon. Facemask in place, snorkel introduce to mouth, breathing begun. As it echoed round my head in, out, in, out, I remembered Dustin Hoffman in 'The Graduate'. He'd come to life again, only this time he had a lifejacket and a polystyrene ring and had changed sex. There is something Neanderthal about trying to walk in flippers, especially size eight, down the steps. I kept bobbing a bit, still grabbing the steps. I found out I couldn't go under. Something was working but I didn't know which. I pushed off, don't forget to breathe, look down, find the coral.

After some time I became entangled in the rope. My flippers were on the wrong side of it, shortly to be followed by the rest of my body. I'd gone in the wrong direction and the swell had taken me that way. I swam towards the others. When I brought my face up ten minutes later I was no nearer. Still no coral. I used my flippers. Suddenly I could see fish, then coral. Then other flippers. It had only taken twenty minutes and I'd managed to travel twenty metres.

After my setback in the morning, I thought it better not to take my underwater camera with me. If I didn't remember to breathe, no amount of photography would help.

I felt I was just like the others, except they hadn't got a Michelin man suit on or a life vest or a half moon. They looked quite soignée, all swimsuits, bikinis, snorkels, masks and fins. The sort you see on postcards.

Bursting with confidence, I made my way back to the pontoon and asked if someone could get my camera. Just then, Helen, Stuart and Andy (the Prestonians) appeared to go in the water. They got my camera and Andy said he'd take pictures of me underwater. It was getting better by the minute. We all set off and I managed to make my way back, via my usual round-about route, you understand, to the reef.

Andy said he'd go beneath me so he could get a shot of me actually in the water. There was a big flurry and he dived down. He got two. Then I took over the camera. I've only eight left now. I forgot all about time and stayed out for – well it was an hour, because I nearly missed my heli-flight back.

I dripped myself to the changing rooms (the toilets), decided not to purchase my official picture with Betty and the large ring and trust Andy sorted it for real.

I'd missed the semi submersible but what the heck, that was for wimps, not nervous swimmers using every buoyancy aid known to man.

If I snorkel in Thailand, perhaps I can dispose of the half moon – no, the Michelin suit. I'll have a life jacket and half moon then I'll look half human at least.

The trip back over the reef was gorgeous, but I've just had an even better view on the plane from Cairns to Sydney. It went way over all the reefs not normally accessible. Fantastic.

The pilot of the helicopter, was the owner of the company and in his mid-fifties. We landed back three quarters of an hour before the boat and his very young Brazilian wife was waiting for him with a baby boy, Liam, about six months old. He then dropped two of us, his passengers, off at our hotels.

He tells me the company targets Brits and Aussies and Europeans in general. The Chinese market is no good to them as, and I quote, 'They eat too much and spit on the boat'. The Indians don't want to pay full price and don't understand it's non-negotiable. He also thought the Americans tight with money. First time I've heard that. Not willing to spend is how he put it.

Despite our reputation as whingers, Brits appear to be popular with the Aussies. Could be common language and nearly everyone is a relative of a Brit, somewhere. An awful lot of stick though re cricket, e. g. cricket lessons begin for the Brits on the upper deck. That's the sun up there, brings the daylight if you haven't seen it before.

So that was it, Pat's awfully big adventure is over.

A postscript to it, I have found is that I have a very sore, slightly bruised throat. This was where the life vest kept pressing against it by the force of the water and I think the sumo suit. Still it's better than friction burns.

The hotel I've just left in Cairns, sub-tropical gardens, had four pools. The freeform pool which had shale-like stones at the bottom (this was actually a solid floor) natural colour and an undulating shape surrounded by trees, shrubs, plants, boulders and stones was the one I used mainly and I had a view of from my bedroom. Beyond the pool was a terrace for drinks. Also there was a small freeform children's pool.

Through the gardens to a full size pool, which deepened halfway across and then shallowed again. Beyond that was the BIG ONE. The diving pool, 2.8 metres deep. I kept well away from that one. Just to show how seriously committed they were to the holidaymakers' needs, they were all open twenty-four hours a day.

I feel when you are away in a hot climate, there is nothing more exciting than swimming in the dark, late at night. I only did it once, but the point was, I could.

I felt quite decadent.

In Cairns itself there is an open-air pool, right by the beach. One for children too. At 10pm both were being used. It was lovely to watch. They seem to have the right idea about enjoying themselves over here.

As we flew back over the reef yesterday the pilot said that a hammerhead shark – yes, that innocent one, the one we're all told is harmless – had attacked a Dutch tourist recently. The first attack in many years, as they're proud of their safety record. The woman, he assured us was ok as they 'took her to hospital and sewed her up, she'll be right.' He seemed mightily unconcerned, not quite how the Dutch woman would feel I'm sure.

The hammerhead attacked because it was the breeding season. I still think it should have hammered not bitten the victim.

As we came along the shoreline we zoomed in to the river mouth to see if there were any saltwater crocodiles in the pen. Sadly there weren't. I have to admit I didn't pursue this so don't know what happens to them.

In Oz, petrol is 30p a litre, diesel 33p; it had come down as the war started. Here in New Zealand petrol is the same but diesel is 23p a litre. It's like another world.

I'm on my way now to Queensland to meet Lynley. I've stayed overnight in Christchurch (I arrived at 1pm) and am due Queenstown midday. Yesterday was a long day. I'd a two-hour time change (where I lost time). I left Cairns at 9.30 my hotel, arrived Sydney 3.30. Got some tax refunded – that's never happened to me before – and waited around Sydney for four hours. As I said, lost two hours and finally reached hotel after midnight.

I reckon I will have spent at least nine days just travelling on this trip minimum. Just as well I came for sixty-two days.

I haven't seen Lynley for about fourteen years. If you remember, she's Paul's ex-girlfriend, a Kiwi. I spoke to her yesterday, and she sounded quite excited. Hope I like her mum, and vice versa.

The flight is only forty minutes long, which sort of makes up for yesterday.

I've been checking up on the white water rafting here and some of the rivers appear to have vertical falls in the middle. One it seems created by the 1978 earthquake. I know New Zealand has active volcanoes but where do earthquakes come in? Have I not been paying attention? Seems not.

Just coming in to land, we're over mountains at the moment and only just at that. Still, the pilot knows what he's doing, we're flying down a valley, mountains on each side, very, very close, and then we land. A very skilled piece of flying.

See you soon,

Love Pat

What Kind Of Lettuce?

Dear Sue and Peter,

Lynley met me before I'd even got my baggage, so as you'll appreciate this is a small airport. It was raining and she was disappointed as the mountains were in cloud. The scenery was idyllic and I couldn't even see most of the mountains. Two more weeks and the autumn colours will be out.

Lynley looked no different. Don't think she recognised me though! Was I such a big shock? Was I dark-haired last time she saw me? I think I was.

I'm staying with Lynley and husband Dale (an American) in their garage. What's happened is, they bought a fabulous piece of land, with mountain views, it's very much Little House on the Prairie with pine log houses all over. Her mother has the front house and Lynley the back, which is where the garage comes in.

Actually it's like a chalet you get on a holiday park and very cosy. This year they hope to start building their home, which is why they're not going to visit the US this year.

The rain is coming down relentlessly, which I believe is quite unusual. It's their version of the plague of flies. Lynley had had to go back to work as she has to work weekends because it's a garden centre. She's taken some days off next week for us to do some touring.

When she lived in London with Paul, she was a

gardener at Kensington Palace. Some days she had to do duck patrol, which meant escorting the ducks from their nest under the bushes to the lake. She had to make sure no birds swooped on the ducklings. There's job satisfaction for you.

This morning at the airport hotel, the waitress was called Joy. A misnomer if ever there was. That's the trouble with this type of given name, it can all go horribly wrong.

Just as well Joy didn't have the Indian family dining at her table, who were in Cairns the other night.

They enquired what the Mediterranean salad contained. The waitress said, cucumber, tomatoes, mixed lettuce leaves, feta cheese. What other cheeses had they? Off to the kitchen, returned, rattled off about four others. They decided. Then, what sort of mixed lettuce leaves? Back to the kitchen and she recited about seven different types of leaf.

I left them at it. This, after all was only the starters. I wonder if they tipped her and paid a portion of her shoe soling bill!

There is a lot in the New Zealand media regarding the SARS virus. So far no cases there and they want to keep it that way. The local paper has found the hospital lacking. They can only cater for one case, after that they panic.

It was reported in the Sydney *Morning Herald* that the virus combined with the Iraqi war is as big a threat to tourism as 11 September and the collapse of Ausett (Oz's other major airline) combined.

Cabin staff from New Zealand refused to fly to Hong Kong this week and several Qantas staff have done the same.

Another article headline saying 'Qantas to provide masks' is as misleading as an Alistair Campbell header. What this means says the article is that Qantas will provide masks only for passengers who think they may be sitting next to someone incubating the dreaded disease. If doctors are struggling to identify this virus how does a layman/woman innocently going about their business of getting from A to B, make this diagnosis? Definitely a Blair/Campbell publicity stunt.

Many Aussie ex-pats were flying home from Hong Kong as though they were in a war zone. Talking to the press about how they were relieved to be 'out' or 'safe.' Does this seem like an over-reaction? What on earth will they do if terrorists bomb them?

A woman reported seeing all these people in Armani suits wearing green facemasks in Hong Kong, and said it felt weird and eerie. True, but quaint with it.

The same newspaper reported the Aussie Deputy Prime Minister as giving the go ahead for the first GM crop trials, while at the same time ignoring a report by the gene regulators that GM canola poses health and environmental risks. Canola is oil-seed rape to us

Are all politicians, no matter which country, lacking that basic instinct for survival of the species? Does it only come into force when they want our votes?

Living in their ivory towers and air-conditioned limousines, they don't seem to realise that their families will be just as affected when all crops are contaminated, as Joe Public's.

When I thought of writing to you both, I thought it would be all elegant prose and dry observations. Instead I find I'm writing a full-on assault of the senses in every sense of the word. I even wonder if you're still reading by now.

Tomorrow I'm due to go jet boating down the gorges and canyons of the alpine rivers. It's forty-five minutes of high adrenaline – but my knee is now very swollen. It looks like fluid. I, who hardly ever do any housework, have got housemaid's knee. How about that for irony?

Earlier today I saw two straw bale houses. That's what they were made of. In the first one they built there is a window in one part of the wall inside where the straw bale can be seen.

One is finished in battleship grey and the other is white. The finish makes them look like they are adobes. They have a rounded look to the walls. They are sealed of course after the bales are put in, I believe it keeps warm in winter and here it can get to minus six, and cool in summer, which appears to top at about thirty degrees or so. This is South Island but I think North Island is hotter.

So, I'll have to see what tomorrow brings. I think I damaged my knee further by climbing back onto the pontoon at the reef. It doesn't take much and the pontoon is like studded metal, so it doesn't become slippy. The price one pays for one's ambitions.

Love

Pat.

I'll Put A Bra On
The Bra Fence

New Zealand
11 April 2003

Dear Clare and Michael,

Despite my knee developing a life of its own and swelling profusely, I was off, not quite at the crack of dawn, but we had jet boating booked for 2.30 near Arrowtown.

We wandered round Queenstown, getting new films, visiting the God of ATMs and generally pottering. We went up in the gondola for the great view of Queenstown and the Remarkables (truly remarkable mountains).

I'd seen there was a restaurant up there with a view similar to the gondolas, so we ambled in for lunch. It was a buffet definitely angled at the Asian market, curries, stir-fries but I managed to find a venison ragout after a superb salad and fish bar. The desserts were pretty good too.

We were running out of time for the jet boating so managed to change it for 3.30.

This meant time for the free chair lift. It may seem wonderful, but allowing for the leg and as it kept moving, as chair lifts do, I was in a quandary. Do I go for it with good or bad leg first. It was solved for me. Put your feet on the marks and it will meet you.

It was a near thing, a lot of wobbling about and shrieking and I realised why there were so many on the viewing deck to watch the chair lift. This could have been used as a family day out. Entertainment provided by various nationalities, weights and sizes. Women with funny knees likely to provide the most camcorder events.

The chair lift led up to the Luge and there was a scenic route and a fast route. You got your own helmet and a quick intro to the intricacies, park, neutral, brake. I wisely chose the scenic route. Even then I was overtaken, but although I only wanted to go at a steady pace I think my machine was a little lacking. It stopped completely on one downward slope and as I got to the end, in full view of everyone, it died again. Humiliation was complete when another 'luger' left his and gave me a push. The other instruction I was given was to stick my feet out and pedal it. I could no more have extricated my foot and pedalled than gone to the moon.

Of all my adventures that was the most disappointing, a real let-down – so off to the jet boating on the Shotover River, the richest river in New Zealand, possibly the world – full of gold. Lynley and I decided we wanted to go in the front and strangely enough no one stopped us. There was the driver/pilot/death wish driver/ whatever, and us two. We were the only two to have seat belts. I felt somehow that at the front was the biggest thrill, otherwise, why would we need belts?

It's forty-five minutes, through the gorges and canyons and the boats are such that they can manoeuvre in four inches of water. Even if the gorges are wide enough, he gets you against the rocks with just millimetres to spare. They promise you a big rush of adrenaline and you get it. When the driver makes a turning sign you have to hold on tightly and he does a 360-degree turn at speed and you finish up inches from the rock face. He does four altogether and the last one is the most spectacular as you come in to land. There's a lot of screaming and laughing hysterically and it does take your breath away. I have since found out there was a death recently on the Shotover River. Would I still have gone, had I known? Oh, I think I would.

On land again you have not got your 'land legs' for about five minutes. You also have a vague feeling of queasiness. Fortunately the adrenaline seems to override it.

For most of the time I had my bad leg suspended, as going over the shallows you hit stones and rocks and they really jarred. I must say though its no worse, but it's not better either.

Tomorrow we go to Milford Sound and the Fjords, we're staying overnight. On the way back I go to the glow-worm caves.

There's no real crime in Wanaka and Lynley doesn't lock her doors day or night. Doesn't it take you back? Then again I don't thing I was born when that was the case in our part of England.

Yesterday I spent my first day visiting friends of Lynley's mum (Jean) and Lynley's. Every kiwi house I've been in has been in a different state of development. Lynley's brother, just back with family from Oz were living with Jean and negotiating for a piece of land. Not in Wanaka, but Alexandra, about one hour away. Two reasons for this, the youngest child cannot get in pre-school here and house and land charges are about a quarter of the price of here.

No matter how grand the house, something was ongoing. A beautiful house on many acres, river frontage, only got a loo two years ago. The skirtings were being stained in the workshop (he's a builder) prior to fitting today. Further down on the same land, Lynley's brother and girlfriend were living in another garage, but this time without water. It was the next project. They would get the existing kitchen from the big house as soon as the new one was built. And then there's Lynley, who hopes to start her main house this year but still only has a water point in one place in her current abode. Everything is recycled where possible. New Zealand prides itself on its green credentials.

Land here with a great view, i. e. mountains and lake or river commands, very high prices. Mountains only is a bit less. You don't get lake or river-only views as they all come with mountains (whether you want them or not). Prices are cheap compared with the UK.

It is a fantastically beautiful part of the world, roads are so-so, no motorways of course, so nearly everything is forty-five to sixty minutes away. The first traffic lights are three hours away. Don't remember seeing a roundabout either and I never saw a sign for a police camera. The roads being so-so are compensated for by the most wonderful scenery and, as most people know – I know you do Michael – this is Middle Earth in Lord of the Rings.

Lynley says Queenstown has a lot of Oriental Asian-owned properties – used as second homes of course. If Lynley travels for two or three months, they always let out their garage and her mother lets out her house. There is a call all year round because of summer on the lakes and rivers and skiing in the winter.

Tomorrow I'm going to put a bra on the bra fence. I'll have Lyn take my picture as I'm doing it. This is a fence which is growing bras. I have yet to find out its history.

In the Cardrona Valley is where Goodyear and others come to test their tyres, as there are frosty conditions when everywhere else is sunny. Also car manufacturers test their new models. No one can see them, but Lyn remembers the new VW in Wanaka when they'd never seen it before. Must have had time off for good behaviour.

Apparently there is an alpine parrot called a kea and it's a very naughty bird. Lyn says teenage keas hang around in gangs and get up to mischief. There was a competition for the world's smartest animal and the kea won, but couldn't be classified as it was a bird.

Sometimes they put garbage all over people's windscreens when they are in the mountain car parks. Also, they can pick on just one car, say a Range Rover, and fifty birds can be on it taking it to pieces. Another trick, they climb up house roofs and then slide back down, just like children.

When skiers leave their backpacks unattended they can open them and hurl everything out, designer sunglasses and the lot flying all over until they find the food.

Lynley insists they are very funny (so long as it's not your car) and I will love them, because they're very naughty, is she inferring something?

Both here and Australia, they seem to be more obsessed about our royal family than we are, mainly women's magazines. Every one seems to boast a cover of some royal, mainly Diana, William and Harry. Despite the level of support for total independence, someone, somewhere is a royalist.

We had a nice leisurely drive back today. We visited the original bungee jump bridge and people were jumping as we arrived. They varied in age, young couples going together, a middle-aged guy waving to his wife, a young girl, quite a few young guys.

There were suggestions made to me and I have to admit if they'd put me in a body harness (as opposed to your feet taking the strain) I would have been tempted. I thought of my knee and knew I daren't risk it. I'm booking the doctor tomorrow. Want it sorting for Thailand. On visiting the doctor she'd said she was glad I hadn't jumped, as she'd had a lot in recently with detached retinas – and I was only worried about my knee.

When you're jumping you can choose to miss the water, touch with your hands or actually go in. I'd got to the stage where I was considering which I wanted to do. Going all the way in was never an option though!

I must admit I'm missing my massages. I haven't had one since Bali, as Oz and New Zealand are just as expensive as UK.

Lynley goes back to work tomorrow, Thursday, but she's off again on Friday. I'm going to book tomorrow to fly to the glacier and land on it. What I do after that remains to be seen. Depends what they offer me. Unless it's shoes with crampons it'll be a case of, who, me? Walk on that ice with this knee?

Today I saw a Takahe, a New Zealand bird like a small Dodo, thought to be extinct until rediscovered in 1948. As there are only domestic animals (as in pets) and goats, deer, sheep and cattle, the large New Zealand birds no longer need to fly. I heard a bellbird yesterday as we left the boat at the fjord. It sounds just like a bell sounding very sweet. I couldn't see it, it's very small, but it was note perfect.

The fjord at Milford Sound is picturesque. There are some impressive waterfalls, one higher than Niagara and the Sound is too deep for any of the cruise liners to anchor. They come in now and again, but soon mosey off. We went out into the sea and on the way back we saw some small furry seals basking on a large rock. Lynley says they must be the most photographed seals in the world. They calmly laid there while we snapped away.

By earth standards, the fjord is young and the mountains are still growing. You can see where the landslides have occurred and brought down vegetation and left a scar down the side.

Although it's called Milford Sound, it is a fjord not a sound. Fjords are made by a glacier, so it was wrongly named. Originally it was Milford Haven Sound as the man who discovered it was Welsh. Instead of changing it to Milford Fjord they just perpetuated the error and dropped 'Haven.'

Last night I visited the glow-worm caves. You go to Te Anau and get a boat at the lake and spend thirty-five minutes crossing it. You're escorted to a room for safety guidelines and information about the glow-worm.

You'll probably be aware, as I am now, that it's not a worm at all, but a larva. The glow occurs at the end of threads and is caused by a chemical reaction inside the larva. Now they say it's a larva, but if you'd seen the way it galloped along the thread to get its prey, you'd think it was a worm. In the film we saw the brighter the glow, the more in need of food it is – so it attracts mainly moths and flies, which can't get away once they touch the thread and as I said the larva speeds along inside the threads for dinner.

We went over metal spars above whirlpools, and roaring torrents. It was mainly limestone so the water had made some impressive holes and chasms over the years. The Cathedral part was very high so it must have been coming through for thousands of years. Then it was boat, walking and finally boat again. There was no recording or photography allowed and the glow-worms duly twinkled, sort of coming and going. It reminded me of a Christmas display of clear bulbs that fade and brighten. The cynic in me wondered if some of it really was courtesy of Woolworths. Had the glow-worms, rediscovered in 1945, disappeared or were not the display they once were and had technology taken over? I say this, because I was near one worm and it had a distinctly green tinge to its glow, perhaps the fuse bulbs, and I couldn't see any thread. I also couldn't see any moths presenting themselves for hors d'oeuvres. As I said, I'm a cynic, I'm sure they're the real thing.

At the caves I met a retired Australian scientist who was visiting New Zealand for the trotting – sulky racing – i. e. horse, cart and jockey racing. When I recited all the things I'd been doing, he remarked, quite dryly, 'It's amazing what we will do to prove we're not getting old.' So that put me in my place.

When we got off the boat at the end, a group of Japanese tourists were exiting. We were coming from three directions. As some Japanese left, some of the others were in danger of being separated and I kid you not, the look of sheer panic on one of the sheep's faces was not my imagination. She pushed forward and shuffled frantically to make sure there wasn't room for a piece of paper between her and the one in front. Until then she'd looked quite normal. I'm finding I'm now taking a perverse delight in this innocent game I've begun to play, as I assert my rightful place in the queue.

Talking of sheep. New Zealand is slightly famous for its sheep. Well I've hardly seen any. A bit like camels in the outback. There are only 1,000,000 people in South Island and the sheep outnumber them.

But I can't find the sheep. Deer, plenty, cows – quite a lot. The odd goat, some nice looking horses – sheep, the odd field or two. In comparison North Wales is overrun with them. The local ones near Wanaka provide the best merino wool. As a consequence they are a very dirty grey colour. I actually like it, Lynley hates it. Ashamed of it. It's because there is so much oil in the wool, it attracts all the dirt, dust and soil. I think they look like very naughty boys who've been playing out in the mud and will be in trouble when they get home.

News from the front. The bra fence came into being when someone put the odd one on and publicity brought more. Some women complained as they thought the guy who owned the fence was demeaning women. He thought it was a bit of fun and the women were being spoiled sports.

I leave it to you, who's right? Either way, I tied my bra, I think it's fun, and we certainly haven't got anything like that in Preston.

Love Pat.

Duck Farts

12 April 2003

Dear Sue & Peter,

Today is Luke Day. Lynley's nephew is just two and quite a character. So today Jean, his gran, and I are in charge. After physio we can do what we want, so long as it includes parks, swings and slides.

One of the nice things here is it cannot include McDonalds. There isn't one, certainly not this end of South Island. Dunedin may have succumbed but I'll have to check.

There are some very civilised café bars and cafés with everything home-made, but a sophisticated. Deli type menu. Ritual Espresso is my favourite and yesterday on 'Pat's day out in Wanaka' they saw me three times. Think they thought I was their Diner in Residence.

It all started with my visit to the doc's. Arrived at 9.10. Doc out on emergency, please come back at 10.20. Good excuse for breakfast at Ritual. The best French toast I've ever had, with bacon, sautéed bananas and maple syrup. Certainly not for the dieter. I ordered a weak latte and I could tell from the colour it was strong, so I asked if they could weaken it. 'That's only one shot in there. Do you want half a shot?', a bit incredulous and after I got it, one guy passed and said, 'That's just milk.' To me it was pale coffee colour if I'd been buying a dress. It certainly wasn't white.

Back to the doc's. Waited until 10.45. Nice women, seven months pregnant, had a good check for DVT and pronounced osteo-arthritis with a question mark. They had X-ray facilities which I wanted on site, but she said I'd be better off seeing my GP at home. I nearly asked for an X-ray but decided against. Why?

Sent me to physio, conveniently located next door, with some painkillers. I left physio and went into town (two blocks) and the hedonist I am turned me into House of Travel. Can I go to the glacier, as it's the last of my must-dos? Can you go at 1.00, she says, today? It's a glorious day and they'll have you back for your 3.00 hair appointment.

At this point I decided to ring Jean to let her know I hadn't been kidnapped. Dale (House of Travel) rang her, as she knew her. Told her I'd be back after 5.30.

It was now 12.15, so I raced up to Ritual, had a big bowl of freshly prepared fruit, yoghurt and honey, plus a smoothie and awaited collection.

Alistair (ex-Home Counties) was the driver of the jeep and the pilot. As there was only me we took a two-man helicopter. I was out for over an hour and we landed once.

I would like to say I got out at the glacier, but knowing the trouble I'd had getting in due to the short legs and bad knee, I declined. I just opened my door and breathed in fresh glacial air – well, it's as good as. Then it got really good. I'm glad I took a heli because we got so near to the glacier if I had opened the door at that point, I could have touched it. A lot of it looked like a sheet of ice, but the really interesting parts were like those wedges of cotton wool where they unravel in folds. The difference here was some of the folds were definite blue, some white and where they had already moved, they ranged from white, mucky white, grey, dirty grey and charcoal grey. As though someone had tipped a bag of coal down them and the dust had left a residue.

To the side (or really in the middle of the mountain) quite a way down was the most beautiful lake I have ever seen. Reminiscent of Lake Louise in Alberta . The turquoise colour was very bright and nothing to do with the sun. It was totally hidden of course and could only be seen from above.

Alistair took me all around, just hovering and on the whole journey he never seemed to go faster than walking speed.

The glaciers all had different shapes and he said they were moving about a hundred metres a year. I said, at that rate, I was surprised we couldn't see them moving. Where they dropped over the edge the folds began to break down and it had a look of a frozen landslide.

In keeping with my techno-less image, my camcorder lay uncharged at home, and my camera I'd just had checked the night before (the counter wasn't working) decided that the test shot in the camera shop was the last one and mid-flight I needed to change films.

I tried to rewind it but would it go? No. I opened the camera in desperation only to see a wound-on film now fully exposed. I must have wound for about five minutes. So I sat there enjoying a most wonderful sight and not one lousy piece of film to record it. Alistair tried a bit of positive thinking by saying that I'd not have seen so much if I'd recorded it. Oh believe me Alistair, I would.

When I took the film in to the shop, they got it unwound for me, but said it had been tightly wound. They put a trial film they use and took twenty-five photos and then wound back and guess what, it wound back perfectly. Why oh why won't it do it for me? I even followed all the rules, quite unlike me.

Anyway back to land and I'd just time to nip in the chemist for my painkillers and Ritual for a drink before the hairdressers.

I'm always filled with trepidation approaching a new hairdresser's and Carmen's name did nothing to reassure me.

The upshot of it was – it's great. She coloured to the darkest colour (perfect match) and also cut it. I looked good, had twice as much hair as when I went in, and everyone's admired it.

I finally arrived home at 5.50, just nine hours after I left, bearing two bottles of recommended wine for my hosts.

This, as everyone told me, was meant to be my relaxing day after the trip to the Fjords. Still there's always tomorrow.

Jean had cooked rack of lamb (à la Jamie Oliver) roasted veg and Maori potatoes, a darker, almost black less sweet version of sweet potatoes. Her son had bought her the cookbook for Christmas so even they must have slavering exuberance inflicted upon them. You'd have thought NZ being a nuclear free zone, could have avoided Jamie Oliver as well.

Luke, Jean and I went to collect Booby who is Jean's best friend. Her real name is Ruby but Luke has trouble and had decided she's Booby. Today I learnt two new things, one courtesy of Booby.

DUCK FARTS

We went to Lake Hawea to have lunch. The views (this must be getting boring) were spectacular. We dined inside a hotel with views and after drove to their special spot, which is very remote and of course quiet.

I learned how to do duck farts. Actually, I knew how to do them; I just didn't know the correct name. We were skimming stones across the water. Now you don't have to think very hard about this, imagination is at a minimum. As the stone hits the water at each point, it's a duck farting. So there, something to tell your children/grandchildren. Duck farts.

The other thing I learned today was how to peg out washing in the country. You use the Maori washline.

That is, you take your pegs, approach the wire fence all round the back of your property, and begin to peg. This is how all Maoris do it on their properties. Jean thinks it could be racist to say Maori washline nowadays. She thought it was funny as I looked for the washing line, I knew there had to be one as Lynley left me some pegs.

I was feeling quite at home as I watched my wash lazing happily in the sun, and on return after lunch it was dry.

This is the hottest day I've had since I've been here. Good sunbathing weather. I went out camcording the lake and Lynley's property but the sun was very low. I have a feeling I'll be coming back from this holiday with memories and postcards but not much else. But what am I thinking? Of course I will. I have twelve enormous sandfly bites, obtained while writing this letter in garden.

One of the pictures I've had developed is of the quad biking. I look like the fatter one in 'Chips', a programme my children watched when young about the California Highway Patrol on motorbikes. In another one, I look the business.

Regarding costs for medical treatment. I paid $NZ 42 for the doctor, NZ $59 for my fancy aspirin, so they don't upset my tum, NZ $35 per visit to the physio. If that's all it is I don't think Amex will be getting too worried. It's about NZ $3 to the £1. Lynley says they get a subsidy for the prescriptions, but I can't because I'm a tourist. If only the UK had the same mindset.

Jean makes her own jam, bottles fruit and belongs to the Herb Club. If I hadn't been in the Fjords I had been invited to the Herb Club. I haven't found out what they do, it probably seems obvious to everyone else.

She also builds her own wall and does concreting. In fact most of the women in her group do strong, manual work (round the garden and house.)

Ruby, aged seventy, goes up the mountain and down each day to walk her younger dog. The older, wiser one, stays home and guards the house when she can be bothered. Despite my activity holiday, the latter dog is one after my own heart.

Just sent off another parcel to England. Not wanted on voyage stuff. If I keep this up, soon I'll only have the clothes I stand up in – and pigs might fly as well.

Tomorrow, my last full day, I may go to the old Gold Rush Mines which had the Chinese as inhabitants. Jean is taking me, so I've told her to choose where she wants to take me. It may not be the mines, but I don't think it's glacier walking either since I had a 10.30 physio appointment today and she had a 4.30 physio. Both of us with knees which have never given us any trouble until now. We'd only make one good one between us.

See you later.

Love,

Pat.

Double chins and a sparrow

14 April 2003

Dear Michael and Clare,

After my mystery tour today (to the goldmines) I have to inform you, I am still talking to everyone I know – and some I don't – because we found zilch. Nothing, not even a glimmer. The £5 entrance fee covers your gold-panning session and general instructions on how to work the heavy equipment. Jean was quite good at that.

We had to hack it out of the rock by shovel (Jean was quite good at that too) and then we took it away to play in muddy waters and sift it through. I was doing this, but it was not to Jean's liking and as she'd expended more energy on this than I had, I felt she could nag me a bit.

Eventually I got fed up and though Jean said she was going to throw it away, I found her later sifting away at it. Still nothing. You could stay as long as you wanted. I had.

It was then that Jean informed me that the actual mine and mining equipment, plus the houses had been built on this site recently, after the original site some miles up the road had been flooded when the dam was built. The mine was rebuilt for a film set.

Now I had given this project fifteen minutes of my time, bent over a trough, imagining gold in every swish, to find out, as I pointed out to Jean, that there was never a chance of gold in 'them thar hills' and it was disappointing to put it mildly.

It was only when I put it to her that she realised that it was never a claim.

The reconstruction was authentic to show where the miners, forty per cent Chinese, lived and worked. It was the 'gold mine' bit that was a fraud.

Just to prove me wrong, while having our lunch the young lad who'd been in our party proudly came up to show his two glass bottles filled with water and his gold. Now I hadn't got my glasses on and can read newspaper print at a push without them, but I couldn't see anything. I looked for a glint, a flash of light to confirm his and his mother's optimism. I made all the right noises though and said how he'd be able to show it to all his friends in the US. They'd been at it at least an hour, so I dearly hope something was there. It's back-breaking work, which is why I only gave it fifteen minutes. Breaking and back, housemaid's and knee are not words usually synonymous with me.

Eccentric, enthusiastic, opinionated, different, these I feel are me. Oh yes, and the bank manager said 'arrogant'. In fact what he said was 'the most arrogant women he'd met considering I owed him money'. Note the use of the word *him*, and *he* called *me* arrogant. I owed the bank, not HIM. I should hasten to add this was in 1992 before I transferred to by current bank – the RBS – where I am extremely happy.

As I write this, I'm sitting in Lynley's garden facing the sun, with views of the mountain and next door's little house on the prairie. I'm getting a suntan, it's 5pm and the neighbour's house has smoke rising straight up from its chimney. I expect the Indians at any minute or a guy in a check shirt to appear with an axe to chop wood, followed by a woman and a small boy (never a girl if you remember your westerns) asking him to be careful, or that supper is ready. And another thing, how come in all these westerns they only had one child? Did they know something I didn't? And as I say, always a boy. Were they into genetic selection in the 1800s?

While we were eating at lunch at the mines, sparrows were hopping around. Then I noticed one sitting on a rock and I swear it was so fat it had double chins. This was one well-fed bird. On our way back we passed through Luggate. Yes, Luggate, but the locals have added an accent on the official sign coming into town from either direction. And it's now Luggaté. Jean said at a musical evening the other day a group were introduced as the Luggaté quartet. I'm sure they played better. Well if it were me, I'd want to live in Luggaté. The Hyacinth (Bucket) in me would not allow me to live in Luggate. It must have been somebody like me moving in that finally got them motivated. It's been Luggate for donkey's years.

On our tour and instruction at the mine were four Americans, three Irish, Jean and I. A real melting pot. Everyone else kept at the panning longer than we did. Either they had more tenacity than us or we grew wiser quicker. Later Lynley and I went to Capriccio's, the restaurant where Dale is the chef. We had a view over the lake and as it was my last night we had a good 'go' at the menu. Big surprise, I had lamb cutlets again. But I had beef carpaccio to start and raspberry romanoff (shared with Lynley) to finish. Lynley had smoked eels to start and pasta with smoked salmon. She should have been well cured by the end of the evening.

Yesterday, Liquorice, one of her cats, had to make real friends with me. So far she'd tolerated being stroked, but she was a nervous cat. Well, as Lynley was away on business, she must have decided I was the best bet for food. She did everything but open the correct cupboard door. She purred, talked and generally insinuated herself against me. I found the right stuff but I must have put it in her sister's bowl, as she looked at me and wandered round my legs. Once I'd transferred it, she was really fine, but I think she was sure Lynley had abandoned her to a virtual stranger. She hasn't really taken to Dale as he forgets to feed her when Lyn's away. Lyn gets her mother to oversee it. Very sensible.

Lynley has laughed at her mother's sightseeing trips with me. As she said, her mother's been taking me to the alternative sights.

Jean was busy telling me about how everything, where possible, is recycled. I showed an interest and the next minute we were at the town's 'rubbish dump' as at Preston or the 'recycling centre' as in Wanaka.

It's just like Help the Aged. Everything is in a warehouse on shelves. Toasters, lamps, books, toys – the lot. I took a picture (one that got exposed) of a young guy in dreadlocks and his pal sifting through the ski box. Loads of skis. They're very proud of everything they buy there. Chairs, beds (inc. mine $10 brand new) futons, curtains. Anyway Lynley thought it funny that on my second day I'm inspecting that big tourist attraction, the Wanaka recycling centre. Only her mother would have thought to take me there.

Well, today I leave Wanaka. It has been a great visit. Everyone has been so kind and helpful. Nothing too much trouble. They've all rallied round to make sure I'm entertained, but as you'll have read I escaped a few times. I find it essential. I think it's to do with my need for space and independence.

Hope to go into Christchurch tomorrow morning to have a look round and will post this. I think I trust the New Zealand post more than the Thai post.

I've just been reunited with a suitcase, and I've just sent another box home and I'm still fifty per cent overweight – and I've still three weeks to go.

Oh yes, at the airport hotel I'm staying in tonight in Christchurch, I had dinner and, the waitress said did I want gourmet potatoes or french fries? Of course I chose the gourmet – and boiled potatoes arrived. I questioned this and was assured they were they. What on earth would they call pommes normande? Exotic potatoes? Superlative pots. The mind boggles. Let's hope it doesn't catch on in the UK.

Love,

Pat.

Have you got your trundler?

15 April 2003

Dear Sue and Peter,

Britney rides the skies again. I had a three-hour flight. Christchurch to Sydney. But now I'm on about an eight-hour to Bangkok. I've got an aisle seat but that's the best they could do.

I've had a go at getting the two spare seats in front to the side of me, but they're for the crew rest time. I offered them mine, but no takers.

When I get into Bangkok it'll be 3am by my body. I hope no one expects me up tomorrow. Caz and Paul are at another hotel and I think they've already arrived. Vic flies in for Wednesday.

I wonder how Paul and Andy are going on in Laos and Cambodia. Perhaps there'll be some brotherly bonding. But what is more likely to happen is there'll be a bit of a skirmish and no one will have to have a long memory.

This morning I made a major decision not to have breakfast at my hotel. I caught the bus outside after an 8am morning call and arrived in town fifteen minutes later.

Christchurch is prosperous. The suburbs from the airport leading into town had some fabulous houses. The streets were very leafy, full of trees. House designs varied, Regency, Edwardian, modern, thirties style. But everyone of them looked good. No two the same. It seemed like a very upmarket Surrey town.

The centre was OK. A nice cathedral, but next to it a monstrosity I can only describe as an aluminium vase with cut-outs. I don't know if they were after a Sydney opera house effect, but it looked the sort of thing towns which are down at heel put near parks. But this was just stuck to the side of what appeared to be the town square and its lovely cathedral. Someone should be shot.

Just as we were coming into town there was a university and I could see a rowing club and then a river. Very like the Cam at Cambridge. I've since found out it's called the Avon and you can punt on it. It meandered through parks, plenty of ducks, it was idyllic. It all looked very English and then among all the other tall trees, I could see palms. Very tall palms. This was totally different to the alpine area.

Then there was a large old school, covered in Virginia creeper, just turning red. In front were massive playing fields with rugby posts in place. Christchurch is called the Garden City – that could be where the vase comes in.

All buses in Oz and New Zealand have wheelchair access. Like all of New Zealand this bus was immaculate. All the seats looked brand new and certainly nobody had put chewing gum on them or introduced them to a Stanley knife.

Just as we passed the river and park two women came by power walking. None of that nonsense in the alpine region.

I sat on the bus watching them and itching, itching you note, not scratching. The bites I had got in Wanaka made me feel like a flea-bitten old crone. Missing teeth would have completed the picture.

At breakfast there was baroque music playing in this modern café bar, the latest newspapers scattered around and I thought I'd come home. This was my sort of place. If they'd said gourmet potatoes they would at least put garlic in them.

People on the plane are talking about masks (due to SARS) and not being able to get them. The fact that I am smugly sitting on four doesn't bother me. They're for my family when we leave Thailand. Pull up the ladder folks, I'm onboard. Actually it's not really that bad, as I say I only have four, I didn't buy the whole shop. The chemist where we got two of them in little Arrowtown in the Alps had a woman's bust in the window wearing one. I duly took a picture – which tells its own story.

The flight yesterday from Queenstown to Christchurch was awful. I was in row three, just where the engines finished, and the vibration and noise they made was bringing on a headache. I eventually got moved and it was marginally better. And this flight was only fifty minutes long. I think it was the Vanguard from 1964 I went on my honeymoon in.

Origin Pacific was the airline and Qantas must use them for very short haul. I'm *sure* they bought that Vanguard I went to Majorca in; there can't be two that noisy.

Jean, Lynley's mum, belongs to a herb club as I said. It appears they cook with various herbs, have talks given to them, make chocolate, face creams and cosmetics using the herbs. So not as boring as first thought.

Talking of herbs. I had to bring the Stilton shoes out to go to the goldmine. The area is covered in wild thyme, which we were walking on, and when we got back I put the shoes away. This requires double wrapping in plastic bags. As I wrapped them, this delicious smell came to me. Thyme – in fact, Stilton and thyme. If I go on like this I'll have the makings of a great meal.

Oh yes, in New Zealand, gourmet pots are small new potatoes. Well they were still wrong because these were medium-sized.

While I was in Christchurch I got my last letter photocopied. I also wanted my very important photo from the bridge colour-copying.

Eventually I found this massive shop/office. Loads of important copying machines, loads of space (enough to run a small car boot sale) and four assistants. I presented my fifteen sheets for copying and one photo. It was forty minutes before I emerged blinking into the sunlight. While I'd been in there the temperature had risen five degrees outside. I could feel my roots beginning to grow.

The assistant's first two attempts at my photo had me not looking thirty, but older and as though a heart attack was imminent. Florid was too mild a word.

I then saw a sign that said all copies had to be paid for, as customers' experiments were their choice, and colour copying was not an exact science.

I called it quits and we went off to the copier. I turned my back and thought I heard it going through quickly – quicker than normal.

When I looked round I realised this was the sound of the machine mashing my first page. Fourteen others were still sitting there sunshine-fresh and the girl was frantically trying to smooth the first page. It had started to look like tissue paper.

I smiled, said it was OK and would she do 'one at a time?' I don't think she understood this concept. Still, eventually they were done.

I should have left then but I needed my 'you don't look older than thirty' photo laminating. She had one go and it wasn't warmed up. Allowing how important this photo was to me, I'm surprised I let her carry on.

Anyway it came out the other side and the surrounds were sort of pleated and bubbly.

She said she'd have another go. I was getting decidedly jumpy and said did she have to? But by then it was through. It didn't improve, but most importantly it didn't get worse.

I watched with bated breath as she guillotined it. I got it back in my sweaty palms, paid a vast amount of money and left, laughing with relief.

If that girl ever had a high-pressure job, she'd be off to the Priory for rest and recuperation for stress after the first two days. Judging by the others, the amount of work they had to do was minimal. They just wandered. Hedgehogs walk faster, or should I say, trundle faster.

That's my new word, 'trundler.' A sign in the supermarket at Wanaka as the gates swing open, says, 'Make sure you've got your trundler.' I said to Lynley we call them trolleys – Lynley says they call them trolleys. She's never heard of a trundler before. But that supermarket had.

Don't you think it's the perfect word for those terrible ones that go where they want and give you an instant hysterectomy as you try to manoeuvre? All those pelvic floor exercises for nothing.

It's also a very good word for what I do on an 'off day'. I trundle round Tesco's. It puts a whole new spin on Win A Trundler Dash. Just doesn't sound the same does it? Whoever could trundle at speed? The whole term trundler dash is a contradiction.

I'm still two and half hours to Bangkok and I'd forgotten my New Zealand time difference. If we arrive on time, it will be 5am by my body. Yes, I'll definitely make Bangkok for tomorrow night, the day won't exist.

Love,

Pat.

This way to the Great Wall

The Grand Old Duke of York

Charlotte, me, Yen, Forbidden City

Frozen Summer Palace, Suzhou Street Shopping Centre

Chen, Myself and Yen

Eastern-Western Yang Shuo

Street games, Yang Shuo

Misty Mountains on River Guilin

As I pictured myself when asked to let go of the ladder when snorkeling in Bali

Sea fishermen, Samur, Bali

Monster in the making, Bali

The Bright Young Things, plus a woman of a certain age

Simpson's Gap, nr Alice Springs

'Chips' in the Outback

Ants' nest in the Outback

Starving dingo with kangaroo kill, Outback

Jumper caught as he leaves the original Bungee Jump bridge, nr Queenstown NZ

The Bra fence, Cardrona Valley

At the front, myself and Lynley

Straw bale house, Wanaka, NZ

Milford sound NZ

View from Lynley's 'garage', Wanaka, NZ

Panic hits Arrowtown, a tiny village in the alpine region, nr Queentown, NZ

Embarking, Thai snorkelling expedition

Almost Soignée

Thailand, Lagoon island

Rush hour in the Mekong Delta, crossing single pole bridge after school

Saigon goose crosses family to other side

Yung Tao, Vietnam. Christ of the Andes, Vietnamese style

Paradise or What?

20 April 2003

Dear Sue and Peter,

Diamond Cliff Resort and Spa. The quiet corner of Patong Beach says the legend. It fails to add because everyone is buggered.

Diamond Cliff Resort and Spa is just like communism.
Discuss.

I can sum the above statement up in one sentence. Both look good on paper, can't work in reality/practice.

I am in the process of transferring to a more user-friendly hotel. The idea that a complex could be built on a beautiful cliff face in one of the hottest, most humid countries on earth and still be classed as a holiday destination is fatally flawed. And I'm just afraid the fatality could be me.

It's so bad they have an open-air minibus, seats nine, to take you around swimming pools, fruit shop etc.

As Vicky was joining me, I had to have another room with two beds. We were booked as deluxe. Our view, albeit on one side of the balcony is the sea, the other is the menial staff clocking-in building and canteen. All the staff come and park their vehicles of various sheen and dilapidation opposite. Yesterday afternoon a full-sized petrol truck covered in rust (allowing it had petrol in it, this enough was worrying) was parked there for one and a half hours.

I don't have this view at home and I certainly won't pay for it. Mind you Kuoni have a great deal of the blame to take. Both Caz and I have paid the same for our rooms, she has Paul in hers but now the hotel are now asking for an extra £22 per night for Vicky. Kuoni told us £45 for the twelve days.

The problem as well is, whenever Kuoni ring me, the person has such a heavy accent I can't tell what they're saying. The reverse is probably true, but I'm the paying customer. Eventually, I agreed to pay just the £45.

Met Boon, Kuoni rep. He has negotiated us another room, hardly any steps, just up the 1:4 gradient. With a bit of luck, if I like it, I'll be able to get a Disney Cart to take me up the hill.

On my return to old room (via cart) I did a quarter-mile detour. No matter which way I come, there are over a hundred steps and with this knee that's no joke.

You can see the architect now, selling to the mugs who decided to purchase it. These rooms will hang off a cliff, suspended waterfalls cascading. All different views of the ocean (except those with rusty petrol tankers.) They will feel they are in paradise – and for those of them unfortunate enough to succumb – they will be. A lift? No, that would spoil it, so old-fashioned.

There were many Kuoni clients, who tend to be the better-off end of society, often middle-aged, waiting to complain. One women about my age said she was exhausted. She'd never been to Thailand before and I don't think she's coming again.

Admittedly Kuoni advertised it in the brochures as 'Not for people with walking difficulties'. When it was booked, I hadn't, but I would suggest that it's not for anyone who wants a relaxing holiday or even anyone who needs to breathe to live – and the last I heard Phuket was not chosen as a holiday destination for its mountaineering possibilities.

The Diamond Cliff Resort and Spa could do for Phuket's tourist industry what SARS is doing to Hong Kong's. Only this will be permanent.

One of the management asked me later what they could do to improve the hotel. I was quite brief – sell it.

There's a free clinic, with nurse and free medicines. I consulted her about my bites and gouges I got in New Zealand.

She smiled and I wondered if she'd understood. She had a nice uniform on and the clinic was very spacious, clean and dare I say it – clinical. The Kuoni rep said they mainly dealt with bites and stomach upsets.

Efficiency wasn't her first name and when I asked if she had got anything for the worst ones she didn't seem to have an answer, she thought I might need an antibiotic, but this was only after I'd told her about how sore the area around was. I said I'd wait another day as they were improving. I asked had she got any ointment (as Boon suggested) and with great reluctance a little pot was offered. I asked to pay and she said, no charge. I felt the whole interview was customer-led.

I think the management must have instructed her to look efficient, but to hang on to all her pots and potions under pain of redundancy. They'd do well in the NHS.

I have to wait until midday to see the new room and if it's acceptable. I hope so; I can't stand all this faffing about.

When I checked in yesterday before the others arrived, they'd only one room booked and that was for me. They were umming and ahhing and their lobby is open plan, i.e. non-air-conditioned. This was lunchtime and I began to feel tetchy. Eventually I said I wanted to go to my room and I wanted to go *now*. I don't negotiate well in heat I told them. They could solve it without me.

They looked alarmed (Caz said nobody ever gets mad in Thailand). I wasn't mad, just assertive.

They took me up to the registration room. Because of the bad planning, they have to have a whole room kitted out, to explain the complex to you. Takes about half an hour. A fresh pineapple juice in its fruit is brought to you. For all I know they could have laced it with Prozac – it didn't work.

You get a kilogram of fruit per day. You take your basket, à la Red Riding Hood and you go all the way back to reception up the 1:4 hill and up and down the hundred steps, plus endless walkways to your room. I think I'll order it and they can deliver. At least at Tesco's I got a trundler. Talking of Tesco's they're here, all over Phuket, and Boon was very excited by this. They will have forty in Thailand by next year. They even stay open from 6am until midnight. This must have been something he thought could be an unusual concept in UK; why even Colwyn Bay has twenty-four-hour. Or is it Bangor?

On arrival the first room was great, but just one king bed. I'd asked for two beds at reception but the room wasn't ready.

So back we went. There were overhead fans in reception, but only over the guest relations desk and tour desks. None where the tables and chairs for guests were. So I got a big chair and hauled it noisily across the lobby and sat it under a fan at the entrance. The staff looked amazed and laughed and one clapped. Strangely enough my room (the awful one I'm now vacating) was ready in seconds.

I've noticed in India and here also, that as I reach forty-two days travelling I get tetchy in so much as I don't suffer fools. I expect service and react accordingly and it always starts with taxi drivers and airports.

Easter Saturday

I am sitting by the ocean view pool. Misnomer, as I would have to be six foot six to stand in the pool and see an ocean. Still, the pool is fine. Lots of jacuzzis, fish spouting waterfalls and I can't drown in most of it.

Another big pool is very dramatic, as befits a cliff side resort, it has a waterfall cascading about thirty feet into it. Some of the seating under the water tips you back at an angle, I have to admit I could lie there under the palms all day. It is very secluded but still part of the pool which has bridges to go under and the like. Pity it's mainly out of my depth i. e. it comes up to my eyebrows.

The last few days have been traumatic to say the least. I don't think I would ever come back to Phuket. Maybe other parts of Thailand but Phuket is expensive, even by English standards.

I was told by Boon that £3,500 is what the average Thai lives on. That makes their standard of living about a tenth of UK yet most meals in OK restaurants cost about £10 for two courses. Often they add tax and service charge (seventeen and a half per cent). Massages in the main street are still cheap, but of course at the hotel they're £22.50. Usually we pay

£4.50 downtown. Tuk tuks (or as I'm wont to call them put-puts) are £1.50 each way into town, but their petrol is only 25p litre. No wonder the charges have been rising a hundred per cent a year for the past few years. They think we are so rich, but as I see it, my money has to provide for when I get home and our high cost of living. They don't seem to appreciate that when inflation rises here for us it will eventually filter over to them, just like what happened in India. If I tip £1.50 (100 baht) to everyone, they only need sixty of those a week to equal the national average wage.

I'd heard Vietnam and similar countries were becoming the new Thailand. I shall make it my business to investigate. The beaches I know are as beautiful.

Yesterday afternoon we went to Karim Beach. Quieter and cleaner than Patong. Patong has a look of Blackpool on heat. As Vicky says, it looks rough – and she's only twenty-nine.

The sea was quite rough and having allowed the daughters to test for steep drops (there was one) I ventured in to paddle only.

Now as you know, I'm quite a sturdy piece of work but the surf could knock me off my feet, and there were serious undercurrents. So I went cowardy-custard-like and sat in the shallows and waited for the surf to come to me. And did it come! The girls went off for lunch and I was still there when they got back. Not quite where they left me, as this surf meant business. Every time it hit, I moved.

As I sat there gaining weight and rolls of fat, I hadn't realised I was taking in serious quantities of sand. I had three bust lines, four tummy rolls (and only one was mine that I knew of) and a grave problem where my love handles should be.

I started to offload, I must have looked like a cement mixer on speed. Sand pies were being ejected at all levels. I could have built three castles and resisted invasion for years.

We eventually left the beach, still weighed down by sand that could not be shifted – we were hot, sandy, sweaty and exhausted, so I let Caz go in search of a tuk tuk. Poor love, she returned after about ten minutes.

Twenty-four hours later I'm still finding sand where I didn't know it could get. We're not going back to the beach until I go out to Phi Phi island snorkelling.

I'm just getting too hot again, time for a dip. Oh yes, despite sitting in the surf for one and a halfhours with only factor eight on, my tan is no better. By Welsh standards, I would be deep brown.

When the girls met me they said where's your tan? After three days Hong Kong, eight days Bali, nine days Australia and ten days New Zealand (temp. around twenty-five degrees) nowhere, nowhere (except, I have on good authority, Cornwall) beats North Wales for a tan. People have always thought that I was mad when I claimed this, but now I'm walking proof.

Easter Monday

Yesterday it heaved it down. It didn't bother me too much but the beach lovers were none too pleased. I went for my hydrotherapy session and I took the bad knee with me.

I had won this after my second room choice (the one with the rusty petrol tanker outlook). They have a lottery style machine where bits of paper are blown around and you put your hand in and grab one. When I first did this, I got a picture of two champagne glasses. The girl and boy who were organising this looked puzzled and asked me to try again. This time I won section 'A'. Sparkling wine, meal for two (sorry Vic) or hydrotherapy session twenty minutes. My excuse was that I had a sore knee and needed the session. It was very relaxing and smelt sulphuric. Well I presume it was meant to smell like that. Either that or the drains were worse than usual. I've booked my snorkelling session to Phi Phi island and the all day canoeing to the caves. Just the half-day safari to book now. I'll have to do these, as I've decided I'll not be coming here again.

I've been with my basket for fruit. I got two mangoes and two bananas. I was going to have some grapes, but they looked in the condition where I throw them away – and there were fruit flies all over them. I think telling the girl I was very fussy about my fruit missed her entirely. Anyway, my basket will not be going a-walking again, despite the fact we have a whole table set up for the eating of fruit. Linen napkins, in the shape of a boat, knives and forks, plates and orchids. Seems a waste doesn't it?

The first night we all went out, Caz couldn't find where they'd been the night before for a foot massage. So we eventually got tired of looking and went in a small place.

The heat greeted us and I said I must have air conditioning and they said the back room had it. So Vicky and I went in the back room for Thai massage and Caz and Paul stayed at the front. I could see a small cockroach in the room we went in and Vic said there were three big ones looking at her in the loo. Well we weren't going to eat there, so we lay on the mattresses. Vicky got undressed down to her knickers, so I followed suit. The ladies appeared then and started laughing. They gave us Thai boxing shorts to put on and told us to put our tops back on.

They went back out laughing and told Caz and Paul that 'Mama get naked' which had them all falling about.

Anyway I got even with them because as they were having their massage, Caz said to Paul not to move as there was a huge roach by his head. Now I feel this roach was on my side as it didn't happen to me. Then again roaches don't like air conditioning.

Twelve-year-old Doctors

Later Easter Monday
22 April 2003

Dear Clare and Michael,

I decided today to have my leg X-rayed. I knew from Paul that dental treatment is a fraction of UK prices.

In fact, one thing we have discovered is that the infrastructure (barring taxis) is still the old prices. Paul looks like Tom Cruise for £750. Even his temporary crowns look good enough to keep. And that's his whole top set.

So I duly took myself off to the main hospital. Here a receptionist took my name. Within minutes I had a laminated ID card with my name spelt correctly.

Next I saw the nurse. Things got a bit more difficult here, as this was someone given their own uniform and her attitude went with it. She'd caught the promotion bug. She told me I could see the orthopaedic specialist tomorrow. I assured her I was only here for seven more days and I just wanted an X-ray – Did I want to see the doctor? Yes, when would that be? In one hour. Too long says I. I was just about to say I'd come back later and suddenly the doctor could see me in fifteen minutes. Fine.

You know, you watch these American series and there's always a senior nurse, who's awkward, feisty, wise-cracking and not user-friendly, and this nurse was it. But she was Thai.

I'd had my blood pressure taken and it was high.

Even I agreed it was high. She said they'd take it again in fifteen minutes. Two minutes later she took it again and both had gone down by ten. So I assured them as I got cooler it would keep dropping. She didn't look convinced. After all, it's thirty-seven degrees and humid here, although it doesn't feel too bad, but it is hot. I've felt it worse than this for humidity on the US East Coast. I melted.

So I went in to see the doctor. This twelve-year-old-looking girl came to collect me. She sat in the chair opposite me and discussed my knee and my blood pressure. I tried to steer her toward the knee. Bugger the blood pressure. I'd another week and Vietnam threatened to be hotter. I couldn't be worrying about my BP. Knees definitely. I was banking on the X-ray being cheap and infinitely quicker than the UK.

So we talked knees and she said she thought she agreed with the New Zealand GP who said osteoarthritis. I was still hoping housemaid's knee.

I then waited outside X-ray for, oh, I guess four minutes and then they took me in and did two X-rays and I was out again.

In the meantime the twelve-year-old girl was treating a girl about her age.

I waited by the nurse-with-attitude's station and the little girl went to collect my X-rays. Back in her room and I'd had a glance as she got them out. It looked good.

Anyway, no arthritis. She couldn't raise an opinion as to what I had, but I don't think twelve-year-old Thai doctors know the translation for housemaid's knee.

So there I was, clutching my X-rays and wandering round Patong. I wondered if I were the only person in the resort that day carrying their own X-rays. I'd like to place a large bet I was. I duly presented them in Preston to my doctor as 'my holiday snaps'. His first words were, 'Where did you get them?' I think he thought I'd been raiding the X-ray department of the Royal Preston Hospital.

And what did this hospital treatment cost and how long did it take? Thirty-five minutes, start to finish and just over ten baht (60 = £1) per minute. I paid £3 to see the doctor and £3.15 for my X-rays. No one had to refer me, I walked in off the street into civility. It looked like our hospitals, the difference being the speed, the efficiency and of course the cost.

If my knee doesn't improve after I return, I'll have to have a scan or similar, but I didn't like to push them here.

Tomorrow Caz and Paul go off to the really posh hotel (six-star I think) and they have their own island for ten days. They only need to come back for Paul's final teeth fitting. It's about twenty miles away but they have a motorbike. It's very quiet, so they'll come into Patong for the nightlife.

I've got myself a 'little man', in the same way one has a 'little woman' to do one's dressmaking. He's copied two tops and a skirt. He's currently doing two more skirts, a dress and a blouse. Total cost £120. I could have had him copy designer clothes for the same cost. Oh yes, he's altered two tops as well. Everything is ready in twenty-four hours and delivered to your hotel. I just have to have one fitting for the some of the others.

Everyone has admired the skirt and top I've got. I'm very pleased and think I may have started a new trend. The Thai girls are admiring it, including the twelve-year-old doctor.

One of the girls at the beauty centre at the hotel is going to do her toenails in my summer colours. Should I patent them?

As I drove here by taxi, I noticed a big advertising hoarding. It said, 'Don't risk your valuables with fake drugs. Consult your Doctor or Pharmacist about your erectile health. Pfizer.'

So that's what they're called here. Your valuables.

In the *Bangkok Post* there was a picture of a bride in full meringue dress including ten-foot train. Her friends were adjusting this wearing facemasks and through the veil you could see her facemask. Something to tell the grand-children then. I remember when we had to get married in facemasks ...

There's a Court's (you know, cheap furniture people) in Phuket. As it's so far out of town (towards Tesco) I couldn't be bothered stopping the taxi to find out what they were charging.

Halfway through my Phuket stay I went with Vicky to an ATM. I then realised I hadn't got my cash card.

Now, I don't think well in heat and now was a time for some very serious thinking. I got out my receipts. The last one was two days ago at the Siam bank. Now Patong Beach Road goes forever. The number of ATMs is legion. I was almost sure I'd not collected it at the last one. It gave everything back in the wrong order. Instead of returning your card before or just after the money it did the receipt first. I was *almost* sure.

I remembered my Amex card and thought I knew my PIN, although it was two years since I used it. Desperation must have given it to me and we extracted money and made plans to inform about my lost card.

We passed the Thai military bank and just towards

the end of the drag I saw a bureau de change and next door to it Siam Bank ATM. It was recessed from the road by about fifteen feet and there was a queue.

I waited, sweat quietly dripping from my forehead. When it was my turn, I asked the young man if they had any connection with the ATM. I explained what had happened. He asked me had I got ID. I was carrying a photocopy of my passport. Out came his keys, the back was opened and out came my RBS cash card. So simple, so easy. In the UK there would have been a tossup as to whether I qualified for a Stannah stairlift before my card reappeared.

There was quite a queue by now and I gave him my photocopy and he returned it and the card. I couldn't conceal my delight, everyone in the queue (and there were a few nationalities) was pleased for me and I said, so you see there is a God, and melted, or was that dripped off into the night?

Each time I went down that road afterwards I couldn't believe my luck in finding the ATM, it was quite well tucked away, and during the twelve days, I must have used nearly all of the others.

When I went to get my one and only basket of fruit, there were papaya there that were bigger than any marrow I had seen. Now I understand why Umaporn, my Thai student, used to laugh when she saw the papaya I bought.

These days when I'm asked my room number, I have to give it serious consideration. I think I've been in more bedrooms this holiday than a top class hooker. Even at this hotel I've seen three.

See you later

Love,

Pat.

In Search of a Suntan

24 April 2003

Dear Sue and Peter,

No matter how long I'm out in the sun, my tan stays the same. Yesterday I was lying full length in a sea-kayak at midday in an enclosed lagoon. The sun was beating down and I had no sun cream on my legs. They looked no different last night and certainly not this morning. How come? Don't they have a hole in the ozone layer in this part of the world? Lynley said it was massive over New Zealand and I'm only round the corner, so to speak.

Tomorrow I'm going to Phi Phi Island snorkelling, hope springs eternal.

This posh notepaper is courtesy of Caz's new hotel. Vicky and I visited today and went over to the hotel's own island. No beach hawkers (thank goodness that will never catch on in Wales) a restaurant, free loan of snorkelling and beach sports equipment. It was just a hundred degrees, no breeze.

There was a table tennis table set up in the shade under the palms, and a Japanese girl and boy were playing, rather gently. I think they were honeymooners, judging by their pale skin, and they didn't know what else to do when there were other people present. Anyway it was too hot for diving for the ball. This was a bit like knocking-up in tennis, so not so far away from their private antics either then.

The boat to the island takes ten minutes. They give

you life jackets, which doesn't fill you with confidence. Once on the island you have to find sun loungers, partially in the shade, but more importantly, not too near the ants' nests. There are red ones, small and medium, but mainly black ones as in the UK and then half-inch tropical ones. Vicky got two vicious bites today when she ventured too near their territory.

We snorkelled from the shore which was great, and the usual yellow, black and white fish were all around our feet. I'm getting quite blasé about them. I've seen them at all the coral I've visited. Once again the sparrow of the fish kingdom. A bit like a twitcher, I'm now looking for the more exotic. I don't want shark, but manta ray and dolphin will do.

Caz's hotel is very flamboyant. Like walking into a James Bond movie. You look through archways at vistas which look like you'll drop into the ocean, water is strategically placed. I've even seen tadpoles in the pools, among the water lilies and lotus plants. But the décor is based on the Flintstones – I really mean it. Great boulders, granite. It all looks rather like this notepaper, but in rough stone. Their bathroom has a bath that takes half an hour to fill, a stone cubicle shower and a toilet cubicle. The bathroom is entered from either the hall or bedroom. The wash basins are beaten steel. All the walls are curved as though you're entering a cave. Some cave. The bed is made of massive tree trunks and has a large mosquito net. There's also a spare bed, which Vicky will use when she has to stay for two days when I leave. All the veranda furniture is cut, thick, wooden logs.

After we decided we'd had enough of the island – you can only float around for so long in a rubber ring with fish tickling your toes – we returned to the hotel to the swimming pool, which extends over the sea. Once again it's made of slabs and has a 'deck' just twelve inches below the rim for you to laze in with your book while the water laps your nether regions. Ice creams and sorbets are brought free of charge on a regular basis, along with water and ice-cold refresher cloths.

Today Paul went playing golf!! He's in a competition on Sunday and he was practising. He gets a female caddie for £1 a day. I don't care if they'd given me Mel Gibson, Tom Cruise, Michael Douglas and his dad, I wouldn't have turned out in a hundred degrees with no shade to play snap, never mind golf. He must have a death wish.

Caz then told us about shopping at the new Tesco. It's a mall and she'd got some new sandals and jewellery. Vic and I couldn't wait to get there.

We hired an air-conditioned Mercedes from the hotel carpool. It duly arrived, all dark blue and impressive. Vicky got in first and started batting mozzies as though it were an Olympic event. It was swarming. I got out, she quickly followed. The driver said he'd got another car. We agreed, but no mozzies. A sleek grey one turned up and it was perfect.

When we got to Tesco (I can't believe I'm writing this in Thailand) the driver said he'd no change for the 1,000 baht I'd given him. Such was Vicky's eagerness to start her retail therapy (remember she hadn't done any for eighteen hours) that she said not to fuss, she'd pay the extra 250b. So the little sod got a tip. Nearly a day's wages. I'm willing to bet he'd change. They just try it on.

I got two pens and a packet of Maltesers. I must be slipping. Vicky got a handbag, a pair of sandals and a necklace. We saw our Kuoni rep in there, boy is it a small world. It's about six miles from our hotel, and he must only go once a week with his family. We will never go again, it's a vast store, I went down four aisles and there he was. He had two great little boys and a lovely little wife. Once again I was the biggest.

We're having a quiet night in. We had dinner at the Italian (part of the hotel), which is down the road. Once again the Disneyland cart takes us there. Somewhere you expect Judy Garland to jump aboard and start singing.

Yesterday I went canoeing. I even paddled my own canoe and once again I've got pictures to prove it. If I've done it, there's photographic proof. I think I'll make a collage – Pat at a certain age.

They took us across to some islands where there are lagoons inside. They can only be reached by canoe and then only at certain times of the day, depending on the tides. If it's too low there's no water in the lagoon, too high a tide and you can't get under the gap to access it.

On one island the caves as you go through are full of fruit bats. Once inside the lagoon you can see mudskippers, crabs and small fish. There was a sighting of a very large jelly fish (a dangerous one) but it had disappeared by the time our canoe got there.

There are also mangrove trees in the lagoon and their branches rise above the water. I was relieved to hear no crocs lurked around their roots as in Queensland.

The sides of the lagoon were very high, about eighty feet in some cases. The rocks were limestone so of course the water had worn its way in. Round the outside of the island at its base there is erosion and the stalactites hang down towards the sea. A bit like a table with a cloth on and the table legs showing.

When we canoed to an island, we got an oarsman, or paddler, whatever. Mine was called Tong. He was a lovely guy. A little girl, older than the doctor I think, sat at the front and shone her little torch at the bats. At another cave, the rocks looked like they'd diamonds set in them.

One of the entrances was so small with sides and top overhanging so much we had to lie fully flattened, hands and legs well inside the canoe. I've tried to film it as we left, but don't know how it's come out.

Once inside the lagoons (we visited three) despite the fact there are kayaks whizzing (perhaps not whizzing, gliding I think) all over the place, it's very peaceful. Some lagoons go round corners, so they seem very mysterious.

We finally arrived at another island, lagoonless but with a great beach. We had an hour there and after hopping in and out of three kayaks, a final journey to swimming was fine by me. As we arrived I told Tong I wanted to kayak by myself. He kitted me out in my life jacket and launched me from the beach. I knew exactly how to do it, but I did keep going round in circles. Then I started in a straight line. I got so excited, I immediately returned to circles and that was how my bid for aquatic freedom ended, ten feet forward, five circles backwards. I did manage to get out to sea and Tong followed in another kayak with my camera. I asked him how deep (I'm always impressed with depth) and he said three metres. Once I know I can't stand up in it, I think I'm being very daring. I hadn't asked him to bring my camera but he was a very thoughtful type of person. Now if anyone deserved 250b, it was he, not some smart-alec in a mosquito ridden Merc.

There were some nice couples on the trip, a Swiss chap and his partner, who hailed from Nelson, but who now taught English in Switzerland. An Aussie couple who left the UK in 1962. Bernadette, a divorcee, with Matthew, her nine year old; we sat together most of the time. She'd been three weeks in Oz and now two weeks here. Matthew made friends with the young crewmen and he was teaching them English.

After my solo kayaking, Tong had placed a beach mat plus headrest and all my bags (as normal I had two, everyone else had one) where I'd chosen in the shade of the palm trees. When choosing such a place, one has to bear in mind a few things. Proximity to ants' nests, size of ants, ripeness of the coconuts, odds or evens of their falling. How quickly will I no longer be in the shade? On all these points it seemed good. Nothing moving on the ground, no cigarette stumps lying around. Coconuts still young.

I had a little paddle, it shelved evenly but steeply. Definitely paddling agenda here. I returned cooled nicely and sat down on my mat and towel. Tong had provided water. I could learn to live like this. Someone to cater for my every whim before I even know I want it.

I glanced at my shoulder and saw something move. A big ant. I reacted with my customary coolness in creepie crawlie situations and panicked. The only quick-moving thing I might tolerate on my shoulder is a gecko, because I think of them as friends. As I panicked it fell down inside my cozzie. I brushed it, but I was sure it was still inside. The couple nearest me, watching my war dance that wouldn't have disgraced an Apache warrior, were the Aussie couple.

She saw what was happening, and by this time, one shoulder strap was down and I didn't care who got a peak at my Rubenesque figure. She asked me, could she hold my towel? It only just met and I wriggled out of my swimsuit. As it came down at the back, she saw the ant and it was just starting to fly! I wriggled into my other swimsuit (you see there's always a good reason to take two bags) and tried to put the ant at the back of my mind. The good news is, I was not bitten. It was probably just as scared as I was. No – that's not true. Nothing would be as scared as me. Then Tong, always perfect timing, said it was time to head back. I'm surprised he let an ant near me.

Still, nobody's perfect.

We'd had lunch on board and as we arrived back to the port, ice-cold cloths, ice creams and bottled water were thrust at us.

I had the chance to buy for £3 my picture as I boarded the boat, framed and trimmed with shells. It looked OK. I looked young enough, thin enough and I wasn't wearing my hamster look as the girls call it. This is where I smile and my cheeks look like a hamster who's stashing his nuts. So, another keepsake from the 'Pat doesn't look her age on that' parade. Actually now I think of it, I look like the lady captain of a lower grade golf club. I just have that look.

One of the caves we entered was called the oyster cave because all the walls were made from oyster shells. I think they were a few millennia old, but it was a little difficult, it got lost in translation. Just a guesstimate then. They definitely weren't the 'crack open and wash down with a nice Chablis.

Friday

As you know, I went snorkelling yesterday. I nearly drowned myself and this was snorkelling from the shore.

We visited Phi Phi Le first and I got my life jacket on and off I went. I did OK and took some nice pictures, in proper deep water. Then you visit (you and the world's mother) Phi Phi Don. There's a big hotel there and it has a few streets just like Patong with the usual shops and cafés. There were backpackers in droves. We'd gone by speedboat and there were about another twenty anchored plus other vessels. One looked like a cruise liner.

As usual I'd taken two bags – well I've got to carry my personalised snorkelling gear in something – but I left one on board and set off for the shops. I found a sun visor and a little boy about eight said 250B and I wasn't going to barter.

I then realised I'd left my money in the other bag. I raced (well ambled) back in the hundred degrees to the boat, only to find it had gone. They'd said we would have lunch in thirty minutes. And exactly thirty minutes later they returned. Too late for the little boy to clinch his deal. I felt really bad. This could have been his big sale of the day – and I hadn't bartered with him. His parents would have been so proud of him growing up in the Thai tradition.

Anyway, lunch in thirty minutes, if you remember, and we piled back on board and very soon we approached a beach. There was only one other speedboat anchored. There was a restaurant and just as we arrived the other boat left. This meant there were about fifteen of us in the restaurant. The buffet was laid out. Very similar to the canoe buffet on board.

The restaurant belonged to the Phuket Adventures so we didn't have to share Phi Phi Don with all the others, and believe me they were swarming. It was like Blackpool at a hundred degrees, the only thing missing was the rock and the Big One.

When we left after lunch, I looked back and we'd still been on Phi Phi Don but round the corner in a different bay. Then finally we stopped at a very small island, nearly too small to see on the map. And then I did think it was Blackpool. It had deckchairs, striped just like UK ones with sun umbrellas up. The majority were taken by Thais who were there with their children.

Because I'd done so well at Phi Phi Le with just a life vest, I thought I'd try without one here as the coral was reached from the shore. At Phi Phi Le they'd thrown bananas and all the fish had raced to eat them. There were hundreds, and we were among them. It was great. And this time I got some pictures of me just with a life vest and not all the other paraphernalia.

So, I ventured out. There were lots of Thai children there with their life vests on and the waves were battering them around a bit. It seemed OK and then I started falling over big rocks and the sand was full of sharp stones. Back I went for the life vest and beach shoes.

I never got out beyond my depth, but because I was wearing the jacket it wouldn't let me stand up. So, I ended up with a mouthful of seawater (and I'd forgotten how nasty that can be) and was having trouble taking out my snorkel and repositioning it. The reason for this being, the tide was coming in and it was now battering me about. The swell was quite heavy and we all know I'm no lightweight.

I eventually staggered ashore, removed the jacket, grabbed some pineapple and watermelon provided by the tour and headed back. I found I could feed the fish in two feet of water and there were umpteen round me. Not all 'sparrows' either, some of the rarer more exotic fish. I hoped to have captured them on my ordinary camera.

So ended my snorkelling. After major and minor triumphs, it all fizzled out rather ignominiously. Instead of going from strength to strength, I went from weakness to strength, to even greater strength and then back to weakness. Even swimming in my depth had a downside. Fortunately not literally.

Tonight I'm overnight in Bangkok and arrive in Saigon at 2.00pm. I really do hope the hotel's fantastic. I should think Cable Travel in Wales are breathing a sigh of relief as I come to the end. I'd only been left twenty-four hours when I had to ring them. I bet they thought that heralded a bumpy ride – and as it is I've never rung them since. Still it's not over until the fat lady sings.

You know all the trouble I have with taxis. In Bangkok in particular they don't know one street from another and you pay as they look. I got in one yesterday at the airport. It said taxi meter above it. I asked to go to my hotel by meter. No, he said. I got out, all five cases and bags and camcorder. I asked the next and he agreed. As he started I said, please set the meter, and he grinned and said 'meter'; I could see it still wasn't going and said, set meter, a little more robustly this time. He banged the meter and said 'Oh no, not working.' So I said, take me back to the airport. He agreed and then said, 300b, I was mad, but thought about it and agreed, but for 100b more I could have got a limousine.

IN SEARCH OF A SUNTAN

Vicky got a tuk-tuk from Phuket town to Diamond Cliff Hotel and the driver told her he couldn't operate at her hotel because of Diamond Cliff Mafia. Now I presume he meant the tuk-tuks outside the hotel were run by them.

The Mafia certainly runs Phuket. They operate in Mercs, collecting their protection money from all the stalls. You can see them. I don't think the ones in the big stores are affected. If they don't like someone or decide they've done something wrong (now, in the eyes of the Mafia, what constitutes wrong? Drug pedalling and not passing on profits? Or not paying protection money?), they chop two arms and a leg off and make the man work for them begging on the streets – and sometimes selling cigarettes. They are delivered in the morning by Merc and collected again at night. It's the sort of thing that can give you nightmares if you think too hard about it.

This is not a subject I would have written about until I knew I was leaving. I think I have offended quite a few people as it is. Certainly one tuk-tuk driver outside Diamond Cliff because I wouldn't give him how much he demanded, he drove like a maniac. I think he was trying to terrify us, but he was certainly in a paddy. He looked at me with undisguised hatred as I paid him. I have since refused to be carried by him.

I'll tell you something; I checked my baggage extra well before I left the hotel. The Mafia have long arms. I've told Vicky to do the same. I had made my displeasure known on a few occasions. To everyone I was generally charming, but I'd possibly made a few enemies. Caz says no one raises their voices to Thai people, as Thais never do. If they're swindling the arse off you they don't need to. It's about time somebody did raise a voice.

I find it offensive that Mafia-run tuk-tuk drivers with very little charm, no discernible skills, can charge for their time double what a doctor, a whole team of radiographers and nursing staff can.

Hotels have jumped on the bandwagon and charge £10 for the breakfast (including mine) when it can be bought down the road for £1. A Japanese restaurant, beautiful, big, clean, only charges £1.20 for a lunch buffet. The sheer greed of the people involved in the tourist industry annoys me. I think eventually, Thailand will pay the price.

Someone talked to a beach policeman and it was explained to them, if you wanted to sell designer rip-offs, you had to pay protection money. One man didn't, and the next day all his stock of watches was cleared out. The Thai policeman thought this was OK because the man had been foolish. The theory being if you want to sell rip-off merchandise, you have to pay the price.

Suddenly Preston seems an eminently sensible place to live.

Love,

Pat

The E.R. Look

Another airport lounge (at Phuket)
28 April 2003

Dear Clare and Michael,

What a relief. Finally left the hotel from hell. It's been such an ordeal, not the least which sharing my room.

I've decided forty-two days is just the perfect time for these jaunts. Any longer and I get jaded, or perhaps it's just my leg. Suggestions have been made regarding cartilage or ligaments. The shop (where I slipped) could be hearing from me.

I'm here in my new dress copied from my old faithful that I've been using as my airport dress mainly because it's loose and has giant pockets.

The first two people have passed me wearing masks. They are young German guys. I have mine in my baggage but hope the Echinacea will do the trick. Spoke too soon, the young chap opposite me has seen the other two and now feels OK to get his out. Up to now it's always been the Orientals who have sported the ER look.

Everyone here is warning me I will find Vietnam hot. Yes, but does it have over a hundred and forty steps to your room? I've checked again, and that is how many it was to my second room, plus corridors. All in the stifling heat.

Bernadette, the girl I met on the canoes came to visit with her son and they're next door at the Novotel.

She went back quite relieved, saying they'd nothing like it and she thought theirs was bad.

I took them to the Diamond Club pool, which has forty majestic steps up, a plateau, then forty down. From there, if you wish to go to the spa (which I did to get my hair done) it was another thirty-seven up and ten down and six more up. Boy did that architect have fun. He could have built the 1960s high rises before they commissioned him to start this. I just hope, wherever he is, he's sweating, aching and feeling extremely uncomfortable. If there's any justice, he'll be all three permanently.

The hotel itself was fine. The rooms were immaculate. The chambermaids kept them sparkling even in that heat. They seem to take about half an hour per room – or perhaps that's just because Vicky shared mine.

I am on board now and sharing the flight with a load of over-excited Thais. They act as though they've never flown before. They are videoing everything and one had even appropriated my seat. There was uproar (not from me) and she moved, but there was no way I was giving up my left side aisle seat. This was a first for me. They'd managed to get it right – well, left.

I think the man I'm sitting next to has just asked me to write down my address for him but I'm playing dumb. I already know he's fifty-three, but he's not wearing as well as me, despite the knee. You can tell we're about to take off from the wobbly writing but it could be no different to you. Vicky says I have doctor's writing. I think I have, but I don't have the salary. All the disadvantages, none of the advantages.

I've not really felt like writing while I was in Phuket, suddenly I feel liberated. It's great. Was it the heat or the steps? Could be both and the pain.

We're just airborne, the seatbelt sign has come off and another man has come to claim the chap next to me. They and two women have disappeared towards the back of the plane. There's a lot of giggling and bonhomie as though this flight were put on just for them. They are filling the aisles and still videoing. It's one big party. I feel a bit resentful, but that could be the English in me being a bit anally retentive.

Grief, more are disappearing towards the back, if it goes at this rate we could find our equilibrium badly affected.

The hostesses are having a hard time trying to get through. One chap seems to be the organiser of everything. Seating arrangements, mayhem, you name it. Nice as it is for people to be having a good time, free for all etc, I'll be glad it's only a one-hour flight. Any more could seriously damage my well-being.

Further to my flight 'companions', I know what it's like, a Bangkok market, bedlam, whatever you wish, but it's not an A to B flight.

During all of the meal, they've wandered up and down the aisle, swapping food, sitting on the arms of whoever's chair. There are about forty of them. I'm beginning to feel a bit left out.

I am now ensconced in my Bangkok hotel again. I have managed to get to the post office to get a bigger box to send my excess baggage home in.

No, this is not *déja vu*, you have already read this twice before. It is not an illusion. I was sending Vicky with it, but it's easier to do everything for myself. The only trouble is, I could have got it away a week earlier and then I'd have been guaranteed to get it before Wales. At the moment it'll be touch and go.

It's now taped and ready to be tied. I've copied my other smaller box, which had Thai writing on it, and I'm now fluent in 'to' and 'from'. I don't know how to pronounce it, but the writing is fluid. So it's back to the post office tomorrow before the airport. On my Viet flight I've got 30kg as I'm in the executive part. Just when I don't need it.

Before we left Phuket we went for dinner at the Holiday Inn right in the centre and only about seventy-five yards from the beach. The food was very good and reasonable and although its position to the road should have made it noisy, you could hardly hear anything. After our nightmare hotel it was like an oasis. It had a lift and I didn't see one step. I bet the people staying there felt they were on holiday. I felt I was in 'I'm a celebrity, get me out of here' without the publicity to boost my sagging career, at my hotel.

When I went to the post office this morning the little girl (she's probably about twenty) in her Buttons outfit – white suit, gold buttons, braid and pill-box hat, who orders the taxis and instructs them where to go, told the driver where the PO was. I knew where it was, but it's in the one-way system and a little complicated. My driver nodded, especially when he was asked to wait and drive me back, and off we set. We went the right way out (he'd no choice) did the correct U-turn and then it all went wrong. He then turned left (he should have done a right U-turn) and asked a chap on a bicycle. He put him right, but by this time we'd gone so far down the road he had to go another mile to do a U-turn. After that we kangarooed along. While he searched for the PO I knew it was only a block from the hotel. Eventually we drew up, but it had taken him thirty-five minutes. I was beginning to run out of time to catch my flight.

I then, because I was stressed and hot, got conned into having my parcel sent express. This cost nearly £60, but it's there in three days and I think it's insured. I'm hoping it's something like DHL, but I'm not sure.

Am now on board Vietnamese Airlines and am so glad to be leaving this benighted country.

As we were loading in Bangkok, I donned my mask. Have I ever felt such a wally? It slipped and slithered till I lost patience and I thrust it in my pocket. Don't think I'll be using it again. I got funny looks too. Except for the three I mentioned, Europeans don't seem to wear them. And none of the Thai party-till-we-drop group seemed aware that SARS was about in the airlines.

The news has just come on to say Vietnam is the first country to beat SARS and report no new cases and they've been given the all clear. As I'm arriving tomorrow that's most opportune.

I have been to the night market and got copy Reebok sneakers for Gavin and Jake. I hope Jake likes them. Boys of nearly twelve will only wear what the others are wearing. You see, when I get on my own, I go off doing things again.

Love,

Pat.

Tin Tin

Bangkok
29 April 2003

Dear Clare and Michael,

On my way out to Phuket I had one day to kill in Bangkok and I was determined to enjoy what I knew to be a busy, noisy, polluted but beautiful city.

My hotel was very nice, Amari Atrium, and the staff were great. One lady at the Guest Relations Desk was really on my wavelength. And she summed it up beautifully. She said (on my return after Phuket) 'I know exactly what you mean because I'm always hyper when I travel.' She was right, I had become seriously hyper by the time I returned, as documented.

Anyway first time round, I arrived in the middle of Songkran, the water festival celebration. Being a big holiday when I got to most of the major sites, they were closed. Only the temples were open.

I went to see the largest reclining Buddha. Quite impressive. Damned hot though! As I started from my hotel the Buttons girl got my taxi and it was reasonable.

As I emerged from the temple in the midday sun (see, Noel Coward was right) I saw many tuk-tuks and some taxis going by. The first two tuk-tuks were exorbitant, then one agreed 50b. He then said, first madam we visit shop, then gas, only ten minutes. I was already in the thing, but I put my good leg forward and was out before he could protest.

The shop would belong to his brother and for all I knew, his mother would own the petrol station.

The next one, a taxi, wanted 300b. I told him to get lost in no uncertain terms (my forty-two days were up and my coach was turning back into a pumpkin and the horses into mice.)

By this time I was extremely uncomfortable, hot and in pain but I wasn't giving in. I crossed the road and managed to flag down a metered taxi and when I got back to my hotel it was 85b. Sorted with satisfaction. It's not the money, it's the principle.

The Amari Atrium had a stream running through its dining room, not accompanied by mozzies, I'm pleased to say, as I was seated by it each morning at breakfast.

Unfortunately its massage prices were more than I was willing to pay (but not as I was to find out, anywhere near as exorbitant as the Diamond Cliff) so I took myself off down the road to a local beauty shop.

I had my usual foot massage and thought I'd have my hair done too.

I was persuaded to have steam treatment, and I must admit I thought it was a good idea. What I didn't know was that it was the first time they'd used it and I was to be their guinea pig.

I have noticed that some Thais in moderately menial jobs get uppity once they get a uniform or a promotion.

Unless I'd met the most unfriendly Thai on the planet, that's what happened with the grey-suited 'manageress'. While she was fiddling around (it eventually was forty minutes before anything happened) and musing over the contraption, she managed one weak smile. Even that seemed a strain and remember, my reputation couldn't have gone before me, as I hadn't hit Phuket yet.

When the young hairdresser finally took over, even though she hardly spoke any English, she was very friendly.

Unfortunately, for them, while I was being lightly steamed they'd given me a book to read where I could look at the pictures. It was a hairstyling book. Oh dear, whilst my hair is not my crowning glory I was suddenly seized by the various styles being modelled by all the twenty-year-olds in the book. I could have one of those. It's strange how in the UK I've long ago given up asking for any of the styles in these books, as I know I can't have them. And strange how a bit of steam and heat and being away from home more than forty-two days can take away your logical powers.

I'd found a style I liked which can only be described as 'unstructured.' I'd often tried it out with lacquer at home but nobody ever admired it.

I pointed to the style and said ' Like that – sexy.' She giggled and said 'Oh no, no – no.'

I kept nodding and said yes. She blow-dried away and a very matronly 'bob' appeared. Page boy really. I jabbed my fingers at the style and raised my eyebrows to emphasize.

She kept saying no, no. I didn't think she dared do it in case the management sacked her. Either that or she was incapable of tousling my hair. I showed her I normally had a fringe.

At the end, having blown the fringe over my forehead, she backcombed it, sprayed it with lacquer and arranged it above my forehead sticking up and saying 'sexy.'

I looked like Tin-Tin. It splayed across my crown and I was faced with a large bare forehead. I said thank you, gave her a big tip and left. Sexy. If you've seen 'Something About Mary', you'll get the picture.

I've said it before but that's the last time I'm asking for a style from a book. That night I was going out with Caroline and Paul to the Landmark Hotel for my Mother's Day dinner.

I had about ten minutes to wet my fringe and alter my altar-boy-cum-choirboy look.

Allowing the amount of humidity in the air, I don't know why I bothered.

Caz had rung at 8am that morning. They'd been there twenty-four hours. I'd slept fine, even though I'd had only four hours sleep I didn't seem to be affected by the six-hour time difference. We went shopping. I bought an expensive (by Thai standards) (£30) top in a large department store that I now have given to my dressmaker to put in side pieces. Remember everyone is size ten or less, but I'm not saying how much she's to put in it.

So I set off for the Crowne Plaza to meet Caz (Paul had dropped asleep by the pool and had sunstroke, he was feeling grim when he wasn't asleep) and from there we'd go to the Landmark.

The bellboy (not the Buttons girl) got me a cab and gave the driver instructions in Thai. He nodded and off we went. He didn't speak English but he could say Crowne Plaza and proceeded to mutter it for the next thirty minutes. He seemed to think that this would conjure up the hotel miraculously in front of us.

We hadn't been gone long before I realised he didn't know where it was. We went towards the centre; I recognised it from the WAT district. I certainly didn't know where it was and was slowly losing the will to live when he turned back and we were in shouting distance of my hotel. I saw the same shrines that tell me I'm a block away.

Just before it he pulled in and asked another driver alongside at the traffic lights. The instructions seemed to be nearly complete when the lights changed. Despair.

The other driver pulled over at the other side and we drew up behind. A big discussion followed. I'd allowed fifteen minutes for the ten-minute journey, but I was already half an hour late.

The other taxi driver rang the depot. I got put on to a girl who spoke English and told her where I wanted. She rang off. Five minutes later she rang back and said: 'Holiday Inn Crowne Plaza' and I said yes.

Smiles all round, we headed off in a totally different direction – sideways, and ten minutes later we were there. (I'd tried him with the Landmark, but he didn't know that either.)

By this time Caz had returned to her room. She'd already warned me the taxi drivers didn't know their way round the city, but perhaps I didn't take her seriously enough.

Fortunately, we had a great meal, a buffet with everything but whole lobsters in it. And strangely enough we didn't feel full.

I wouldn't mind but these taxis are the official ones. They're metered and the livery is either blue and red or green and yellow. The former seem to be the clueless ones. Then again I've only been to the airport with the latter and everyone knows where that is.

I arrived the next morning to check in early. The

reason for this is my leg – what other? I need a left-hand aisle seat. If I'm not able to straighten it, I'm in a lot of pain.

The greatest plans ... So they gave me a right-hand aisle seat which exacerbates the problem. I knew the flight wasn't full (SARS etc.) so told the stewardess my problem.

I moved once everyone was on. Great. Later, the hostesses came round with a tray and I took a flannel.

This seasoned traveller had only taken one of the used towelettes issued as I was reseating. Talk about sheepish.

As we were leaving for Phuket I felt like I was on holiday with the Tooting Bec holiday club. There was a group of Londoners in a big group, all vests, shorts, skinheads and beefy, sometimes tattooed, arms. I can see them all now at the Nag's Head, saving since last summer for the big one. They seem nice enough but very in your face and loud.

Bangkok Airways served lunch on a fifty-five minute flight. Plus used towelettes. What service.

Best Room in the House – Not So's You'd Notice

30 April 2003

Dear Sue and Peter,

Another airport lounge, this time Bangkok, and because of being business class (they have no first class on Vietnam airlines) I had special check in. Even with 30kgs and posting a 7kg pack this morning I'm over by 4kgs. Looking bad for my return.

As I sit in the business class lounge, I'm amazed at the condition it's in. The only good thing about it is the comfy armchairs.

The free food is absolutely awful. A bit of fresh fruit and three types of sandwich. Crusts off white bread, stale white bread at that, filled with either cheese, minced chicken or ham. They were also slightly warm, which of course is just what you want in somewhere as warm as Thailand when eating chicken. Needless to say I spat it out (bet they don't get a lot of that in business class.) There was also some sponge cake.

As I wandered through the airport, I saw a fresh juice stall, so for £1.30 I got papaya and pineapple. I'd rather pay than have the rubbish they serve free down here.

After I'd been down in the executive lounge looking at the offerings for a couple of minutes a woman came down the escalator and asked had I checked in at the desk at the top? Well of course I hadn't. So I gave her the permit card and then she had the cheek to ask to see my boarding card. It says row 1, seat C and you can't get much nearer the cockpit than that, so that shut her up. And this was all before I spat out the warm chicken. Imagine her horror if she'd known about that.

I said you can't get nearer the cockpit than row 1C, but you can in Bangla Road, Phuket, if you sit on the barstool in the bar of that name. But I think even I'm too old for the oldest game in town.

No wonder that woman checked, only the desperate would leave their trolley, haul their two bags down the escalator for stale sandwiches and indifferent air conditioning.

Various Americans (male of course) are coming down and having quite a reunion with old acquaintances further in the lounge.

I think I'm in the non-u part as I can be seen by the hoi-polloi in the main building. It's probably the done thing to move where you can't be observed. As far as I'm concerned this was as far as I was willing to drag my cases. They're quite light for me, but just watch me on the way back, anything that weighs heavy will be going in hand baggage.

I had a limousine to bring me here. Might as well arrive in style, only double the taxi price. The driver coughed and snuffled his way to the airport. I wonder if he was incubating SARS. If he were, I've worked it out I'll be home before I develop it. But would I be better off in an NHS hospital or would Saigon be a better fate? There are so many other things for them to kill you with in the UK. MRSA, wrong drug treatment, wrong limb removed (they'll only need to hear about my knee and start treating me for the wrong thing). As you see I have no faith in the NHS and with four very good reasons. That's why I keep wanting them to discover what's wrong with my knee before I get home, then I can confront them in the UK with my diagnosis, but will they believe it?

So, I've tried New Zealand, then Thailand and I'll see what it's like in Ho Chi Min City. Do they have MRI scanners in Vietnam? I'm about to find out. Hope they have good cheap massages.

Well, as we left Bangkok it poured down, that seems appropriate. I do hope Vietnam is better. Just like China, you can't get the currency before you get there, and there are no published rates. So I won't know how much the taxi will cost to the hotel. I have some baht with me to change at the airport. I do hope they have ATMs.

It was days in China before I knew how much anything cost. Now I know everything was very cheap. The flight to Vietnam was very bumpy. Was it the aircraft, the pilot or the weather?

Saigon.

The room I was going to get on arrival was meant to be the best available, including the Presidential Suite – well, it took me two hours and only then because they offered to let me have the upgrade for US$10 per night. I'd already sent a fax to Sheryl, the travel agent. I'd seen two rooms. The first was awful, the curtains were hanging at one side and the view was a back street with shabby roofs and back alleys. This may be romantic in Coronation Street but I was ready for a bit of TLC.

I asked was this the best available room as I'd seen a picture of an executive room. This wasn't it. The next room was the same as the last but overlooking the swimming pool. Rather gloomy though. I hung on for the exec room. They asked would I like to sit and have a drink at their expense in a cool room. I have been offered this throughout the whole trip for a variety of reasons e. g. shopping trip, irate tourist etc. I must be a worrying sight.

The local agent rang me and said it was too late to contact my travel agent. I asked when he closed, he said 6pm, so I said, you've thirty-five minutes, long enough to send an email. So he agreed. Then I sent Sheryl an email. Well I think I did. The upshot of it was she rang me, but I was already in my current room, one floor up and with balcony onto the swimming pool. I have dark wood parquet flooring and furniture to match. Very French, around nineteenth century. This building was built by the French and used by them until they left after their drubbing by the Vietcong. I'm now in the old part. Since they're nearly empty, why couldn't they look after me properly in the first place?

I told them with tourism at a low because of SARS (they were given the all-clear only yesterday) and the Iraq war, they should be glad to see anyone willing to travel. Why give me such a rotten room when I could have been offered the third one they showed me? I mean, have they got a death wish?

I went for a walk around the area which is just by the Saigon River and finally ended up in a bistro just opposite the hotel run by a young Frenchman called Mark. He said many complaints were made by tourists regarding the Grand. It's meant to be one of THE hotels in Saigon, it used to be called the Saigon Palace.

When I crossed the road to reach the river it was like the dodgems. My taxi driver said there were five million motorcycles in Saigon and I believe him, because all of them plus a few cars were heading for me. I managed to get halfway and I've never been so terrified on a road before. Because it was dark, it seemed worse.

Eventually a man crossed the half I couldn't manage and then took me back. He came especially to get me. Wasn't that nice? Either that or he didn't want the noise of an ambulance and the mess of a squashed tourist opposite his little stall.

The two river restaurants just served Vietnamese food and the language was their own. I can quack in Chinese but I don't know if I can translate it into Vietnamese. Some still speak a bit of French so it's handy.

As a result of my traumas, my knee is twice its size. It is so painful. The worst it's been. It wasn't helped by the fact that I had to trail down to reception (via the lift, but it's still a trip), twice because my room card wouldn't open the door.

Anyway, now I don't have to walk, I've forgotten the pain and I've just got my natural endorphins going by belly laughing at 'Frasier' on the TV. It's an old one, but still good.

Saigon is very French at the centre. There is a big cathedral, Notre Dame, where mass is said every Sunday. It's meant to be modelled on the Parisian one, but it's massive and it's red brick. I hope to visit tomorrow.

They've got modern, huge buildings but they all seem to be for banks – HSBC, Citibank, Prudential. Looks as though Vietnam is going the way of China – or perhaps this part never took to communism. An American lawyer I met at the airport said visiting the South was easier than the North, more free and easy, less questioning.

The shops round here on the most famous street in the city are quite exclusive and all prices are in US dollars. And they're not cheap either.

There probably is somewhere cheap to go as in China, but it's local knowledge you need. So I've four days to get a feel for the place.

I can go and see an exhibition of American atrocities (and French also I think) but they warn it isn't pleasant. No thank you, I watched the news in the sixties and seventies and that was enough.

In a city guide they tell of the destruction of the American Embassy which heralded the end of the Vietnam war. They say, quite smugly, that they, the Americans, now have a more modest consulate. The words used have a triumphal air about them. I suppose, as it's recent history they haven't forgotten. Just as well we weren't the same with the Japs and Germans.

Well, here endeth the social comment on both Thailand and Vietnam.

The streets round here all have tamarind trees in them and they have a look of French boulevards. All très elegant.

Tonight a bikeshaw (or cyclo as they call them) asked if I wanted a lift. It's about £1 per hour, but allowing for the shock of the *en masse* motorbike assault on the street near the river, I don't fancy my chances much in a rickshaw.

As usual when I arrived at the airport, (the sign for taxi said US $4.00 to the city) and the first driver said $8.00. I've got round to snarling now, so I snarled it only cost $4. He said OK $4, I said, too late, and went toward an ordinary taxi and asked the man, $4 to city? and he said yes. The driver put it on the meter and it only came to $2.00.

On principle now I won't use anyone who starts by trying to rip me off, no matter how low they come down. It's not the same at the shops, they start high and expect you to barter.

The French chap, Mark, says Cambodia is very poor. Vietnam's not too well off but it's a lot worse in Cambodia. I shall have to ask Paul and Andy. I know it was going to be cheap.

Well, hope springs eternal. Tomorrow will be better. I'll be able to walk on my leg and Saigon will be great.

Love,

Pat.

From Roedean, England

1st Letter, Vietnam
1 May 2003

Dear Clare and Michael,

I am forgiving the Grand Hotel but only because their massage girl (they don't seem to call them masseuse) for feet is fantastic. Despite my leg I actually fell asleep.

This may not be the wondrous thing it sounds, since I only got up at 2pm. The only place breakfast is included and I can't get up for it, but as we can see I couldn't make lunch either.

My leg was so bad yesterday evening and all through the night I didn't get to sleep until 4am.

Anyway once up I was off to find breakfast and a photocopier. Because of this quest I've learnt my first Viet word. Lau Lau. The photocopy shop I was directed to was closed. The people next door said Lau Lau – holiday. I presume they meant it meant holiday and not just closed. I could be living under an illusion.

I then found another where the copier was in the 'back room'. A bit like it was in UK when people just started having them to boost income, were signed up by unscrupulous salesmen for vast sums until the end of time or until the government gives back the £5million p. a. from pension funds, whichever is sooner.

She charged me enough and it wasn't too good.

The copier needed a good clean.

I then found a post office. It would appear that the speed of service is universal. A young women dressed in salwar kameez started to weigh the envelopes. She wrote down the weight in a corner. VERY CAREFULLY. She looked up the price on a chart. VERY CAREFULLY. She pulled out a plastic box with lots of coloured stamps. She perused them, as though she'd never seen them before. She got out one from a group, replaced the paperclip and started on another highly coloured group. Then she saw she needed another from each of the groups she'd put away. I thought I should tell her by now I needed one more lot of each but I didn't like to confuse her. I also needed seven for postcards – dare I risk telling her? Then it got worse. She realised she hadn't got enough in said box for the letters. Another group was needed from another box. I was beginning to lose the will to live. She made the photocopy girl in Christchurch look like a speeding comet. I eventually left having parted with nearly £7. This seems an awful lot for just four letters and seven postcards in a third world country. A three-course dinner costs a lot less at a top hotel. Wine extra of course.

I went to the French restaurant again tonight and it was buzzing. Many people were from France, the couple next to me were in their twenties and touring for a month. They came from Lille.

Mark, the proprietor, was helpful when I asked who to ask regarding tours allowing I can't walk too far.

My leg tonight is fine; I've not been on it too much. I enquired at reception and they said the international hospital would charge me an arm and a leg; well actually she said $80.00 just to see me and they wouldn't be able to tell me what was wrong. You'd think she lived in England and had no faith in the medical world. So I'm having to wait until UK.

As I walked round today, despite the fact the roads are very wide, the state of the footpaths and kerbs shows it to be a third world.

On every corner and available part of the pavement, the Viets are cooking, mainly crepes. Its smells lovely, but I've not been tempted yet.

I passed a Hindu Temple and saw a Hindu shrine in a large shop. It was on quite prominent display.

On the way in we passed a Baptist Church, so it seems like all religions are allowed to practise.

There was a banner across a building I noticed as I arrived advertising the REGENT SCHOOL, recommended by major embassies. It said, 'Regent student wins place at Oxford University'. As I got nearer I could see 'Headmistress Mrs Steiman from Roedean, England'. As you'll imagine this was not a small banner. And it's not Hong Kong but Vietnam, but probably not how we imagine Vietnam.

A young boy bearing papers approached me and I asked for English *country* newspapers. 'I have English,' he says and shows me the *Financial Times*. So I've explained I want the *Daily Mail* and he says he'll look for it. He was really keen and lovely. They are not pushy like the Thais. Rather gentle with it.

On the way back as I'd shopped for juices at a superstore I decided I would get help. Now there was a cyclo, you know, rickshaw, on the corner and the poor mutt must have misjudged me because he asked did I want a lift.

I negotiated a rate and gave him my shopping, he

then tipped the rickshaw forward. I thought leg, then I thought rear, then I wasn't sure.

So I put my good leg in, but I was worried for the cyclist. He already had my shopping and didn't look big and beefy, rather tall and wiry. A friend of his had seen the problem and together they held the bike while I negotiated myself in. There was quite an audience by now but I took no notice. I certainly wasn't going to give up. My leg was in no state to walk, it was a hundred degrees and I had three bottles of juice (I only had two until they pointed out I get three for two with my grape juice.)

So as I elegantly draped (or was that plonked?) my little frame into the seat, they both tipped me back and we were off. We left the pavement with a crash, which didn't do my back any good and I think his chassis might need a bit of attention tonight. And he'll be wondering why.

I hadn't realised how far I'd wandered. I was a few blocks from the Grand.

Somehow all the motorbikes managed to avoid us and we went serenely on our way. The arrival was far more graceful than our departure as the footrest which is curved just sat on the kerb.

I alighted and the doorman offered his arm. I managed to make it all look natural to me. I then received my groceries. Not quite how the ladies of the past usually arrived at the Grand.

Still it was an entrance of sorts. And it was then I went for my massages. As I left I gave the girl a tip of 4000D. I thought she looked disappointed. The manageress explained this was 'feeble' tip. I'd given her 16p or so. I meant to give £1.60. I couldn't give much more because the massage only cost £3.00. If you give too much tip it makes the prices go up, they think they aren't charging enough. It's a question of balance.

Last night when I was taking my life in my hands getting across to the river, as I got closer I could see all these cyclists and motorcyclists in what appeared to be a queue, but it didn't go anywhere. It was like a holding pen, it was covered. It was only then I realised I'd reached the river and they were queuing for a ferry. I've no idea if the ferry went across or down the river but it seemed very popular.

As I neared the boats which were restaurants I noticed that there was a lot of the floating plant that all Asian waterways seem to accumulate, and among the plants were hundreds of polystyrene boxes of the sort that McDonalds give out. I don't know if people had individually thrown them in or they'd been tipped en masse. As time goes on they're going to have a very big pollution problem. The Far East doesn't seem to care regarding pollution or doesn't realise the harm it's doing. It'll cost them a fortune to put it right.

Comet, the electrical firm would have a fit if they saw how many white goods shops there are. Every other one round here seems to have enormous fridges or TVs. They're all very much into electronic gadgets and telecommunications in this part of the world.

If I'm not mistaken, the very large fridge-freezers are about £140 but I think duty free they're a lot less.

The boutiques are selling beautiful dresses (not my size) at UK prices. I've seen one that's gorgeous and I'm going to go in and see if they can make me one. Like I need more clothes!

According to the *Vietnam News*, the national English

language daily, tourist numbers dropped by forty-one per cent against last year but the revenue was down only ten and a half per cent, so it means that the tourists they've lost were the under spenders. The big spenders must still be coming. Trade deficits are quoted in dollars and then the dong.

I really find these newspapers interesting because they tell us in the West who's meeting whom and trading with whom. We don't hear about it in our papers. The tragic thing is that nowhere could I see a UK presence in the commercial market. There are many German and Japanese companies, but definitely none from the UK. Still we must hope that Tesco takes the opportunity and expands here. It does seem to be our most aggressive supermarket chain. It's all over Eastern Europe.

Strangely enough Americans seem to be the salesmen doing most of the business here. If only our people could see the opportunities and get in on the ground floor as the economy takes off.

Thursday

I've managed breakfast this morning. It was OK. The bacon was cold though and they were so nice I didn't like to tell them.

The only ones who were originally weren't too co-operative (excuse the pun in communist country) were the reception staff. But I did go for them with all guns blazing.

While having breakfast I saw a cyclo go by with quite a big white guy in it. So it seems they were just being careful when his friend helped him to make sure white mama didn't go A over T with two containers of grape juice, one of apple and six packs of Maltesers. They would probably have felt dishonoured if this happened, not to say what white mama would have felt.

In Thailand in the restaurant with the girls they called me mama. On my own I was always madam – something my mother was frequently telling me, usually coupled with 'little'. Well, they can't say that anymore, can they?

I've just been serenaded by muzak of the fifties again. It's just like having the Light Programme on, only without George Elrick (anyone under fifty-five may never have heard of him, but he changed the face of radio broadcasting by daring to da-di-da along to the intro music of Housewives Choice, 9–10am every weekday morning.) The others seemed so stuffy. And remember this was the pop music of my childhood I heard at breakfast during the long summer hols.

So today I heard, 'Diana', 'Dream', 'A summer place' and finally just to confuse the issue, 'Tie a yellow ribbon' (round the old oak tree).

This latter seemed to have snuck in there under false pretences, but I notice it has been played in every Far Eastern country on every muzak tape I've heard. The composer must have a deal going.

I think this hotel (and probably all the others) has been underused recently. When I ran the hot water from my gold and marble taps it was mid-brown but after a few minutes changed to a pale gold colour. Unfortunately I do not think it's gold which is causing this. It's almost like a double warning saying DON'T DRINK THE WATER.

The air conditioning also smelt awful. A reconstituted damp smell. The housekeeping chap who'd been delegated with showing me my third room said it would soon clear. It did, but only after he'd helped it on its way with an apple spray freshener.

I'm relaxing more now I've been here a day or two. If I could have got a doctor to pronounce me unfit to stay (via the knee) when I first arrived I'd have left. That's what I mean about being jaded after a certain length of time.

Caz and Paul should finally be on their own now, although Paul's got passionate about his golf. He's met up with two buddies and as Caz says, he's buzzing. What with that, and the teeth, there'll be no holding him. In the tournament he was in he played off twelve and came six hundred and something out of a thousand. He was reasonably pleased and there was a big dinner and presentation that night and that's when this taxi driver took three and a half hours to find the Evason Hotel. Now this isn't a story he made up, as Caz wouldn't mind when he arrived back, but one wonders whether his pronunciation after so much 'goodwill' left something to be desired. Then again, in the middle of the night down county lanes, who could the driver ask as they usually do? The average gecko doesn't do directions.

You can see him now muttering Evason or as Paul might have said, EWUZUN, for three and half hours in the hope it might just spring up in front of him. I think Caz was lucky to get Paul back at all.

She's already making plans for their two suitcases (large ones) with which they are overweight to return to UK. Did I tell you she's had two cashmere suits made for work? She always has skirt/trousers/jacket and sometimes waistcoat. They're costing over £400 for the two, but in Italy they'd be nearer £2,000. She said the last ones they made her were like designer suits.

This morning I'm off to see if Vietnam Airlines have cancelled my flight on Saturday. There was a notice as I left Bangkok on Tuesday, which apologised for the Monday flight being cancelled.

My Saturday flight being cancelled would mean my leaving on Friday as I have to catch the Saturday BA out of Bangkok. So I can't make any plans for the next day or two until I know.

I notice from the guide that the shopping area is a designated area. After that one presumes there are only Vietnamese shops that would only suit the purposes of the locals.

Mark at the restaurant suggested I go to Vung Tao which is a beach area. It all depends on the airlines. Today I intend to take a cyclo. The alternative is a pillion passenger on a motorbike or a taxi. The bike's out because of the angle for my knee. In the taxi I'll not feel the atmosphere, so it has to be a cyclo.

The street the hotel is on was written about by Graham Greene in 'The Quiet American', which as you know has just been made into a film with Michael Caine. It takes place during the French era.

The advice given re the cyclo driver is to get your hotel to arrange it, pay just a bit more for peace of mind. I was thinking of walking to the airline offices, but perhaps not.

I've just looked at the bumph from the tour company 'Travel Indochina' and it stresses the need to confirm seventy-two hours beforehand, especially if you're travelling Vietnam Airlines. Bit ominous, eh?

Think I may let the hotel do the confirming. After all I've not given front desk anything to do for over twenty-four hours. Time to liven them up again. They'll dread seeing my form loom into view. I wish I knew more than Lau Lau and then I might know what they were thinking. Then again, ignorance is bliss.

See you later.

Love,

Pat.

Lau Lau

2nd Letter,
1 May 2003.

Dear Sue and Peter,

My new word Lau Lau is now working against me. Today is Workers of the World Lau Lau May Day and Vietnam Airlines office is closed. So this morning it took me forty-five minutes to get through to the airport. They in turn gave me V Airlines direct number at airport. *Dung* has confirmed there is a flight on Saturday.

Because I want to see the Mekong Delta before I leave, I shall have to get up at 5am and have my breakfast given to me in a box to set off for the delta so I can be at the airport by 2.15pm. I have got a private car and private boat trips around, plus lunch for $40. The driving time is three hours all told on a good day.

Tomorrow my cyclo driver of today who took me sightseeing earlier has arranged for 'his friend' to hire a new car to take me to the beach. I shall be giving the hotel the name of the hire company and the cab number before I leave. After all, we're only cyclo acquaintances. This friend could be anyone, in fact my cyclo driver could be anyone. His name is Bong; I feel like he could apply for a part in Aladdin and do very well.

Bong took me to the post office, the proper one, where people recognise stamps, and I had my letter weighed. Then he took me round all the various landmarks. I camcorded a bit and he then said would I like to go to the temple, so we went to the Buddhist Temple. I was allowed to record inside. Many people were worshipping.

He then said, 'We go to war museum.' Now I didn't like to offend him, after all he was doing the pedalling or pushing where there was a slight hill. (This is normal, I saw others doing it.) So I was duly dropped off at the museum.

Now this is what I'd been trying to avoid. You paid to go in and were given a leaflet with the Vietcong side of it.

All the atrocities were there. Everything condemning America, but only once mentioning Australia, New Zealand, Thailand, Philippines and South Korea. Plus, of course, the South Vietnam Coalition. But these were called by individual units as though South Vietnam never existed.

As we all went round, mainly Westerners of various ages, there was total silence. No one discussed anything. Even couples said nothing to each other,

Although Saigon is now called Ho Chi Minh City or HCM, Saigon is the preferred name by even the Tourist Board. I should say it's about 50:50 on the hoardings and various firms about the city. My hotel is definitely The Grand Hotel, Saigon. The pens are printed up accordingly. Surprisingly for a newish communist state there seems to be no bureaucracy governing this.

As we went through the streets, we were passed by funnily dressed men on motorbikes. They had brown tunics but funny-shaped dark brown knitted hats. They belong, it seems, to a monastery. As it was a Lau Lau, I think they were on a day out.

I went for my massage again today. Got two different girls, and it wasn't anywhere near as good. The best thing was that I now get twenty per cent discount.

The first girl didn't seem too friendly. I was having the body massage first. Yesterday it was part Thai, part Swedish. Today it was all hell. If she'd worked for the Vietcong however, the war would have been over far earlier.

Now I like quite a strong massage and a bit of rough and ready (as Roy would testify to) but this went beyond anything I'd ever had. Was it because Britain had joined with the great serpent (USA) in Iraq?

There was quite a lot of nipping and if I'd been in the school playground, I'm afraid I'd have been telling teacher.

I've had my back sat on by various people, but after a few minutes, during which she'd expelled all the breath from my lungs and I felt I could get in a size ten again, she said 'two minutes' and pointed up. I wondered if she was going to get a pair of builders boots to finish the job. I'd seen where they walk along your back and wasn't sure she wasn't going to get a balancing pole.

Two minutes later she returned, and without boots, did walk on my back and buttocks. Size eight was looking good for me. I then progressed to the foot massage which is performed with a little wooden squat style pencil.

This time, every time she applied it, it hurt. Had all my organs failed at once? Had the undercover agent for the Viet Cong finished me? When she realised it hurt she then took another out the drawer and this one didn't hurt at all. So you see, it wasn't me, it was them.

So, I'd been pummelled, pinched, squeezed, flattened and poked with a too-sharp pencil. Not too good a day for me.

Also, I'd taken a dip in the pool, it was cold and the sun had gone in. It also graduated quite quickly to 1.5m. So I ended up swimming in ever-decreasing circles.

There's always tomorrow, when I go off with two strangers to the seaside. Doesn't look like it's going to be my week.

By Sunday when I get home, I'll have been up for thirty-six hours and travelling for twenty-six hours minimum.

Anyway your ordeal is coming to an end. You won't be seeing these missives on a regular basis. You'll be off the hook. Your mission will be complete. Still I hope you've enjoyed the stamps.

Today I bought Joanne (my granddaughter) a pair of beautiful silk oriental pyjamas. I got them big enough to fit her when she's nine (she's six now.)

Well I've just changed TV programmes and the Discovery Channel is doing the Falklands War. I can't get away from it.

Last night, after the previous bad night's sleep, I'd just got off and the fire alarm went off at 12.50am. It went on for ages. Allowing I was one floor up from the pool, I wasn't unduly concerned. In a tight corner I'll choose water over fire any day.

After I listened for people moving about I went to the door, no one to be seen, so I rang reception and someone without a great deal of English said, 'Plumber, no worry mistake, plumber set it off. Sorry.'

Allowing his English when I first spoke to him was dodgy, I thought he did OK and eventually I got back to sleep. Yes, it's definitely time for me to go home. Even the things that happen to me are beginning to lose my interest.

When in Australia I was reading (and still am) Bill Bryson's 'Down Under'. I'd saved it for then. While round the pool in Alice Springs (I sure got a lot in in those forty-eight hours I was there) I noticed a chap of a similar age reading it too. When I passed him the next day I saw he was a bit further on than me and I whispered in his ear as I passed 'Don't tell me how it ends.' Well he chuckled so much his beer belly was still moving when I sat down in my corner. Shade, for head and torso, legs in full sun.

I've found the heat in Vietnam bearable. Easier than Thailand and Bali. Everyone warned me it would be very hot, but there's often a breeze that springs up now and again, and just when you can't take any more, there it is.

I noticed at the post office (listed building) this morning that the children and older people selling very mediocre postcards were very persistent. Reminiscent of Bombay. They pester you. So far I've not encountered this in Vietnam.

They were asking for higher prices than in UK, so I told them so, they didn't bat an eyelid. Just say OK, how much you pay? They call it bartering. Anyway, I stuck to my guns. These aren't the poor people of Vietnam, these are the opportunists. The taxi drivers of the pavements.

I realised this in Bali when I was there the first day and got conned by the hotel's official masseuse.

She fed me this story, just casually mentioned here and there about her not being here in the morning as her son was ill. Go to hospital. The next day when I asked her how her son was she looked puzzled and had forgotten what she'd told me. As my mother used to say, you've to have a good memory to be a good liar. That was the day she took nearly £30 (I think) off me for a massage, foot massage and manicure. Remember my bill at the hotel for six and half days of wonderful food was only £35. So now, if anyone says they are sick and starving etc ... I don't believe them. They're conning me. The sick and the starving are at home fighting for survival, not charging UK and US prices to gullible visitors.

See what I mean? I'm ready for home. I've become cynical again.

When I set off, I'm fresh, trusting, believing the best of everyone. By the time the tourist sharks have finished with me, I wouldn't give Tiny Tim the time of day. I'd probably take his last Rolo too.

I see on my Mekong Delta tour that I can sample coconut candy and coconut pulp after I've seen it made. Not if they don't want me to throw up all over them, I can't. I can think of nothing worse than coconut candy unless it's doused in chocolate and I think that's an indictable offence, it shouldn't be allowed.

I dined at the French restaurant again tonight. It seems to be a gathering place for all the French ex-pats. There's a great buzz of accents. Now I know everyone has an accent of sorts, but the French have a wonderful accent. It's THE accent, despite the fact that their 'establishment' keeps stabbing us in the back. I still like all things French, I just wouldn't keep a bust of Napoleon in the hallway, that's all.

I seem to have found my sense of humour again. What on earth did I eat at that restaurant? Perhaps it's not my sense of humour, just a sense of the ridiculous.

Can you see me tomorrow morning meeting my two chaps on the opposite corner to my hotel, taking the number and getting a copy of the rental form or I'm not playing out? It would have been much easier to have arranged it via the hotel but there were no brochures around advertising it. I also feel I wanted to give a break to my cyclo driver for pedalling me round in the heat and up those hills. Actually, they weren't hills, just a steady incline, but you know what it's like on a bike, everything's a hill. Just as well he never worked at the Diamond Cliff Resort and Spa. Double hernia before breakfast there.

Friday morning.

Well, Bong is circling the hotel on his rickshaw. Is this the vulture just sizing up his victim or does he just want to make sure if they hire a car I'll pay for it? That's understandable, as that would be a sizeable investment for them. Speculate to accumulate.

They probably don't realise it, but today they become members of the free market economy. There'll be no going back now. Bet you by next year the cycle is traded in for a motorbike, the next foot on the ladder.

When I got back from breakfast this morning, the maid was half way through the room. They're very keen here and are in at 7.30 if you let them. I had not left a notice on my door either way but it wasn't 9.00 when I returned. She didn't seem any too pleased, but neither was I.

I've left my engagement ring off, it's in the safe along with my credit cards, so I'm not worth much as a hostage or similar. I'm sure I'm going to be fine, but I'm doing the very thing I've warned my girls about for years – getting into a car with strangers. Not only strangers, but strangers who hardly speak English. And in a foreign country. Still, I've got my Lonely Planet phrasebook bought for full English price (as per the back page) from an enterprising young man outside the P. O. He originally wanted double what it said, £4.50. So I told him what that meant in dong (Vietnamese currency) and he accepted. But the little bugger got me anyway, it's a second. Some of the printing is a bit fuzzy, but readable. Still, it came in its plastic container as per usual for Lonely Planet. They more than likely really gave them away. Still, I like enterprise and at least he didn't whinge about paying for his education, his ailing mother or his starving brothers and sisters. I think that's why he got my vote.

The maid is pattering up and down outside. There's someone still with a communist mindset. She'll be banging on about workers' rights next.

There are some funny posters here. They're wide and narrowish. They show two young women at one side, extremely happy with life and the word KOTEX written above. On the other side there's a head of a happy, smiling baby saying above it, Huggies. I presume the same firm make both, but surely they're not suggesting there's a connection?

Well it's time for my day to start with Bong and his friend, so I'll let the maid back in and make her day.

Love,

Pat

Pat Sees the Sea
(but misses the point)

2 May 2003

Dear Clare and Michael,

I duly gave reception the number of my car, but it seemed above board because it was a taxi, a private one, which Bong had hired from his friend Ving who was driving. He'd had it two months, it had 2,580 kms on and he was extremely proud of it. So was Bong and I suppose it is an achievement where the disposable income is so little. So now he'd gone into the private hire business which did not include giving Bong ten per cent finder's fee, as I was to find out.

I tried to tell what a finder's fee was (I mean how many Vietnamese know the English for that?). But it didn't get lost in translation, in fact Ving understood quite a lot, but he wasn't playing ball. So Bong needed me to bung him something for his day not spent pedalling overweight mamas around Saigon. He said his wife would ask him where his money was.

I mentioned ten per cent commission for introducing the business. Good grief, if I explained any more Bong could graduate from Harvard Business School with an MBA. So it ended up costing me more than it would for a tour company to find me a guide including private car and lunch.

I tried to explain to Bong last night that I wouldn't need him, but somehow his English went a bit wooden there. I don't think he fancied a hot day on the bike when he could have a day with bucket and spade, and who can blame him?

If you've got a white mama willing to fund you for the day, build up kudos with your friend and ease your aching calves, you'd find your English had deserted you too.

I like to do my bit for the local economy and feel that today, I've done a big bit to help it along. As with the food chain I'm sure it'll go round eventually.

I had a good look round as we went. As soon as you leave Saigon there are heavy industrial works spewing up clouds of smoke/steam/emissions of goodness knows what. Then the garden centres appear, mainly fantastically cut ornamental trees. A bit like the veg when they're trying to impress (I've got photos). Topiary appears to be a Vietnamese passion.

Nothing to do with SARS, but mainly people in the Far East wear masks when on the roads, whether walking or travelling. One presumes pollution is the problem.

I saw one chap with a Burberry-designed mask. His girlfriend looked equally chic but hers was more feminine.

I asked Bong who were all the young girls, in white satin tops and trousers on their motorbikes. Students he says.

I have just passed the Parklands Saigon Town & Country Club and it looked so good, I think even I might have trouble getting in.

Coolie hats are worn by about fifty per cent of Vietnamese because it keeps the sun off and keeps the top of your head cool. It sounds eminently sen-

PAT SEES THE SEA (BUT MISSES THE POINT)

sible to me, but I don't see it catching on at the beach in Wales.

As you drive along there are hammocks slung between trees or anything else suitable and usually someone is asleep in one as the traffic roars by. In fact Vietnamese can sleep anywhere. You see them all over the place, on a pack of crates in a shop, in their cyclo seat, sitting on a stool by their stall. I remember Thais were much the same.

I've just realised that to allow me off the cyclo driver has to raise the wheels high in the air. This must take some doing with me installed.

I notice all pregnant women wear smocks and if they have a uniform it has been designed to let out. No Posh Spices here. Strangely enough it makes them look curiously old-fashioned. And I'm not keen on the Posh Spice look.

You see all sorts here, but crossing the road were a mother carrying young child and a small child with dad who, in his other hand, had a live goose. He was holding it by the scruff of the neck and it was squawking. The traffic was thundering by, it had probably never seen as much in its life.

We've passed a water park just outside Saigon and then a Disney-like park. It looks suitably exciting for children. Many monster faces about in concrete.

There are whole families on just one motorbike. Well, Mum, Dad and two children at any rate. One thing's for sure, the children won't fall off, they're well wedged in.

We have passed through Dong Hai, which is on a river of the same name, unless I misunderstood Bong – and it's likely.

As we were passing a car, a man who'd been repairing it shot out from underneath on the traffic side. We just missed him. If something had been alongside us, either we or him would have been seriously inconvenienced. A lot of Saigon is being renovated in the Art Deco style. Lots of pastel and vibrant coloured town houses.

I've just found the perfect solution to the road tolls the government wants to introduce. It's here in Vietnam and it will appeal to Labour as it creates lots of bureaucracy.

When you get to the toll sometimes you can give your money to a man in a kiosk. Then you drive very slowly about fifty yards, where there is another kiosk. Usually there is an official standing outside. You give him your ticket and he gives it to another man in the second kiosk. Sometimes you get back some of your ticket.

But my favourite is the one where there's a man outside a kiosk on the right side. You or your passenger (Bong) has to get out and in the free-for-all manage to pay for and get a ticket (it's a hundred degrees remember). He gets back in and then fifty yards down is the other kiosk on the left side with the two men. When Bong went to pay at the first kiosk there were people all over trying to pay one little man on his own, and as I saw it, entirely unprotected. There was no queue and the one with the longest arm seemed to win.

Alongside the main road there are some very lovely old-style colonial houses. Their only shortcoming is they are on this enormously busy highway with all the horn-blasting that goes on and some serious fumes. Despite all this, more are still being built.

They seem to carry the building equipment on motorised bicycles. I've seen metal conduit in ten foot lengths, about twenty or so tubes of it on one bike. Another had two concrete sewage pipes.

Thinking back, the guy with the sewage pipes shot across the traffic in the usual presumption everyone would give way to him – and they did. Also there was a young man walking towards us in the fast lane. We avoided him as he expected us to. Confusion often does reign when a pedal cyclist will just turn out and go the wrong way among the others. No one seems to think it's odd or even dangerous and they certainly don't remonstrate. So they're not me then.

Seems to be a lot of petro-chemical firms at Vung Tao, as it is a major port. There are piles of rubble from buildings either going up or coming down. It has a very prosperous look and I would think in twelve months time it will be yuppie-ish.

They eat sugar cane here and it gets sold roadside in town and country. I've just seen one statue to Lenin and hammer and sickle flags, but I suppose it's because it's been May Day.

As we neared Vung Tao, there was a big, clean industrial estate. In fact everything has a clean look to it.

Bong and Vung dropped me off at Ocean Park. I said they could collect me in three hours. Bong seemed to think he was coming with me. Now the thought of wandering round in a hundred degrees of heat and trying to converse and explain what I wanted to do, I baulked at.

It couldn't have got much worse, the nice town we'd left had given way to a Blackpool Golden Mile effect. I tried to get something to eat, but a coach party – yes, I was among the coach parties and a knees-up from Eastenders couldn't have been worse – had just finished and there were tables of spilled rice, and half-eaten chicken.

They were all laughing and it seemed to be at me. It could have been that I was the only Westerner for miles, but they laughed so much I began to wonder if my skirt was tucked in my knickers.

I tried using my Vietnamese phrasebook, but it didn't work. It could have something to do with the fact I don't get on with coach parties per se. It's always the same mentality.

So I wandered off and found another pavilion. I managed to ask for ice cream and coke. And he brought me a Walls Cornetto – I hate the things in the UK. Why would I want to eat one in Vietnam?

So miserably I looked at the sand and the sea; it wasn't encouraging. Eventually I reached an area with a swimming pool (I have one of these at the hotel) and I paid my money (£1.00) and got myself my own lifeguard and a very uncomfortable wooden slatted lounger. The number on my armband was 01223 and it was fluorescent pink. The depth was 0.8m – 2.2m, so I spent half an hour swimming along trying not to scrape my knees in 0.8m. After I'd had enough I went back to the meeting place.

Bong said Vung would take us along the front so I could see the rest of the beach. As we came to a corner I saw high on a hill overlooking the beach, a figure of Christ, in the manner of Christ of the Andes. I couldn't judge how large it was, but it seemed pretty big even though I was a long way off. This surprised me, in what is still a communist country, such an overt show piece of Christianity.

The next shock was just a hundred yards round the corner. A beautiful resort. Not only had I paid over the odds, I'd been short-changed on the venue. I could have spit.

There were four-star hotels, swimming pools, bistro-type cafés, even massages. It was like going from the Golden Mile to Juan les Pins – the beach became lovely and a bit rocky but very pretty. This went on all the way round until we hit the chic town again.

From now on, the small fish are going to have to swim for themselves. I'll stick with the people with knowledge.

Looking back on the coach parties from hell, I think they were taking bets on how I got there. I should have let them take pictures and charged them for the curiosity value – I could have covered my day's costs.

When I was in my exclusive pool, some tourists came to have a look. One of the women was wearing a mask. Did I look that bad? I smiled at them, they smiled back and looked curious. It's not that I won't tell them why I'm here, I can't. Phrase book or not. Another woman then appeared in a mask, are they selling tickets to see me?

Tonight I just had a face massage, foot massage and hair wash. The whole body massage does things even my physio doesn't. They put the usual supports under my bad leg. Imagine being remembered throughout the Far East as the woman or mama with the bad leg? Then again, I think both Thailand and Vietnam will remember me for far more.

Bad-tempered, demanding, wouldn't be taken for a ride like all the other visitors. Has she no sense of what's right?

Since returning home, it has be suggested that it may have been be some sort of scam the Vietnamese hotel was running. I told them I'd talked to a young guy who'd checked in and also been given one of the grotty rooms when the hotel was plainly not even a quarter full. She wonders if it's a ploy to get more money by making you upgrade.

In the cold light of day I don't feel it was. I think it was just bad marketing. Why not use your nicer rooms for the same grade overlooking the swimming pool instead of the inferior ones?

I wouldn't have complained for at least a day that way. Then again, I showed them run of house, which it said on the booking form and they said it meant nothing. At this moment I await my refund.

PS I did get my refund, plus one for the hotel not used in Hong Kong. Only British Airways to deliver and I'll have a hat-trick.

Another suitcase in another hall ...

3 May 2003

Dear Sue and Peter,

Another suitcase in another hall. With apologies to Lloyd Webber/Rice.

5.30pm

I am sitting in Saigon airport waiting another one and a half hours until I can check in my luggage.

This is because Vietnam Airlines cancelled the flight as I really thought they would. After all it's Saturday.

I got up at 5.30am to go to the Mekong Delta. If Saigon is hot, the Delta is melting.

Le (pronounced Lay) collected me at six. I had my boxed breakfast which I have to admit was OK. Oops, I've just whacked another mosquito, I've got the feeling I'll be bitten to death or melt before I check in.

I'm now on Thai Airways at 9pm. The Thai flight gets me in with just forty-five minutes to catch the Heathrow flight. I know it could only happen to me.

When I came back from the Delta the airport was empty, just me and a guy sitting on a chair.

I could see on the departures board there was no flight to Saigon, curse Dung, the clerk on the phone who confirmed my flight, now he was living up to his name. He was the usual sort of young lad – they say anything to be left in peace. After all he was working May Day. Bet he wasn't too pleased about that.

A reasonably aged chap (around thirty – thirty-five) took up my case. I didn't bother raving, far too hot and I wanted to be in Manchester by 8.40 tomorrow.

I'd told him I'd confirmed it and he seemed extremely calm. He started making phone calls and when he'd finished, I, of course, was a wet mop.

He said Thai airlines had a flight at nine but I should be ok and if not there was another BA flight one hour twenty later. That then left me fifty minutes to get my baggage in UK and transfer to Domestic, plus immigration etc. Not much hope of that.

Lesley is meeting me at Manchester and I don't have her number. It means my ringing Caz to get her number. It just seems one thing after another.

If that mozzie bugs me once more it's for the chop. Trouble is it's not very dignified clapping a lot and bobbing up and down. Especially if people can see you've missed.

On finding no flight, I returned to Saigon city by airport bus, having left my luggage. Well, everything but my camcorder – the guy didn't want to take responsibility for that.

At least this way I saw so much more of Saigon. As opposed to just drifting around the hotel and sightseeing areas, we wound our way through all the poorer areas of the city.

I then hired a cyclo and ended up at Diamond Plaza. This is a vast store on the lines of Harrods. The rich young things of Saigon were shopping here.

There must be a tradition or fashion, but the girls linked arms together and no way would they separate.

They blocked aisles, pavements, anything. Allowing they'd cancelled my flight on me, I found this frustrating, but remember – I'm jaded.

My trip to the delta was wonderful, but you won't be surprised to hear, my tape ran out, but only just before the end. I got a 120 minute tape this time but it doesn't seem to make any difference.

Mind you, I charged it up fully last night. Oh yes, and my camera film decided I'd used that up as well.

We took a small riverboat round some of the delta. Think I'd need a few days to do it all. We stopped on a bank where a family has been making food for forty years, so they must have kept going through all the guerrilla war. They make rice paper. Not as we know it in the UK for cakes, but all types, mainly savoury.

An old lady (she was all of sixty-five) sits in front of a sunken cauldron of boiling water. Above this is a very large griddle. She seems to spread a type of batter over this and runs a spatula under it as it begins to set. It is like cellophane. She carefully places half over a raffia-like whirligig and lets the rest hang down.

As she completes this, her daughter moves them onto drying frames to be placed in the sun. Le showed me some by the river as we went in.

I'm not sure how hygienic it is, but I didn't see any flies paying them attention as they dried.

They flavour them, some with coconut milk, sesame seeds, herbs, spices and they're very crisp. A bit like (only better) than nachos.

I bought yet more postcards and after much bowing between us I went off.

Actually it was quite tricky for me to negotiate getting in and out of the boat, especially when I heard it was two metres at the edge and perhaps six further out.

Although it rises and falls twice a day with the tides, it's a fresh water river at Cai Be where we were visiting.

Another stop along the riverbank brought us to another family. This time there were many stalls but we were going to have coconut juice and rice krispie cakes at a little plastic table.

The family here send their foods all over as they're famous for them. I was taken on an inspection of the whole process.

I had my camcorder going and I had to wait while this young lad (about eighteen) started his fire to begin his show.

I thought I was going to pass out. I would not choose to stand by an oven and giant wok giving out amazing amounts of heat with a heavy (getting heavier by the minute) camcorder and water trickling (my water at that) down my nose, ears, fingers. Not in a hundred degrees and almost a hundred per cent humidity.

Just as I said I have to go, the process started.

He'd had all this black burnt-looking fire cinders, very fine, in the bottom of his wok. He stirred it if I remember rightly, with a big block of wood on a stick. This wood looked singed to say the least.

He'd put Langian skins (dried) in the fire under the wok and now he put in the rice. Within seconds the rice had done a popcorn. It sputtered and burst out to look amazingly like popcorn but in worm-like strands, not round nodules.

He tipped the whole lot into a strainer and the black cinders fell through.

He then passed the rice to two other young chaps,

who were stirring rice with syrup with big stakes. Once they'd done this it was transferred to an oblong tray about two and a half inches deep which was marked down all sides. As it set, it was cut.

Then the women took over, some boys too, and started bagging it. Le bought some for me. They made many other similar types of sweet things. Le said the students loved the ricicles things.

I can't see mothers in the UK with their little darlings making ricicles in this way. After all it's one of the first things they learn to make.

Nothing seems to be wasted. The coconut husks are dried, langian (like lychees) skins are dried but most importantly the rice husks are dried. The latter is extremely big business. You see big boats plying the Mekong full of dried rice husks. All are used for fires.

We went to the market on the river. Each boat which sells a particular product has a few hoisted on a pole so everyone can see. So you have three pineapple, two guavas, bunches of bananas, even cabbages.

Then the little boats come in and get enough for their shops and houses and off they go.

There are still boat people and they do look poor, but as usual, there are lines of coat hangers of clean washing all around them.

I recorded as we went along, people waved and smiled. Some children were shy, but many wanted to be friendly.

At the second stop where they made the ricicles, one little girl was a real scene-stealer. She kept blowing really noisy, slurpy kisses. She was three, and quite chubby for a Vietnamese.

Le, who is as slim as all the Viet are, says no matter

how much she eats she cannot put on weight. My heart bleeds for her.

Looking at the Vietnamese race, it must be genetic. They're even slimmer than the Thais. If anything, the men are on the chunkier side. Certainly none of the women.

I'd just put my 'corder down this morning as we drove to the delta and I looked up and the road ahead was filled five across (it's only one each way and two cycle tracks) with buses, trucks and cars, plus motorbikes.

Our driver didn't ease up. He presumed the others would drop back. Well they didn't. We were just able to go into the cyclo lane (perhaps the cyclists had had more sense) and dip ever so slightly into the ditch.

On the way back a similar incident and once again, we'd to go off the road to live. So I suppose really I should be glad I'm alive and being eaten by mozzies, waiting on an uncomfortable chair for the check-in desk to open.

The chap who arranged this said once I'd sorted my luggage I could go to the executive lounge. As this is Thai Airways' own, I'm hoping it's something special. Remember after this I'm back to just being a world traveller plus, with seven inches more legroom.

We finished our river trip after going down the narrow waterways where there are many villages and family life just goes on as normal.

There were a few bridges over the waterways and some were used by motorbikes, but you would have to have a morbid fascination with death to do this.

There was also one which was a wide bamboo pole at the bottom and a narrow one at the top about three or four feet apart. These were held together so you walk along the bottom one and hold on to the other top one. Makes my efforts getting on and off boats a tad conventional.

As I was saying, we finished our river trip by going for some fruit and a cold drink. This is first where the tape stopped working. The café was made of the most beautifully woven coconut reeds (as grow in the river) it was thatched but inside the underneath was woven in a wonderful pattern. Halfway down, in green, there was a chevron pattern running round and I was told these were coconut tree trunks cut in half lengthways.

They even had clean toilets in a special block. You looked out over the Mekong as you ate your mangoes and in front of the café was about twenty feet of water lilies. Le says the houses and other properties have the water lilies to keep boats from getting too near and stop the bank from sliding into the river. And they're really pretty.

I don't know why they worry too much about the bank. When our boat landed it crashed none too gently into the landing stage. I use the last two words loosely. The wooden stakes, quite thick, disappearing into the water certainly move easily when they're hit, but if this happens too often I presume they've got to have some give.

The main thing is though, I didn't end up in the drink. You'd have thought they were ushering an old granny on and off. Both Le and the driver were involved. Had American Express had a word with them? Said, 'For Heaven's sake don't lose her, she'll cause endless trouble if you do.'

As we set off I said I needed an ATM when we got to the delta. Le didn't think there were any outside

Saigon. And there's me with 2½p.

So far I hadn't seen an accident, which must be the biggest surprise of the whole trip. Anyway not long after we set off this morning, the roads were really busy and it was still only 6am and the police were already there. The debris was scattered over a wide area, about a hundred yards. There was fruit and a crash helmet. Right at the end of the debris was the bike, which looked fairly crushed. No one around and no blood, which of course doesn't mean anything with a bike.

The strange thing was that it didn't seem to slow anyone up or change their driving habits.

Anyone just enters a road, usually without looking. People are just expected to make room for them. That's all right so long as the four-lane highway is not coming toward a two-lane highway when there's only room for three vehicles or twelve bikes. Double white lines mean nothing. I think the only good thing is, there aren't many corners. Cyclists very often drive against the flow. Fragile young girls dicing with death.

I have learnt a new set of words, rya xe means bike/carwash. I saw it so much I had to ask what it meant.

Le, who looks eighteen but is twenty-five, is a graduate of tourism and she wants everyone to love her country.

All around the delta on the edge of the rivers there are many TV aerials, usually about thirty feet high. Le says only ten years ago, there was no TV, radio, CDs. Now they have pop stars and no matter how poor, they seem to have TVs. Fashion is very much at the forefront.

We came back through heavy rain and within seconds of it starting the roadside stalls all had their macs, plastic, in rainbow colours, swinging in the breeze.

Cai Be from where I got the riverboat has some very big houses and looks like it's going to be prosperous. Don't think it'll be long before they got their first ATM.

Cai Lai just before you get to Cai Be, with 190,000 population is more heavy industrial, but still on the delta. A hive of industry.

Lotus flowers grow all over and Le tells me that the woody stalk is cooked and the middle of it is used in salads. I had some last night and also in China. It has a reasonable bland taste.

I love their cucumber. It is so crisp. I could eat it all day and couldn't see my eating too much UK cucumber.

The Vietnamese talk of their freedom from 30 April 1975. It is an annual holiday and everyone celebrates.

Le is also a Buddhist. It seems everyone has a religion. I noticed all these gravestones (Eastern style) in the middle of fields. Sometimes just one, sometimes quite a large group like a cemetery. She said, people are buried near their families. They are born there, lived and raised there families there. When they die, they're buried in the paddy field so their family can light incense for them and pray. It sounds logical. Just looks odd.

I also noticed some beautiful new apartments yesterday. I couldn't tell what the Vietnamese writing said but in the largest printing it said AMERICAN STANDARD. So I presume rehabilitation is complete.

According to the Lonely Planet phrasebook, war veterans are now welcomed back. It gives phrases to use like, I was with ... squadron, I served in ...

Further to my observation re Kotex in my last letter, I saw a TV programme last night, two competing teams, seeming to have to sing or identify songs and Kotex was printed large on front of the stands the contestants were standing behind.

A pop group came on to sing and across the floor, writ very large was KOTEX. So they danced back and forward as the strobe lights played across it.

It makes you think we must be quite twee compared with the Vietnamese.

Love Pat.

P. S. I'm now in a dead and alive hole (plastic seats with sticking tape over rips) called Thai Airways Business Class Lounge, still swatting mozzies.

A Race Against Time

The End

Dear Clare and Michael,

My flight didn't really go according to plan. Are you surprised?

The reason I was sitting in a flyblown executive lounge on a black plastic seat with black plastic patches was because Thai airways were ferrying me to Bangkok. When I left Bangkok I was in the Vietnam executive lounge and it was grotty. The Thai airways lounge (in their capital city) looked fantastic. So of course the same was true in reverse. The black plastic sofas belonged to Thai airways and the beautiful lounge with cream leather belonged to Vietnamese airlines, which I couldn't use.

We left on time and arrived in Bangkok and it turned out I'd only thirty-five minutes to check in again and catch the flight. That was without taxiing round to the parking bay, which went on forever. My blood pressure must have been through the roof by now. After about ten minutes by bus (I kid not) we arrived at the gate. I raced out as fast as my bags would allow. Another long slog.

I knew my hold bags were going to be transferred and the airline wouldn't go without me joining them.

I found BA (masquerading as Qantas). There were two chaps messing about so I told the check in girl I needed to get to the gate before it closed. She agreed I'd have to be quick.

She issued two tickets (London to Manchester too) and I raced off – and guess what, I had to go roughly about as far as I'd come from the Thai Airways jet I landed on.

I'd wanted to spend the four hours I should have been at Bangkok airport having a Thai back massage and buying four boxes of beautiful fresh orchids.

As I raced towards the gate I passed one last stall and they had orchids! I got out the plastic and hurried the girl along as they paged me to go to the gate for final boarding.

I was still being Hoppalong but a fast Hoppalong as I rushed on board with my black pull-along, Harrods bag, camcorder, handbag and four boxes of orchids.

As I boarded the plane I must have put down the orchids near the entrance. At the check in they said I'd got the last seat and although I'd asked the guy at Vietnam Airlines to ring ahead and book me a C seat on the left-hand side by the aisle, he evidently hadn't done. The stewardess this time when I explained my predicament said I should ask the big chap sitting in the aisle seat if he'd move. As soon as I saw him, I knew he wouldn't because he needed all the legroom, coupled with the fact that his wife was sitting across the aisle. Apparently they always did this.

I got sat down and at that moment I was hot, agitated and not at all the soignée traveller I like to think I've become.

After an hour or so I'd relaxed, I had my second dinner of the evening. Tell me, how can you be so hungry just flying around? Could it be all those moving walkways and stress?

I took my painkillers and settled down and for once

in my life I slept on a plane.

I kept waking up to do my leg exercises about every hour but just dropped back again. I was ever so pleased, I'd put my Britneys on after I'd got seated in my inner seat, not without some difficulty. I think the chap in the aisle seat was wishing he'd changed when he had the chance. I only found out later he was wearing his too. And he (or his wife) had chosen the same colour. So there we sat and there we slept, two matching pairs of legs DVT free.

Halfway through the flight, well before sleep anyway, I remembered the orchids. A quick check with the hostess and she came back later telling me my orchids had been placed somewhere cool and I could collect as I left. Phew, after my desperate last minute purchase, what a relief.

So on exiting the plane I got my orchids and set off for baggage reclaim. It was only after about half an hour and no more baggage appearing that I checked with a BA women and she said my luggage had gone to Manchester. I specifically asked for Heathrow, so I got the train and got off at the first stop for domestics. Due to the baggage, enquiring, waiting on the train and the journey it was now getting very near to gate closing time for Manchester.

Once again I raced unevenly for the departure gate, having to clear X-ray luggage machines again. I'd been to the loo, extracted some money from an ATM and this had been enough to put me in the danger zone again for gate closure.

It's surprising how far away a lot of these gates are. You'd think that by now I'd be such a seasoned traveller none of these things would happen to me.

You know what? I think as long as I travel these things *always* will happen.

So I rushed aboard again, got nicely seated and enjoyed my second breakfast of the day albeit on the small size. Actually I couldn't fault it, it was ciabatta bread with nicely seasoned sliced sausage and a just right moist scrambled egg. Reconstituted dried egg, I believe. Surprisingly I enjoyed it. Should I be declaring that I enjoyed airline food?

A thought struck me before we landed at Manchester. Orchids. I couldn't remember putting them in the overhead locker. On arrival I checked, no orchids.

I couldn't remember collecting them after the X-ray machine. Let's face it, this was the first time I'd travelled with orchids. I'd managed to retrieve them at Bangkok but not at Heathrow.

Later in the day I got through to the flight department at Heathrow and a young man confirmed they'd got my orchids (four big boxes, enough to sort out Westminster Abbey) but as they were perishable they hadn't gone to lost property. He thought the 'young ladies' would have received them who worked at Heathrow. I just said I hoped they enjoyed them. So it was not to be that Thai orchids graced the homes of my friends and family.

Like so much of the holiday, my return hadn't run to plan either. I've no idea why I should be surprised at this. Did I ever think it would be otherwise?

How it was done

In July 2002, my eldest daughter Caroline rang and said she was getting married in Thailand next Easter. What did I think?

Well, I thought it was a great chance to visit lots of places nearby, that's what I thought. It was also a great place for a wedding.

I was reaching for the Phillips World Atlas as I came off the telephone.

If I'm doing a thirteen-hour flight I want to make it work for me. Why waste the journey?

A quick glance confirmed Africa, on the way, Hong Kong, Singapore and China nearby. Australia and New Zealand just beyond – OK, quite a bit beyond, but I would definitely be over in their direction.

I could give BA a ring and see what they did in Round the World tickets, and how many stopovers I was allowed.

Africa was a no-go as it wasn't on the 'route' but the rest were.

UK to Hong Kong, into China then off to Singapore, Australia, New Zealand and finally Thailand, perhaps even Vietnam.

I mentally put a figure on how much I wanted to pay for the flights and hotels. I thought forty-six days should do it.

Within days of hearing about the wedding I was heading to Wales for my August break. I wouldn't be back for a month, which is where Cable Travel in Porth Madog came in.

Enter Sheryl, booking clerk there.

I always believe in using independent travel agents. I would never use any in a chain. They cannot always give you the best offer. Their interests are not always my best interests.

So, the first rule of international, independent travel is follow the independents. There's at least one in every town.

The reason for my using Cable Travel was because Mr Cable gave me some very good advice, even though he wasn't in charge of booking my holiday when I went to India. I was returning the favour.

So began the first of many visits to Sheryl. In my mind I envisaged spending £3,000. You may think this to be optimistic for forty-two days' travel, on my own and therefore having to pay full room rate, not shared with anyone else, but I was hopeful.

By the time one of my Chinese students graduated in December and asked was I going to Beijing, the itinerary has stretched to sixty-two days.

It meant leaving on 4 March. Somehow it seemed Christmas would just be over before I was packing for three different climates.

My eldest son's ex-girlfriend was a Kiwi and I contacted her in September to say I was 'doing' New Zealand. Much excitement the other side of the Pacific, but as I was only going for four days it wasn't enough. Eleven days were soon arranged.

So that was how Beijing and New Zealand extended it to nearly nine weeks.

BA and Qantas allowed a variety of stops but had a mileage limit. I could get to New Zealand and arrive at Wanaka in South Island, but the miles back to Christchurch have to be extra. £40 in fact.

At the end of August most things were booked, four days China, two days Hong Kong, five days Singapore, seven days Bali, six days Australia, four days New Zealand, fourteen days Thailand and four days Vietnam. The cost by now had risen from around £3,000 to £4,000.

I checked it carefully. Singapore because I wanted to stay on Sentosa Island was costing £500 in hotel alone. Reluctantly it went. Vietnam, £400 – it went. The costs dropped accordingly.

I had arranged with BA a flight with all stopovers. I then paid £340 to upgrade to a World Travellers Plus on the Heathrow-Hong Kong stage and return. My flights in China were an extra (£400). I tried to keep my room rate to about £50 per night. In China this enable me to stay up to five-star, but only four-star in Australia.

Independent travel of this type is just a logistical exercise.

When I travelled in India two years previously (see my next book), very little of it was pre-booked, but this time because I was going to be away so long I wanted a good idea re costs.

Vietnam was eventually reinstated and I finally paid £3,560 for all flights and hotels, not including Thailand and New Zealand accommodation.

When you think a two or three-week tour, sharing a room, costs around £3,000 this was a good deal. I felt I was getting value for money. Admittedly I had to pay entrance fees, but because most of it is Third World, they weren't exorbitant.

When I was in India I had to tell someone about my experiences and wrote to my children. Unfortunately one of them, who shall remain nameless, mislaid my letters (which were to form a book) due to renovations going on at the house. So this time I wrote to two good friends in different parts of the country and just photocopied the letters. If one got lost it wouldn't matter. I even posted them from different post boxes.

These poor people would find up to eight thick missives (no other word for them) arriving some days. I would ring regularly to see if they were enjoying them.

Usually they were about twenty A4 pages. You needed to go and soak in a bath with a glass of wine to find time to read them. One friend, the mother of two young daughters, was carefully balancing work, mothering and wifing and nursing when one daughter broke her arm, which would mean their camping at their local A&E for the duration, and I'm ringing from Bali to ask her for marks out of ten for presentation. Do you think I'll get it published? Have you any constructive criticism? There was a pause at the end of the line and I realised she hadn't read anything. Not even had time to open the envelopes. She wasn't just being tactful because she thought they were so awful. Life was happening to her and apart from the would-be book, my biggest worry was the air conditioning in my hotel room.

Fortunately they're still friends of mine, they didn't hold it against me, when, metaphorically speaking, I had them pinned up against the wall, with my hand round their throats, demanding a verdict. And I did send their children some very nice postcards from each destination.

The hotels were chosen from brochures which specialise or allow you to book just the hotel At one stage I had so many brochures in my Welsh hotel room, it was in danger of collapsing into the room below.

So, not only had I got flights and over 60 days accommodation, an excursion into China with four flights, a four-day expedition to Vietnam in Executive Class plus and upgrade at the hotel, I'd also got seven feet more legroom on the two long-haul flights. When paying this sort of money I think it's essential. £170 each way. BA only gave me 20kgs baggage allowance, but on the World Travellers Plus it should be thirty kgs.

When Sheryl queried this BA told her that Qantas had no thirty kgs allowances so twenty was all they could give me.

Unfortunately, the chap sitting next to me on the return journey had been to Thailand and Australia and he was the person who showed me his ticket with thirty kgs allowance after I mentioned to him that I thought as we were paying more we should be allowed more.

Sheryl has said BA are not willing to compensate for the last parcel I sent from Thailand because I thought I'd be overweight travelling home.

She has given me the address and I am taking it up with them myself. So far I have received two refunds totalling £62 re the hotels in Saigon and Hong Kong.

If I'd had a choice I wouldn't have chosen BA, but they were the only ones who did a tie-in with Qantas.

For anyone with the time to spare this is a cheap viable way of seeing the world. It's just logistics.

To coach travellers, I apologise if out of necessity (age, disability etc) you have no choice but to use tours – for the rest, it stands.

Terrorists should never stop us travelling, nor any

natural calamities either. Life is here to be enjoyed, obstacles overcome and whatever is batted at you, you bat it back

And my toenails which caused comment throughout my travels are painted royal blue, emerald, purple, royal blue, emerald. They make a statement about me. I don't know what it says, but it's very emphatic.

Final postscript – I neither put on nor lost weight.

Final Thoughts

Portrait of China

China had always been synonymous with the Terracotta Army to me. I am interested in archaeology, geology and palaeontology and had watched, slightly envious, as various political leaders and royalty were allowed unrestricted access to this wonder of the world.

I based my trip to China to visit the army at Xi'an. I was not disappointed but have not gone into paroxysms of pleasure to describe it. Most people know about it and have seen pictures, most probably when President Clinton was allowed down among the army. As this didn't happen to me, I felt anything I said would be superfluous.

As mentioned before, at first China didn't seem very foreign, everyone was dressed in Western clothes and but for the store and business signs in Chinese characters, I wouldn't have known I was in a Far Eastern Country.

But, you only had to stray marginally off the beaten path to see the Chinese way of life. Of course, my first visit was Beijing and although visiting with a family, being a cosmopolitan city took the edge off the oriental image.

My friends are very Westernised; urban city dwellers, used to the good life, educated and definitely upwardly mobile.

My contact for Beijing came through Ivy, a Chinese girl who lived in one of my student houses. While she was studying I took her and three friends to Wales. We visited Snowdonia and the Welsh coast, taking in the castles as well as the scenery as we went. One of these friends was Charlotte, or as I was introduced to her that day, Marian.

The University of Central Lancashire visits Beijing University annually and has an arrangement to take students who have successfully completed two years of their degree. Visas are provided for the students and as long as they pass an English exam after a certain length of time, this is extended to cover their studies.

All Chinese students choose a Western name. I always know when I receive a call from a heavily accented student and ask their name, and they give an ordinary English one, that they will be Chinese. Currently one of the boys is called Kevin, but his name is really Li.

So as I was introduced to Marian she informed everyone she'd changed her name to Charlotte. This has led to a lot of confusion, but we generally know who we are talking about.

Ivy invited me to her degree ceremony in Preston in December 2002. Once again I met up with Charlotte and this time her mother, Yen – her best friend as she told me.

For reasons too complicated to explain Charlotte and her mother Yen, came to stay after the ceremony for three days, during which time we inspected the eateries north of Preston and the accompanying countryside. Included in that was the Trough of Bowland and the part of the Ribble Valley where the Queen has said that if she and Philip could retire this is where they'd choose. If it's good enough for the Queen, it's good enough for my visitors. Fortunately this is only eleven miles from my home.

Yen helped me dress the Christmas tree and although she didn't speak any English, she was soon picking up words and through Charlotte we managed.

Yen was a very smartly dressed woman, extremely fashionable, about a size six. I've said it before but she eats far more than I do. Many people think it's rice that keeps the Chinese slim, but I believe it's all the various teas (including green tea) they drink during and after every course. No milk of course.

Thinking about this, dairy products appear to play no great part in Chinese cuisine as I saw it. No cheese, no sign of milk, I can't even remember a yoghurt. When they made a smoothie it seemed to be just fruit.

Yen dries shrimps in the apartment. Charlotte thinks this is terrible, but I found it intriguing. They are on a tray under the sofa. When I was there the shrimps were at a fairly advanced stage of dehydration. I've no idea what they might smell like at the beginning of the process.

Yen is from Shanghai and their cuisine is different to that of Beijing, so they regularly dine at a restaurant offering Shanghai delicacies, as they did while I was there.

If I'd seen all those HSBC ads before I went to China, I'd have realised why the vast amount of food was left after each meal. Finishing all the food on your plate means your hosts have not provided enough. There was never any chance of my insulting my hosts in this way; I could never ever eat as much as they were doing. You could have fed the 5,000 on what four people left.

Chinese food appears to contain no potatoes, rice being their choice of starch. Their vegetables are fresh and varied, but varied seems too tame a word for the amazing number of them available at any restaurant or market.

Meat, fish, tofu and vegetables seem to make up the majority of Chinese food. Whenever my hosts ordered the food it was always an excellent balance to give you all your nutrients. Puddings as we British know them didn't seem to be on their menus. If a sweet were provided, it was usually fresh fruit. I never saw any dish that resembled anything available from out local Chinese takeaways. In fact I don't remember eating a sauce in any meal ordered by my Chinese hosts, certainly nothing like sweet and sour.

Cantonese people are said to eat six times a day – and I don't think they mean little and often.

I cannot fault Chinese hospitality. It is superb. I feel my hospitality when they visited me was somewhat lacking. At the time I thought I was entertaining them royally. I even let them pay for dinner at the restaurant one night – which we would consider normal. Their rules demand that they take on the total cost of the visit. I'm glad I didn't know that before they came.

While in Preston one night all the Chinese friends of Charlotte and Ivy dined at a restaurant; I was the token Westerner. An older young man who'd been in Preston some time from Hong Kong insisted on paying for everyone. There were about fourteen of us. The camaraderie and atmosphere were great.

Most of the Chinese students who travel to Preston seem well off. Many have an Amex gold card. Money does not seem to be a problem to them. Once again a blanket statement, but drawn on my experiences and my friends at the university and other landlords.

On visiting the Great Wall, I think was rather

jetlagged still. It didn't impress me as much as it should, so therefore I presume that's what it was.

I'm sure by the time the Olympics are staged in 2008 they will have sorted the periphery of this other great wonder of the world. In an open pen, solitary and very forlorn was a black bear, chained up naturally. I've visited enough tourist traps to realise that many of them have surroundings that do not live up to the expectations of the actual attraction. The Great Wall was no exception. It's tacky and scruffy. It seems to be relying on the Wall itself. No effort, after the little cars to transport you upwards, seems to have been made. There are stalls selling the usual souvenirs, but generally it looked like a cross between a film back-lot and an end of season fairground. Either just have the Wall or else make sure the surroundings complement it.

Chinese people are very pleased to see Westerners. Even when they are tourists themselves, they are gregarious, as interested in me as I am in them.

At Guilin, as I wandered about the 'Chinese' bridges across the lake opposite my hotel and into the pagodas, I came across many tourists, mainly Chinese, but some Koreans. Quite a few took my picture and we tried to converse, but it was mainly sign language, much laughing and smiling.

At the visit to the Flute Caves a sign asks you to be socially ethical and not remove any of the stalactites or stalagmites. So it would appear they appeal to our sense of guilt to behave correctly.

Off the coast of China is an island, Hainau, which is sub-tropical and known as the Chinese Hawaii.

It's stated that the Chinese takeover of Tibet was friendly and that in 2002 China gave them US$ 826m.

When visiting the Forbidden City I noticed praise is lavished on previous emperors who were the most beneficial for the people. There are plaques to them stating their achievements, but I notice the dates on these plaques appear to be from 1997 onwards.

One cannot imagine this being done before their country began to operate a more open market policy. They seem to be acknowledging their past and accepting there was some good among it before communism.

As with a lot of the Western world, sewage seems to be a major problem. At Yang Shuo – the East meets West town – as I sat overlooking the river with a coffee at a smart 'European' café bar (or was it an English tea shoppe?) there was a torrent of water gushing out into the river from the town above it. The smell was not something pleasant and I chose not to sit in the open air because of this. The Li River looks clean and certainly has plenty of fish in it, as this is where the cormorant fishermen ply their trade, but the water had definitely not been treated. The actual outlet was a feature and attracted a great deal of attention. To look at it was visually pleasing, you just had to have lost one of your senses.

Many of the adverts in the map I bought were for hotels, hostels – this is a big backpacking centre, my eldest son stayed here seventeen years ago – and leisure facilities. In some, the translation was excellent, some played safe and only used Chinese characters, and some of them looked like they'd done it on the cheap and got the local high school student on the job, but that's enterprise for you.

Just below an advert for the Hard Seat Café including logo is Fawlty Towers, so Basil must get this far.

I'd visited the Forbidden City with Charlotte and

Yen. Very impressive, but once again I was the only European I could see. Many Chinese of course visit these symbols of their past where once they couldn't even tread.

Tiananmen Square is the largest square in the world and the Chinese are extremely proud of it. The guide to the Great Wall, in between telling interminable jokes – I think to copy the slick method of US tourist attractions – told how proud she was of the Square, but she now realised may Europeans only thought of it in terms of the student revolt. Quite a few people on the bus nodded and she said she was trying to understand how we felt, but the Chinese just know great pride.

On the way to the Wall we visited a jade factory which was run by the government, with dire warnings not to buy at other outlets, unless it's an authorised source, as the jade may not be genuine. So that was one official way of parting us from our money. The next was a precious stones factory. Of course you could see how the craftsmen and women, as at the jade factory, cut and polished the stones. A hard sell began when I showed an interest in a sapphire in the latest fashionable colour of this stone. Negotiations, bargaining, they just couldn't close the deal. I had a price in my mind and they didn't seem to understand I wasn't open to offers.

The doors at each end of the showroom remained shut, no matter how many times I strolled towards them. They might have given the impression it was security, but in reality they didn't open until everyone had bought, or in the case of failure – me – the next lot of tourists arrived. So it was another dishonourable mention in despatches for me.

So to the newspapers. In the *China Daily*, 10 March

2003 the government of one of East China's Jiangsu provinces initiated a public poll on the performance of local government departments and officials that have frequent contact with ordinary people.

Nine officials were singled out as 'the most unsatisfactory officials' and were ordered to suspend exercising power for six months and given a ninety per cent salary cut. They were also asked to write a self-criticism and a rectification plan. Such a move triggered hot discussion.

China Youth Daily and *People's Daily* on-line edition and the *Jiangnan Times* reacted with the exception of the latter, who seemed to think the action taken would stamp out malpractice and defended the action taken in their province, the other two were greatly concerned.

This mainly concentrated on the fact that a public poll could be taken as enough evidence to condemn the officials. Points were raised that officials who followed the rules and created resentment could be victimised. The public could be prejudiced. The poll should be questioned. They quote how the law requires via testimony, documents, material evidence and videotapes. The poll as the only evidence is unprecedented.

Another defence of the officials said some could have been named because they refused to go against their principles. A later item again in *China Youth Daily* fully supported the poll and said it was remarkable progress where it reflected public opinion quite faithfully.

So there were four points of view printed, split evenly between opinions. Is this the Chinese version of democracy?

To finance now. The Manila-based Asian Development Bank forecast excluding Japan, Australia and New Zealand that the region's forty-one developing economies would still out-perform the rest of the world with 5.3 per cent growth, despite the impact of SARS.

China was the hardest hit by SARS, but will still be the strongest performer, with growth at 7.3 per cent. The region has high levels of reserves and low inflation, leaving it able to weather the storms.

The ADB also said that Afghanistan's economy is likely to surge in 2003–4 provided security improves and there is international support for reconstruction.

Cambodia, Sri Lanka and Mongolia are due to expand by 5 per cent in 2003, Nepal 1.5 per cent, Pakistan 4.5 per cent, Bangladesh 5.2 per cent, the Philippines 4 per cent.

In Central Asia, Azerbaijan, Kazakhstan and Tajikistan grew 7.7 per cent dipping to 5.8 per cent for 2003/4 due to a drop in oil and gas revenues.

In Southeast Asia growth was 4 per cent, mainly due to SARS, with Vietnam performing the best at 6.9 per cent. Singapore, again hit by SARS, grew 2.3 per cent, Hong Kong saw a drop of 0.6 per cent to 2 per cent, again SARS.

Airline representatives are calling the relief package to Hong Kong of 363 million Hong Kong dollars 'a placebo for a serious illness, that falls far short of addressing the financial pain caused by SARS'. The package is to help airlines, retailers, caterers and franchisees at the airport. Unfortunately the bulk of the offer is simply an interest-free deferral of half of the airport's landing fees for the next three months. Apparently this is far short of what Kuala Lumpur and Singapore have offered.

More than seven million people trapped in rural

poverty in Western China are to be relocated. It will cost US$ 360–600m.

Relocation will be on a voluntary basis and the government will provide assistance to build new homes and find incomes. Thirty-six key projects have been ongoing in the Western region.

Improving the environment is high on the list to regenerate the destitute areas. Ecological projects include protecting natural forests, returning farmland to forests, desertification control and the closure of pastures for the renewal of grasslands.

Top Chinese advisors have warned that rapid urban growth contributes significantly to the 'growing pains' of a city. Better planning is needed. Its urbanisation stands at 36 per cent, but will be 70 per cent by 2050.

Development of labour-intensive industries such as agricultural products, processing, tourism, service and manufacturing industries was a practical way of creating jobs. The employment of rural labourers should be top of the agenda.

A social security network is taking shape as China's market-oriented economic reform advances. By the end of 2002 one province had established insurance for the elderly covering 6.7m workers and 2.8m retirees, plus medical insurance for 6.7m.

Effective trade policies put China on the fast track of foreign trade growth, so says the Vice-Minister of the State Development Planning Commission.

Both imports and exports rocketed by 20 per cent in 2002. A major contribution to the performance was the sharply increased exports and imports of private and foreign-funded enterprises. That was as a result of the nation's foreign trade system recently. China will continue to stimulate the economy by further promoting domestic demand and pushing rural consumption.

As China grows it feels it is a blessing for other countries rather than a threat. Of course this is only their opinion.

There has been talk that it has forced down prices globally by grabbing a greater share of the market with its low priced exports.

China already imports more than the rest of Asia including Japan. In 2002 car sales exceeded 1m for the first time and are expected to rise by another 20 per cent this year.

Volkswagen and General Motors are among the biggest winners, because even when the cars are assembled locally many of the components are imported. China is now VW's biggest customer outside Germany.

Sydney Morning Herald, 4 April 03. After joining the World Trade Organisation at the end of 2001 restrictions in trade and investment are easing. BMW said last month it had formed a venture with Brilliance Alliance China Automotive to produce three and five series sedans in NE China. It is half owned by BMW and will produce 30,000 cars per annum when production starts later in 2003. BMW are taking advantage of cheap labour and the demand by China's growing middle class.

China drew more than one third of all foreign investment in developing countries, said the World Bank. It overtook the US last year as the largest recipient of foreign direct investment.

Back to *China Daily*, 10 March 03.

Experts have been robustly defending re lowering prices globally. They feel that as a destination for exports from other countries it is also opening wider and significantly lowering its tariff levels after joining the World Trade Organisation.

In this sense they say China is importing deflation. They think the impact of its exports has been overstated. Chinese exports account for a mere five per cent of the world's total. A professor from Peking University says, 'It's understandable that a fast-growing China will draw worldwide attention. Of those who regard China as a threat, some have an ulterior motive, but most simply do not understand China'. On closer analysis of China and other economies it revealed, '. . . there was no need for other countries to worry that China's increased export of products, made by cheap labour, would squeeze their market share'.

As the money supply continues to grow rapidly, mainly as a result of an 18per cent increase in savings, banks sought to maintain strong financial support for growing businesses.

To increase domestic banks' competitiveness they need to speed up the shareholding reform, so that they can operate in accordance with the market demands.

At present, foreign banks are not fighting to recruit personnel from domestic banks, but as their business expands in an all-year-round way in the coming years, they will offer higher salaries and other favourable treatment to compete for quality personnel.

And finally, as proof that China is going full-tilt into the capitalist society comes an article reporting Mastercard is eyeing huge business potential. Nearly ten per cent of the population of 1.3 billion are now eligible to apply for credit cards. That includes the 7m that bought car or home last year, the 16.6m who travelled abroad and the 65m households with an annual income topping US$ 1,200.

Competition between rival card companies in the Chinese market is still three to five years off and will not occur until more of a buyer's market emerges. Once financial institutions are permitted to issue cards for international use, in accordance with the country's WTO commitments, the pressure will build, even with domestic banks, to compete.

So the Chinese will be, like the rest of us, eventually slaves to the plastic. Cash will no longer be king.

A Glance at Hong Kong

If I'd gone on a dedicated long weekend to Hong Kong I would have looked at it from a different perspective.

Many people were using it as a stopover for Australia, as it splits the journey roughly halfway.

In my case I felt it was a staging post, I suppose mainly because Bali beckoned, with South Pacific and all that. Also, Hong Kong cannot be said to be restful.

It's way up front 'in yer face' stuff. The Asian Tiger at its fiercest. The fact that it is vastly overcrowded gives it an appearance of never being still.

Although it has progressed from being the sweatshop of the world, its people appear to be permanently on the move.

It would seem after the Chinese took it back that life goes on much as usual, but I imagine the tax on maids though could only have come from a Communist mindset. In the same way that employers then passed it on to the maids, one could say that they were responding in kind.

I chose a hotel in Kowloon, price was important, but I wasn't to know the SARS virus would start there.

It would have been simpler to have had one at the harbour facing Hong Kong Island. That said, being in Kowloon brought me nearer to the day-to-day lives of the people.

Most apartments seemed to have an air conditioning unit on the outside wall. Allowing how humid it seemed at twenty-four degrees I would imagine this is essential in summer.

As Hong Kong is so small, the only way to go is up, so skyscrapers proliferate. On Hong Kong Island itself, as you climb ever higher, the beautiful mansions begin. The higher up the mountainside, the richer you are, and your status is assured.

Even though ninety-eight per cent of Hong Kong is Chinese, English and Cantonese are the two official languages. Since 1997 the official language of China – Mandarin – is on the rise. Just to confuse the issue, many other dialects and languages are spoken.

The largest foreign community is the Filipinos with 150,000 working, as described earlier, as maids, but also as nannies.

Religious freedom is tolerated but very often there is a blurring of the different religions – as in Sikkum province in the Indian Himalayas – where people can practise, say, Taoism but also attend a Christian church for communion. They may also practise Buddhist traditions and find no anomaly in this. This could be why the young man training to be a Buddhist wanted to enjoy being a Catholic as well, and I wasn't aware of the nuances.

In the thirteenth century the Mongols were invading and Sung Dynasty loyalists brought the ten-year-old Emperor, the last of the dynasty, to Hong Kong – overnight. From this it is claimed that he was the only Chinese emperor to set foot on Hong Kong soil, albeit just overnight.

Until China ceded Hong Kong, followed by Kowloon and finally the New Territories for ninety-nine years to Britain, Hong Kong was just another part of China, not distinguishable in any particular way.

Western traders from around 1513 were the Portuguese, but other trading maritime nations, mainly the Dutch, English, French and Spanish were not far behind.

It was silk, porcelain and tea that interested them and until 1757 all foreigners were restricted to Macao, a Portuguese territory. After that, traders, but never their families, were allowed to live outside Canton, whose Chinese name, by which it is now known, is Guangzhou.

I realise why everyone in China was asking me was I going to Guangzhou and were surprised to find I wasn't. I hadn't realised its former name. On my next trip it will be on my itinerary, but this time ten days only allowed me to take in three cities.

It was while taking the above goods out of China that the British, on being asked to provide only silver in return, offered opium. Only now and again I'm not proud to be British and this has to be one of those times.

By 1729 the Chinese were alarmed at the spread of opium. They forbade importation of the drug, but ways were found around this. Then in 1839, a fanatical imperial commission laid siege to the foreign factories in Canton until the traders surrendered.

Almost a year's trade, 20,000 chests, were found and destroyed. The traders had to sign bonds agreeing to desist from dealing opium forever, under threat of death.

As the British continued to press the Chinese, tensions rose between the traders and the government. This in turn led to the Opium Wars and as a result of superior British firepower a series of treaties favouring the traders emerged. The most important of these forced China to cede Hong Kong.

And so, we return full circle to the Hong Kong we know today. The most fortunate part of which is, it no longer relies on opium for its economic engine – and is recognised the world over for its dynamic trading power and adaptability.

Hong Kong is a true survivor.

A History of Bali

Bali felt exotic, slightly mysterious, but due to travel programmes, books and newspaper articles, not as mysterious and exotic as it once was.

As Bali has the highest literacy rate in Indonesia, almost ninety per cent, it's not surprising that there is a rite honouring this. Once a year a special god is honoured when books are given to her to be blessed and no reading or writing is done throughout the island.

On the day devoted to the divinity of prosperity and financial success, no business is conducted. Another day honours metal objects, usually daggers (kris) but now more often cars and motorbikes. They decorate items with ritual offerings and palm-leaf ornaments.

Other days celebrate domestic animals, musical instruments, precious metals and stones, mainly gold, silver and jewellery, puppets and dance costumes.

The coconut palm is of importance to the Balinese because it provides everything from floor mats, fruit oil, fuel, building materials and containers both for drink and food. As I found later this is common throughout the Far East.

Bali has one major active volcano (to the right as you look at the map) and, for good measure, five others, all equally active, just to keep you on your toes. And just enough reason to stop one emigrating to the good life Balinese-style.

The only newspaper I managed to get hold of was the *Bali Advertiser*. Under the heading of Announcements, Special Events, Letters and Opinions were the following.

Adverts for container space took up quite a bit. One was for space to Southampton, England. Other adverts advertise a service to find you an agent for shipping, at the best rates, of course.

An alarming increase in HIV/AIDS cases was reported. A figure is given for Indonesia, but Bali figures were 251, which seems an awful lot for a small island.

They also reported fifty-three cases of Dengue Fever in March 2003 in Denpasar. The Health Office in co-operation with the Rotary Club is making a big poster emphasising the importance of eradicating the mosquito nests. They fear the outbreak will explode if they do nothing.

Also in the 'For Sale' section are two separate ads for the sale of a book. One is 'International Best Seller novel by Margaret Atwood, winner of the Booker Prize, will sell for Rp40,000' (about £3). The next is 'No 1 international best seller Violets are Blue by James Patterson'. They want £4 for that.

Someone also wants a pizza oven for homemade pizza. Could be the start of the Balinese version of Pizza Express.

A supplier of ecstasy pill got just eighteen months imprisonment.

The condition of Bali's environment since the 1980s tourist boom is getting worse. The concern seems to be that the mangrove forest is being used for recreational purposes as opposed to being green belt. And the beach at Suwung is turning into a shopping complex. Sewerage management does not appear to have been discussed.

An Australian, writing in the paper during his sojourn in Bali while travelling round Asia for twelve months with his family, reveals just how much he paid for his shots before leaving Australia, Aus$ 2000 for the four of them – about £400. They'd had to wait for these as the US Defence Dept had bought up all supplies of Cholera in case they needed it for the looming Gulf War.

The final article in the newspaper was what looked like a regular item called Anakku Anakmu: 'Thoughts for living with your child'.

Thought 202 – Avoid 'do it or else' situations whenever possible.

Thought 203 – Don't use sarcasm with your child. Sarcasm always alienates.

204 – Don't promise what you can't deliver.

205 – Teach your child what to do in case of fire.

206 – If your child catches an edible fish – eat it.

Most of the insights I have gleaned on Bali come from various articles I have read, guidebooks and verbal information.

The Balinese, despite our concept of a peaceful, Utopian existence had a rough time of it from about 1815 until 1965 when an abortive coup took place in Jakarta. As a result, massacres took place on Bali and about 100,000 people were killed, sometimes whole villages. This was only the year after a major famine.

Back in 1815 a volcano erupted on Lombok killing over 12,000 people on both Bali and Lombok.

Krakatoa, the more famous eruption sent only fifty cubic kilometres out, but Tambora, the Lombok volcano, sent out almost four times as great an ejection, at 180 cubic kilometres. The final death toll allowing for later mudslides and the volcanic ash that covered the crops resulting in starvation was 35,000.

There followed a series of plagues, many epidemics of various potentially fatal diseases until, in 1871, smallpox left approximately 16,500 dead.

In the meantime the Dutch were keen to colonise Bali. Given the above, one wonders why. It became clear the Dutch were worried the British might establish power there.

They claimed sovereignty only after the Rajas had committed ritual suicide. As the Rajas couldn't surrender, it was expected that they took the honourable way out of self-sacrifice. Their family followed suit.

From around 1839 the Dutch felt in control with skirmishes occurring with fatal regularity, as they increased their hold.

In 1904 the Dutch launched a military expedition, after blockading the coasts of Badung and Tabanan. Then in 1906 came an episode which heaped shame on the Dutch. Troops marched on Denpasar and watched as the Raja of Badung began a puputan (ritual suicide) which eventually included his whole family and courtiers.

As more people surged out of the palace the Dutch troops opened fire into the crowds. The mound of bodies reached higher and higher. The corpses were then looted and the palace sacked.

At a smaller court in Pomecutan, there was more ritual suicide, including the Raja's wives who leaped into his funeral pyre (strangely enough he'd died of old age) rather than surrender. The new Raja and family chose suicide as well.

The above happenings eventually turned round Dutch policy in the East Indies as public opinion in the Netherlands turned against the government.

When learning about the Dutch East Indies Company and the trade in which the Dutch engaged and various battles in history, I don't remember any of this being taught.

By 1908, 600 years of rule by the Rajas of Majapatut was over. They had been wiped out.

The Dutch felt some guilt for the situation in Bali, as well they might, and they started a programme of reforms. As they didn't understand the caste system and the way Balinese society worked, their decisions would cause repercussions for many years to come for the Balinese.

In the reforms the social positions and roles of each individual Balinese were fixed, which in turn threw the political units, farming and labour into turmoil.

1920 onwards saw tourism on the increase and many people migrated to Bali, many artists, dancers, musicians, even sociologists and economists.

These people were where we in the West got the idea of the idyllic life of the Balinese. Their writings and paintings promoted their interpretation of this and inferred that Balinese arts and design were influenced by European immigrants.

Although it is thought some of this may be true, nineteenth century Balinese artists had been experimenting before the arrival of the newcomers.

In 1917, an earthquake, followed by a mouse plague that ate the crops, then Spanish flu left Bali devastated again.

The Great Depression of the 1930s affected their exports and halved the value of their currency. Pigs and copra were the main items for export.

During the Japanese occupation in WWII the occupiers played the race card by fostering Balinese feelings against the Dutch. Local people hoped this would be backed up with arms to regain their island from the Dutch after the War.

The Dutch were finally forced to leave between 1946 and 1949. The Balinese were fighting each other with Nationalists on one side facing the pro-Dutch on the other. The latter were the rich higher caste who had gained from the Dutch fixed caste system.

It's hard to imagine the gentle, warm people who welcome you to Bali today with the rivals who were willing to torture their opposition, but that is what happened.

With Soekarno, President of Indonesia, from a Balinese background, Bali hoped for economic and spiritual support. What they got was rampant inflation and corruption.

The Socialist Party was banned, so there is strong communist support, especially where land reform is desired. In 1963, just before the bloodbath in 1965, Gunung Agung, the volcano, erupted during a ceremony held only once every hundred years. The people felt is was a sign they should revert to past values. For four days the volcano erupted; smoke and ash blotted out the sun, molten lava poured down the mountainside destroying villages. Thousands died from the immediate eruption and the famine and disease which automatically followed.

Before the October 2002 terrorist bomb, the last threat to peace on Bali was in 1998 when there were riots in Jakarta. Busloads of Javanese were said to be making for the island as the President's family owned many hotels. They intended to burn and loot the properties.

On hearing this, hundreds of Balinese, armed with

their kris (daggers) were waiting at the ferry terminal. The simple measure of refusing to let them disembark solved the crisis.

To come to the bomb. Bali has had peace since 1965 and despite the would-be Javanese bus invasion, the current generation are not used to conflict.

I have found them to be gentle-natured. Some, of course, are on the make and take every advantage of you they can, but that is true all over the world. Everywhere people are upwardly mobile any way they can.

I have been told by an Australian that the bomb was aimed at Australians, the Balinese just happened to be entertaining them at the time. That, of course, is just his opinion; he felt it was in retribution against the Australian government.

As I've said in my letters, the Balinese are worried as their economy is suffering badly. People have families to feed and there is nothing they can do to change the situation.

The island has a prosperous look to it, lush vegetation, beautiful houses, happy, clean children. As with all Eastern countries the school uniforms are immaculate to behold – and as usual education is highly prized.

At the end of Sanur where I stayed, there are no high-rise hotels. A government regulation decrees no building can be higher than a coconut palm – fifty feet to you and me.

Houses on Bali are often picturesque. They are divided as a human body. They think of it as an organic unit. The most sacred part, the head, is where the shrines are to be found in the north-east corner. The arms are the sleeping accommodation, the courtyard in the centre is the navel, the legs and feet are the kitchen and granary, whilst the gate is the sex organ and the anus is the refuse tip.

The layout is the same whether rich or poor. No cement or other fixative is used when construction is in stone or mud brick. The two surfaces are rubbed together using water and they fit perfectly. Doorways are ornate with usually a religious symbol carved.

It is just as well I was not born Balinese, as the following makes me feel queasy just writing it.

Puberty brings all the angst presumably as in the Western world, but in Bali comes tooth filing. Pointed canines are considered too similar to those of witches and demons. When they are filed the six evil qualities of our nature – greed, anger, passion, intoxication, jealousy and stupidity – are diminished. As the cost of the tooth filing ceremony is high, it's sometime left until just before marriage.

On marriage there is a theatrical aspect. Economy also comes into it. Elopement is considered good fun by the Balinese. The groom kidnaps the girl, adjourns to a friend's house with her and enjoys a pre-wedding honeymoon. The groom's standing is higher for doing this as it's considered heroic. Boring is how they think of a man who allows his parents to negotiate for him. Usually the elopement has been planned in advance and the father play-acts his horror. The wedding ceremony takes place forty-two days later.

Babies are not allowed to touch the ground until they are 210 days old. They are then given a name and their hair is cut.

The beautiful instruments of Bali are called gamelan. Each morning, at my hotel, an old man and a young man played during breakfast.

In the rites of cremation, the base of the tower is shaped like a turtle entwined by two snakes as a symbol of the foundation of the world. In 1992 there was a ceremony for the mother, wife and stepmother of one of the royal families. It was reputed to cost one million US dollars.

Cremation ceremonies are whole village affairs. There is a party atmosphere as preparations are made. If the body has been buried, it cannot be brought into the house, so its soul must be called back from the graveyard. An effigy is made which contains soil from the grave and this is placed in a little pavilion and, to guide the soul home, a lamp is placed outside.

The corpse should be washed, but this is done symbolically using a drawing of a human figure on a board if no corpse is available. Otherwise I presume someone, goodness knows who, is responsible for washing the disinterred body before cremation.

The ceremony finally begins as the sun is at its zenith. Towers vary in size and have tiered roofs depending on the importance of the deceased. For those who are cremated immediately and not previously interred, their body is placed on a platform. This platform represents the space between heaven and earth.

The procession is rather chaotic. Up to a hundred men may carry the pyre and they spin around at crossroads to confuse the soul, so that it never returns or disturbs the living. At the cremation ground, two birds are released to signify the soul's release. No grief is displayed now as the blaze begins, as this would disturb the soul so much it wouldn't be willing to leave. There is another ceremony three days later to cleanse the pollution brought by the death on the living.

Despite the bomb, having to sign a dsiclaimer and going against government advice to visit, I feel Bali is still good for visitors. It is still THE holiday island.

Australian Picture

It's true I never wanted to visit Australia. It never appealed. New Zealand did, but Oz – never.

I take it all back. I had the time of my life. I only spent nine or ten days there, but I packed a lot in and it was great fun.

It's vibrant, exciting, a bit flash, cosmopolitan, friendly and up for it. All the usual clichés. The sheer friendliness of the people. They're very confident, gregarious and open. I felt completely relaxed and at home. Very welcome.

Sydney of course runs at a different pace than anywhere else I visited in Oz. I can live with that.

Aussies seem to exist quite happily at their end of the globe and generally seem to not bother whether the rest of the Western world is marching to a different tune.

As the Iraqi war was starting I talked to a dreadlocked taxi driver who, like all the other Aussies I talked to, did not support his government in backing the war. Not one person I spoke to supported it. They were not at all pleased and seemed to feel they were being dragged into something and because of that felt they would be a terrorist target now.

Although the character of the Australians changed as I moved further north, the openness and friendliness never did. Very, very laid back. Very proud of their country.

As I flew across the continent I didn't get the vast

spaciousness of the country. It was sort of pocket versions all the way.

As I read Bill Bryson and he came to Alice Springs, he said how much he disliked the place. I was really disappointed. Then he was forced to return and was enchanted with it as I had been. A real gem. People seem to go for a visit and are still there years later.

An advert in the Alice Springs paper is for the Central Australian Aboriginal Alcohol Programmes Unit (CAAAPU) Alice Springs. They want various staff and state that sobriety is a condition of employment.

The town council has also installed security lighting at the skate park and is looking at options concerning shade and drinking water. There's a public meeting to discuss skateboarding issues, with members of the police, YMCA, schools and Aboriginal organisations.

At Alice Springs everything has to be brought in by road. A rail line is being built, but it's been twenty years in the making. Because of the transportation costs everything is dear.

You see these vast road-train trucks thundering down the highways. It's fortunate many of the roads aren't busy and they're straight or you'd need to pluck your courage up to pass one.

The famous Ghan (railway line) connects Alice Springs with Adelaide, but apparently does not take freight. The new line linking Adelaide via Alice Springs to Darwin is due to open by 2004 and there are celebrations planned all about the route. After waiting twenty years I'm not surprised.

Fifty years ago Oz only had half the present population. In the 1940s it struggled. The war altered the old society structures; women who'd served in the war or worked in jobs reserved for men didn't want to return to the home.

The old ways were not acceptable. Ex-servicemen also felt the old order wasn't for them. A social welfare programme was initiated taking in housing, education and a government-owned airline was set up. The biggest change however was in immigration. A spectacular programme resulted in two million migrants between 1945 and 1965. Half of all migrants had to be British, but there was no restriction on where the other fifty per cent came from. The migrants were 'assisted' which if I remember rightly meant whole families were sailing to Oz for £10 a head. Most people in the UK knew somebody in the late '50s or '60s who were emigrating.

Now, one third of all immigrants are Asian. In an average year one million make inquiries but only approx 75,000 are granted entry. Over half of these already have family in Oz, twenty-five per cent are skilled workers and just 13,000 are refugees. So far Oz has absorbed 435,000 refugees since 1945, making a higher proportion per capita than any other industrialised nation. It has been for many years and will continue to be so in the future, the biggest 'hot potato' in Australian politics. Views on immigration are many and varied, but nearly all are controversial.

In 1945 Oz had a predominantly Anglo-Saxon makeup, with ninety-eight per cent having a British background. Then Germans, Greeks, Italians, Yugoslavs and Dutch who spoke little English founded their own communities, with shops and newspapers.

But there was little friction and these immigrants were the workforce behind the major development of the '50s and '60s.

In 1948 General Motors set up Oz's first car plant. The success of the cars was seen as a sign of progress.

US finance, European immigrant labour and an affluent Australian consumer.

By the 1960s instead of being a nation of farmers it was becoming a manufacturing country. Cars and white goods became available to most of the population. By the mid-sixties Oz was seeing unprecedented prosperity and other than the US, its people had the highest standard of living.

When Britain joined the Common Market it was the first signal (for Australians) that ties with the old country were gradually being severed.

Oz was left out in the cold for its trade. They needed someone to fill the gap and that was Japan and the United States.

By the 1960s the white-collar workers exceeded the blue-collar workers for the first time. A booming middle class was beginning to emerge.

Oz, long regarded as the workingman's utopia, found itself one of the most middle-class nations on earth.

Things changed when Oz entered the Vietnamese War. It sent nearly 50,000 conscripts over ten years, lost 500 and had over 2,000 wounded.

Then came feminism, student power, black power and the sexual revolution. At the same time the migrants were changing English conformity and began introducing European food, open-air cafés and a truly cosmopolitan lifestyle.

Suddenly Oz started looking at things differently and by 1972, elected the Labour Party. Labour won another election in 1974 but faced a world recession caused by the oil price crisis.

Oz had never had to deal with issues such as inflation and unemployment for over thirty years. The government became involved in scandal, at one point attempting to borrow four billion petrodollars from a doubtful source. Whitlam, the Prime Minister, refused to resign and the Queen's representative in Australia dismissed him and called an election.

Some considered this an illegal act, in spirit, if not in the letters of the Constitution. Whitlam's rival, Malcolm Fraser of the Liberal-National Country Party, won the following election and vowed to take politics 'off the front page'.

In 1983, Labour again took power, and during the next thirteen years governed by consensus in that it brokered historic deals between unions and business that gave unprecedented industrial peace.

In the meantime the Oz economy was sliding constantly. It started with a series of devaluations of the Australian dollar. It became know as 'The Pacific Peso'. The Prime Minister warned the country that it would turn into a banana republic if economic changes weren't made.

Labour maintained a degree of social justice by keeping the welfare system, but pushed towards free market policies. All the time Australia was linking itself more closely with Asia economically and diplomatically.

The latest figures available show that comparing the year ending 2000 with the year ending 2001 Australia imports in minerals, lubricants and fuels increased by over twenty five per cent but total imports only increased by seven per cent year on year. Exports were up just over five per cent.

For imports the main markets are the USA, followed by Japan and China. For exports Japan is way ahead of the field, followed by USA and Korean Republic.

Tourists, at nearly 5,000,000 per annum, consist

AUSTRALIAN PICTURE

firstly of Kiwis, closely followed by Japanese. The British follow in third place at 650,000 or so.

Australia comes over as a 'can-do' sort of place. I like that type of mentality. It makes you feel good about yourself and the country. You can't imagine anybody being depressed there, at least, not for long.

It could be all the sun, but something gives them a sunny disposition and it's catching. As they say in references,

'And I would recommend this person to anyone.'

Well, that goes for Australia too.

Impressions of New Zealand

I suppose I can understand why Kiwis are the most travelled people in the world. For those of us fed up with big city lives and hectic day-to-day existence, New Zealand is like a backwater. A paradise of beautiful scenery, quaint towns among the mountains and lakes and a quality of life not seen in the UK, by most of us, for many years.

To native New Zealanders this is probably claustrophobic when they are young, hence the travelling. One guy who came over to the UK and stayed said there wasn't enough going on in New Zealand, the place was too small, and he came from the big smoke, Auckland.

This, of course, is what makes it an idyllic place to so many people and the perfect place to raise a family and enjoy a superior lifestyle.

There's skiing, any number of water sports, sailing and one of the most spectacular accessible mountain ranges in South Island.

It seems to have everything – and a laid-back life as well. As I've described earlier Christchurch was a beautiful city and quite cosmopolitan. The sort of place you'd probably want to settle in.

Wanaka was small and perfectly formed, but might be too small if you didn't need all the sports available within driving distance. The trees give it an Italian look in places.

Although NZ has the usual high tech facilities I still

feel it is like the UK in the late '50s. Everyone seems to know everyone else, which is fine and friendly, but not everyone wants that. Neighbourliness seems to be the order of the day.

New Zealand lived up to my expectations, but I have to admit, I thought it would be bigger. By that I mean its cities. I expected more and bigger towns, yet I know it hasn't a high population. I suppose I expected it to be more like central England, not the Highlands of Scotland re population.

I honestly hadn't understood when our Kiwi friend said it wasn't big enough. I thought he was just doing the 'grass is greener' bit.

New Zealand did not support the Iraqi War. All its citizens I spoke to were talking about it and were anti-war and fully behind their government. Very much a pacific people.

In 1882, a refrigerated ship, the Dunedin, was filled with sheep's carcasses. Arrival in the UK was three months later. The meat arrived safely and so started a trade for New Zealand that would be extremely profitable for years to come.

Profits were higher in England than on home soil. Realising a good thing, the farmers began to breed sheep, not just for meat, but wool as well.

As the century closed, sweeping land reforms broke down large inland estates and provided money for the first mortgages to put people on the land.

Improved working conditions led to the world's first compulsory system of industrial arbitration. Even the aged poor were awarded a pension.

With the exceptions of tiny Pitcairn Island and Wyoming USA, women were awarded the first right to vote on an equal basis.

At the beginning of the twentieth century the affluence of the farmers increased because of dairy farming expansion and of course, the frozen meat exports.

Later New Zealand turned down, rather politely, an invitation to join the new Commonwealth of Australia. After that they were upgraded by the British Empire from 'colony' to 'dominion'.

The election of a dairy farmer as Prime Minister in 1911 confirmed New Zealand's position as Britain's offshore farm.

With WWI came a new sense of nationalism, at the same time emphasising the ties to Britain.

A hundred thousand men joined the Australia-New Zealand Army Corps (ANZAC) fighting in Africa and Europe. Almost 17,000 Kiwis died. As there were only one million New Zealanders, the figure is disproportionate in the Gallipoli expedition where 8,500 ANZACs alone died. This gave New Zealand a higher standing in the British Empire, but at what a price.

The Great Depression arrived and New Zealand saw Britain's demand for its products fall. This led to serious unemployment and then several violent and bloody riots.

As the world economy recovered in 1935, a new Labour government could take full advantage. It established a Social Security system. The same government led New Zealand to war in WWII. Almost 200,000 Kiwis fought, not only in the Pacific, but in Italy, Crete and North Africa. Five per cent died in battle. Surprisingly even the tiny Cook Island sent soldiers to the World Wars.

With each World War, New Zealand's identity and nationhood increased. In 1947, the government formally got full independence from Britain.

After the last war, the biggest immigrant group of 30,000 was the Dutch, eager to leave their country for the boom times across the world.

In 1951 the ratification of the ANZUS (Australia, New Zealand and US) security pact showed the world that Australia and New Zealand realised they couldn't rely on Britain for their defence arrangements.

When passenger ships in the 1950s began their trade again, it was time for New Zealand to leave its time warp that judged its society compared to the Old Country. Still, until the 1960s and '70s society was narrow, closed and very much controlled, but by the 1980s gone were the old ways of shops closing rigidly at 6.00 pm, no liquor in restaurants and weekend closing. (Because of a strict forty-hour, five-day week most families spent the weekend together.)

New Zealanders began eating out and it became part of the nation's culture. New Zealand wines are now ranked among the best in the world.

On a visit to the wineries I noticed savvy winegrowers plant a rose bush or tree at the end of each row. Any pests attack the roses first and so the grower gets advance notice and can take evasive action.

In the early 1970s, New Zealand had to diversify quickly, they were left confused when, in 1973, Britain joined the EEC. They had lived long and well with our trade, rightly so, as they bred excellent products, but they had never had to market themselves.

When oil prices soared in 1974, debts began to accumulate. Trade barriers imposed on the UK by the EEC sent the cost of industrial goods through the roof.

By the end of the '70s and into the '80s inflation up to 16.5 per cent caused farmers' costs to rocket and the government had to increase subsidies. Economic deregulation took place under the Labour government in 1984 and continued into the '90s.

In more recent years New Zealand has had a reputation for its anti-nuclear stance. Despite the ANZUS pact, the American nuclear-powered or nuclear-armed vessels were not allowed into New Zealand ports. This resulted in the cancellation of the pact.

New Zealand has since declared its nuclear-free zone of 200 miles around its coast and pledged to renegotiate the ANZUS pact with the US to force it to keep nuclear armaments out of its ports.

By 1983, Australia and New Zealand had a new trade pact to guarantee free trade between themselves and today only one or two areas are not free.

Comparing the end of 2000 with the end of 2001, imports hardly rose at all. Exports however, rose over ten per cent, so they must be doing something right. Their main area is still food and live animals, as might be expected.

As with Australia, New Zealand also has turned its trading attentions towards the fast-growing economies of the Far East. Australia is still its biggest trading partner, followed by Japan. One third of all exports go to the Asian markets – more than Europe and America combined.

One third of imports come from Asia. Japan and Singapore are the long-term partners but now the other tiger economies of Korea, Thailand, Indonesia, Taiwan, China and Malaysia are on the bandwagon.

I have not touched on the Maori issue. I never saw any in South Island, but I was mainly in the alpine region.

Only during the Labour government of 1984–90 was acknowledgement made of the validity of the Maori claims for fishing grounds, land and other assets which the Maori claim were taken illegally. The Treaty of Waitangi in 1840 is the basis of their claims. Land claims, where the government owned the land, were generally granted and they gained a large fishing concession.

Tension is still continuing over these issues and unlikely to be resolved to please everyone. These tensions are perceived to be the growing pains of a new nation.

But, finally, New Zealand is a great place to visit and for people thinking of upping sticks it may just provide them with a bolthole from the rat race. As a holiday venue it cannot be beaten – I can even forgive the sand flies.

Visions of Thailand

What can I say? I was miserable, but I put that down as much to the appalling hotel, (where we only had one key between us – security they told us). In my mind if we were fit to be trusted with one key we were fit to be trusted with two.

I had such high hopes. I had always wanted to visit this country. It was up there with the Great Barrier Reef, the Seychelles, the Maldives, Mauritius, the Pyramids, Petra and the Terracotta Army. I'd seen the pictures, heard great reports from others including my family and couldn't wait to get there.

As stated, I'm sure I'd been away too long, I was definitely becoming jaded. Also sharing a bedroom after so long on my own was not easy – I once had to spend twenty minutes including the minibus journey obtaining another key to access my own room – through no fault of my own – in the heat of the day. I was also in tremendous pain.

Despite all the above, I do feel in Patong Beach, where we were, the locals have reached a point where they feel we should please them as opposed to the reverse.

That's a blanket statement of course, some local people were great. Very kind, very friendly and not out to take you for every penny they can squeeze out.

I think also it was the feeling of confrontation every time I boarded a tuk-tuk.

Seeing the man every day with only one leg and

no arms begging or selling cigarettes did nothing for my peace of mind. This was the man, it was explained, who had annoyed the Mafia. Every morning he was delivered by Merc and every night, very late, he was collected.

When my daughter gave him some money the stallholder nearby said she'd be better giving him food as the Mafia took all the money. It's all right saying that, but how on earth does he eat it?

There appears to be, throughout the country, great devotion (yes, that's the right word) to the royal family. Every building including back street parlours, hairdressers, tailors have pictures of the King, wife and children. They are usually surrounded with tinsel and flowers. Framed in the larger establishments like hotels. One taxi driver had a picture just above his seat on the roof, I could see it was royalty and when I asked he said it was the Queen Mother and he looked at it like a lovesick teenager. Royalty seems to be regarded with reverence.

There are extremely large portraits at every traffic island, on hoardings and anywhere there's room. Some pictures are formal, some casual, even showing the King cycling. It is as though this is part of their identity – who Thai people are.

I am sorry I did not have a chance to visit the north of the country, away from the tourist hordes and the cynical attitude of the Thais who provide the service industry in the resorts.

Reports from backpackers and other travellers assure me Northern Thailand is another country than that in the south.

The south also has other problems, which naturally are not publicised, but if you get a newspaper you can catch up with the news on the terrorist front.

Due to its proximity to Indonesia, Southern Thailand appears to have regular incursions from that vicinity. Reported in *The Nation*, 29 April 2003, an English language paper, while I was there, was a military-style raid by two groups of men armed with automatic rifles which killed five marines. They stole thirty military weapons.

This was approximately 250 miles south of Phuket. Apparently the raid sent shockwaves through the five southernmost provinces, which are mainly Muslim.

In the past year this region has suffered twenty violent police deaths and the mob lynching of another two on Saturday.

In the latest attack the electricity was shut down before the firing of rifles at the marine sleeping quarters.

The raiders had already cut down trees to obstruct roadways and planted grenades to slow down pursuers.

Apparently there were confused responses from the government. The Prime Minister accused armed separatists who trained in the Middle East and were looking to attract financial support from unnamed Muslim countries. He did not elaborate. He thought the groups had crossed from Malaysia to launch the attacks. But the Defence Minister, on the other hand, described them as 'ordinary bandits' despite carrying out what appeared to be a well-planned operation. The area all this happened in is right on the border with Malaysia.

Under local news in the same paper, same day, a naval officer who survived the attack alleged the attackers spoke Malay.

A leading academic at the Prince of Songkhla University in Pattani thought the attacks could have

stemmed from disputes among powerful cliques in the area. He maintained that allegations were made re Middle East trained militants without any proof.
'It's getting to be the standard official line'.
Immediately beneath this article, still under 'Local', the police lynchings are discussed under the headline 'Justice will be done' and the heading 'Ninja gangs are baseless rumour'. The lynching of the two policemen in which more than a thousand people were involved was described as 'outrageous crime'.

The policemen had been detained in the village headman's house on suspicion of being Ninjas. A group have been robbing houses in the south and locals dubbed them Ninjas for the speed at which they work.

The initial findings suggest that local people mistook the police for the Ninjas. It was a misunderstanding, says the permanent Secretary for the Interior. Some misunderstanding.

As a result of this, it's been suggested only southern officials (e. g. police) work in the southern province, where they will understand local languages and cultures.

In the meantime a reward has been offered of about £8,000 for the capture of the 'Ninja' gangsters, but this is only for anyone who captures *all* of the gang. At this moment nobody knows how many are in this gang, so it looks like the reward is safe for the time being.

Pawnshops are preparing for a surge from parents as the schools go back. It was expected that they would borrow approx £6 million over the next few weeks. City pawnshops have lower interest rates than government maintained pawnshops. Government shops charge two per cent per month, city shops charge 0.75 per cent for low amounts.

The Thai Queen will be sixty next year and 10,000,000 postcards are to be distributed to people to send their best wishes. The cards are expected to be ready by March '04 and are expected to be popular, with a take-up rate of fifty per cent. The birthday is 12 August.

As I mentioned, Courts, the furniture people opened in Phuket. Perhaps it is my ignorance, but the newspaper reports the company as covering furniture, electrical appliances and computer software. The decision to choose Phuket as the first location was because it has a rapidly growing economy, with strong demands for homewares amid less competition than Bangkok.

Thailand, called the Kingdom in the article, was Courts' fourth target in the Far East, after Singapore, Malaysia and Indonesia.

As a wrap-up to Thailand, I wonder for how much longer it will be the peaceful Kingdom it wants to be. The violence, bombing and attacks are played down, but are very much on the doorstep of some of its biggest tourist areas. They aren't exactly front-page news and I suppose you can't blame them for that.

Vietnam Snapshot

I have visited here for four days and just one part of the country, as you know.

The people are very friendly, like most in the Far East. Once again in common with the region they are upwardly mobile or, if not, aspiring to be.

A recent programme on Channel Four examining globalisation noted that Nike had been in Vietnam for fifteen years. Whatever happened previously, they now only employ people aged sixteen and over in their apparel department and eighteen or over in their shoe department.

They pay three times the national wage, which enables families to extend their houses. But the most important factor, because the wages are so high, families no longer require their children to work to eke out a reasonable living for them all. More Vietnamese children are now in school than ever before.

As more companies set up, competition for skilled staff is pushing up wages. People from the North are filtering down to where the jobs and high rewards are.

Agriculture, where according to one woman you work fourteen-hour days for one third of Nike wages, does not appeal to the masses. This once was all they had, but now they have a choice.

Another woman had been made a manager. Her husband also worked for Nike. He earned the normal three-times average wage. Her wage was three times his. As she fed a bottle to her son (about fifteen months old) her ambition for him was to be a doctor.

A comparison was made with Taiwan, which was once the sweatshop of the world in the '60s. Now it has the same economy as Spain. Many Taiwanese are millionaires. Abject poverty has disappeared.

Although Starbucks and McDonalds are on the streets of Saigon, as the presenter said, it is a question of choice. Nobody has to eat there. If we can have these companies, why not in Vietnam?

The nice part was that a Vietnamese company had set up a company called Cha for Tea, based on the Starbucks presentation and principle. It now had outlets in the Far East and continues to expand. If you can't beat them, join them. I shall feel everything has come full circle if I see Cha for Tea on a high street near me.

There are no signs of British companies taking advantage of their growing economy, with the exception of insurance companies.

Despite their common past Americans seem to have it sewn up. American businessmen are everywhere – and expected to be so. I hadn't noticed any other nationalities but in so short a trip, only so much is possible.

The *Vietnam News* (the national English language paper) of 30 April 2003 reports that despite SARS, drought and the Iraqi war the Vietnamese economy has weathered the storm.

A drought has affected the coffee crop of 40,000 hectares in the Central Highlands, which is their largest coffee growing area.

More than 730,000 people are suffering water shortages. Two underground reservoirs are drying up. Floods are forecast to hit the region in the coming months.

Industry grew 15.5 per cent over the last quarter with the non-state expanding 19 per cent. The trade deficit reached US$ 1.2 billion in the same quarter. Foreign investment is $580 million. The Deputy Prime Minister said that for the rest of the year, they should build on gains to see more export markets, especially for tea, rice, engineering products and maritime products. GDP increase last year was seven per cent.

Quote: 'The cabinet also noted with satisfaction that in the past four months much progress was made in the settlement of citizen's complaints and denunciations.

The number of complaints lodged straight to central agencies from localities has reduced substantially and "hot beds" in social affairs are no longer to be heard of.' Unquote.

The paper reports that more than 20,000 poor people, mostly ethnic minorities, have received free medical checks and treatment under a charity drive by volunteer doctors and health workers from HCM hospitals.

They also carried out 1,150 cataract operations and repaired facial deformity (mainly cleft palate and harelip) in 550 children.

Quote: 'In the 28 years since Southern Vietnam was liberated, the Cuu Tong (Mekong) River Delta has overcome many setbacks resulting from the long years of war to become a rich agricultural region.

The delta is known as the country's rice basket and supplies fifty-two per cent of the country's paddy rice. It is also the biggest producer of seafood accounting for fifty-five per cent of national supply.

Since the end of the American War local residents have faced harsh weather conditions, natural disasters and a shortage of money while tapping the region's natural resources.

Shortly after Liberation Day in 1975, local provincial leaders built an irrigation and drainage canal system to transform the rice fields and ensure bigger crops. The winter-spring crop is now the biggest crop of the year, supplying ninety per cent of the country's rice export.' Unquote.

It goes on to say a vast land clearance programme in the Plain of Reeds which had been a swamp had turned 700,000 hectares into high-yielding fields. Vietnam is now one of the world's biggest rice exporters, and 200,000 hectares of low-yield rice fields have been turned into shrimp farms. By 2005 shrimps will bring an export value of US$ 1.5 billion.

Vietnam exports more than 300,000 tonnes of fruit per year, mainly bananas, langians, pineapples, mangoes and oranges to mainland China, Taiwan, Singapore, the US and EU, most of it from the delta.

Vietnam and India have been co-operating together on various projects – agriculture, rail transport and science and technology. The most important results have been in IT.

The Indian government have backed an operation, Aptech, which is using US$ 2.5m in non-refundable aid to carry out six software projects and is also co-operating with Vietnam's Technology Finance and Promotion Co to set up IT training courses in Hanoi and Saigon.

India is also awarding 120 scholarships each year for Vietnamese to study IT in India.

Saigon has granted licences to 3,000 enterprises, capitalised at almost US$ 300m this year. Textile and garments posted the highest increases in revenues, up thirty per cent, closely followed by leather and footwear, then rubber and plastics. The chemicals industry was just over twenty per cent.

I hope none of our car-hating Chief Constables get onto this, but Hanoi's traffic police department penalised 23,000 motorists/motorcyclists caught violating the Law on Road Transport, confiscating 188 driving licences and worse still, impounding 2,700 cars and bikes.

In the newspaper is a large advert with a leprechaun in the middle advertising Sheridan's Irish House: Live Music Nightly, Whiskey in the Jar, Guinness, Gaelic band Saturdays. So the Irish theme pub has got legs of its own.

All round the major hotels are the expensive boutiques. The prices, all in US$, wouldn't disgrace Fifth Avenue. The décor is very Western, minimalist and tasteful. The fashions are extremely beautiful but slightly oriental.

The paper also reports from Bali, where the Australia stressed the need for tight border controls to curb terrorist attacks like the Bali bombings, as Asian ministers held talks on the island on ways to combat people-smuggling.

Australian Foreign Minister, Alexander Downes told delegates from forty-five Asia-Pacific and observer countries that the marked rise in people trafficking had created political, economic, social and security challenges. He said the business is worth US$ ten billion worldwide annually.

The paper also reports an article in the *International Herald Tribune.*

Quote: 'The fact that 1.5m Britons will have the chance to vote electronically in local elections using the electronic voting system, security experts on both sides of the Atlantic say it its fraught with danger and an invitation to fraud.

In all the electronic elections held so far in Europe and US experts say the systems used were vulnerable to attack and could be manipulated in undetectable ways that would have made it impossible to determine that the results of an election had been changed, either by accident or design.' Unquote.

What price democracy?

It says something though if Communist Vietnam feels it should report this development. Time for us to worry perhaps?

In the Business pages of *Vietnam News* it was regretted that the Minister of Posts and Telematics was licensing five telecoms firms to provide services. They say they are officially bidding farewell to the decades-long corporate monopoly in telecoms. I think it's fair to say, Vietnam like China is well and truly in the capitalist world and enjoying every minute of it. They probably wished they'd done it earlier.

At the ceremony, the Minister said it marks a step in their development, unleashing competition and stepping up the spread of its economic integration. He hoped the companies would set Vietnam up to become a major telecom player.

In the Arts section of the paper, a Saigon City Gallery travels back to the time of Southern liberation. Visitors will feel like they're back to 30 April 1975. It will feature historical events and daily life from 1959–75 during the American War. The painting displayed on the page shows a young girl, crouching in the paddy fields with a rifle, but she had a nice pink scarf around her neck, looks like silk, the rest is battle-type dress.

One quote from Nguyen Thanh Thuy, Student

HCM Fine Art College was: 'Looking at the paintings, young people like me, who have grown up in a unified country will get more of a sense of how our life of peace ... is derived from the sacrifice, blood and tears of the elder generation'.

As the war is quite recent in their memories I suppose it's understandable that it is frequently referred to, but Vietnam does, despite that, appear to be moving on at incredible speed. It looks like being the next Asian tiger economy.

From what I hear, Cambodia is still as Vietnam was fifteen years ago. Perhaps someone should take the telecoms revolution to them.